ANTHONY J. GRUBBS

THE PLAYWRIGHT'S PERSPECTIVE

INNOVATIVE DRAMATURGY AND ITS POETICS IN EARLY MODERN SPAIN

UNIVERSITY PRESS
OF THE SOUTH

2021

Published in the United States by The University Press of the South. Printed in France by Monbeaulivre.fr

E-mails: unprsouth@aol.com; universitypresssouth@gmail.com

Visit our award-winning web pages: www.unprsouth.com

www.punouveaumonde.com

Anthony J. Grubbs.

The Playwright's Perspective. Innovative Dramaturgy and its Poetics in Early Modern Spain.

Second Edition. In English.

xx + 244 pages. Bibliography and Index.

Cover Art: 'El Caballero de Olmedo.' Lope de Vega (Liceo Theater, Salamanca, Spain).

1. Theater. 2. Spain. 3. Lope. 4. Calderon. 5. Torres. 6. Naharro. 7. Bances. 8. Cueva. 9. Performance. 10. Comedia.

ISBN: 978-1-931948-95-1 (First Edition: USA, 2010)

ISBN: 978-1-952799-32-7 (Second Edition: Europe, 2021)

In memory of
Professor Robert C. Gibson

ACKNOWLEDGEMENTS

I am indebted to Professors Nancy Marino and Catherine Larson, both of whom have offered unwavering support and invaluable mentoring throughout my career. It is their example that I strive to follow on a daily basis. I also want to thank Professor Bryant Creel for his valuable remarks and guidance after reading an early draft of this manuscript. I also appreciate the comments and editorial suggestions of Professor Carmen Ruiz-Sánchez, Anne Marie Gibson, and Lisa Ann Doonan.

This monograph would not have been possible without a grant from the Program for Cultural Cooperation between Spain's Ministry of Culture and United States' Universities, which facilitated extensive research at the National Library in Madrid, Spain. My gratitude also goes out to Diego Sainz de la Maza and Rafael Flores Zimmerman for their assistance while I was researching in Spain. I am also appreciative of the support that I received from the College of Arts and Letters and the Humanities and Arts Research Program at Michigan State University.

I want to thank my parents for always being there for me and supporting my professional and personal decisions. Last and most important, my wife, Carmen, and daughter, Lucía, continue to be my strongest supporters and brightest lights in my life.

TABLE OF CONTENTS

PREFACE

Innovation and conflict have always characterized early modern Spanish theater. The dramatic text, transformed and reincarnated with each interpretation onstage, was in a constant state of flux in the Golden Age. As a result of the influence of Aristotle's *Poetics* and the literary theory established during the Italian Renaissance, especially by Franciscus Robortellus's *In librum Aristotelis de arte poetica explicationes* (1548),[1] which demonstrated how an Aristotelian approach to tragedy served as a similarly useful approach to comedy, most scholars in sixteenth-century Spain tended to contemplate dramatic theory in a more formal, theoretical, and rhetorical manner. In subsequent years, several theater practitioners began exploring the implications of performance and audience reception from a different perspective, liberating dramatic theory from the arguably uncompromising precepts that had previously dictated literary and theatrical practice. These playwrights stopped reflecting on past theory and concentrated on present theatrical practice, turning to audiences for cues as to their expectations, for example, whereas Alonso López Pinciano's *Philosophía Antigua Poética* (1596) grounded literary theory in Aristotle's *Poetics*, Félix Lope de Vega Carpio's *Arte nuevo de hacer comedias en este tiempo* (1609), based on his enormous success on the boards, upstaged his more classically oriented predecessor. Later attempts at reestablishing Aristotelian precepts were even less successful, as dramatic theorists and practitioners mostly ignored the *Tablas Poéticas* (1631) of Francisco Cascales, for example, in favor of dramatic forms modeled after Lope's *comedia*.

The relationship between Golden Age theater theory and practice, illustrated through the study of representative works by six playwrights, is the topic of this study. The impact of practice on

---

1. See María José Vega's book *La formación de la teoría de la comedia: Francisco Robortello* for a comprehensive study of the formation of Robortello's theory of comedy, to which, she suggests, all European literature up to Romanticism–and arguably even modern literature–is indebted.

theory is as irrefutable as the impact of theory on practice. In fact, many prominent playwrights wrote treatises (re)affirming their decisions to stray from traditional norms and to create new dramatic art forms. Without exception these defenses were written after the playwright had enjoyed success and introduced his—and, in the case of Golden Age Spain, the theatrical world was overwhelmingly populated by men—particular pioneering contribution to the theater. By examining the ways which theatrical practice was influenced by performance and audience reception, their impact on shaping theatrical theory becomes clear, not only in the well known case of Lope's *Arte nuevo* but throughout sixteenth- and seventeenth-century Spain.

Of course, all playwrights continually face the challenge of creating original works for a dynamic and demanding public who must be kept at the forefront when writing a play, since they are the receptors of the message that is transmitted by means of the performance of the dramatic text. This realization, however, does not downplay the importance of the script, but elevates all three aspects: the text, performance, and reception, to equal ground. These factors have led me to concentrate on the connection between performance and reception in this study of early modern Spanish dramatic theory, and although performance and reception can be dealt with in a mutually exclusive manner, it is more feasible to look at them collectively with the dramatic text—as Pedro Calderón de la Barca suggests in his prologue to the *Autos*—in the attempt to reproduce the entire dramatic spectacle.

Scholarship dealing with early modern Spanish theater is vast and far reaching, to say the least, with a long history of varied and dynamic approaches.[2] In the sixteenth and seventeenth centuries, the dramatic landscape shifted and new theories appeared, causing a heated and on-going dialogue between the supporters of innovation and the defenders of tradition. Emilio Cotarelo y Mori's *Bibliografía de las controversias sobre la licitud*

---

2. Laura Bass's and Margaret Greer's *Approaches to Teaching Early Modern Spanish Drama* and Jonathan Thacker's *A Companion to Golden Age Theater* offer good starting points for an examination of sixteenth- and seventeenth-century Spanish theater as well as comprehensive bibliographies.

del teatro en España compiles a comprehensive collection of the dramatic treatises of the time and is the logical starting point for any study of early modern Spanish theater theory; Marcelino Menéndez y Pelayo's *Historia de las ideas estéticas* is another indispensable reference. Federico Sánchez Escribano's and Alberto Porqueras Mayo's *Preceptiva dramatica española del Renacimiento y Barroco*, and, more recently, *La crítica ante el teatro barroco español* by María José Rodríguez Sánchez de León offer ample fragments of dramatic treatises dating from the seventeenth to the nineteenth centuries. Furthermore, both Melveena McKendrick and Ignacio Arellano address Golden Age dramatic theory in their histories of early modern Spanish theater; in his *Historia del teatro español (Desde sus orígenes hasta 1900)*, Francisco Ruiz Ramón also gives a general overview of the dramatic trends of the time, and Marc Vitse's *Éléments pour une théorie du téâtre espagnol du XVII siècle* also proves invaluable. A lively dialogue still exists regarding the impact of the theory in early modern Spain, and the number of critical studies that treat the implications and importance of the dramatic treatises of Golden Age Spain is also enormous. Marvin Herrick discusses the influence of Terentian Comedy in Europe in *Comic Theory in the Sixteenth Century*, and Raymond Grismer's *The Influence of Plautus in Spain before Lope de Vega*, specifically discusses Plautus's comic legacy in the Iberian Peninsula. C. J. Metford further describes the often negative criticism that Spanish theater faced. Jesús Pérez-Magallón demonstrates how changing attitudes toward theatrical practices transformed theory in "Del *Arte nuevo* de Lope al arte 'reformado' de Bances: Algunas cuestiones de poética dramática." Other studies that deal with the treatises of the specific playwright-theorists will be discussed in the corresponding chapters.

Scholars have also concentrated on other factors besides the commentary of supporters and detractors of the theater. The theater-going public in Spain was varied and of different temperaments. Many commentators of the time described most audiences in less-than-flattering terms—arguably the most famous example is found in Lope's *Arte nuevo*, where he describes them as rowdy and unruly—an understatement, to say the least.[3] Otis H. Green addresses this disdain in "On the Attitude toward the *Vulgo* in the Spanish *Siglo de Oro*" and other, more recent studies on the theater-going public include work by Jean Sentaurans, John Varey, Catherine Connor, and Jane Albrecht, to name a few. José Hesse's *Vida teatral en el Siglo de Oro* discusses the general theater scene both on and off stage. José María Díez Borque's extensive work encompasses the entire dramatic spectacle, dealing with both local and foreign spectators, the staging of the plays, and the actors' performances. Descriptions of the dramatic spaces, especially the *corrales de comedias,* have been put forward by Hugo Rennert, Varey, William Shoemaker, and, John Jay Allen, all of whose efforts and insights have resolved uncertainties common in the past about the staging and the actual construction of the *corrales*.[4] All of these factors in conjunction with modern-day performance and reception theory continue to offer new insight into challenges of composing, staging, and viewing theatrical works in early modern Spain.

While in the past most early modern Spanish theater scholarship was based primarily on close readings of the text, this changed toward the end of the twentieth century when Performance Studies became fundamental. The historical and social factors revealed by the texts were never forgotten, nor was their importance diminished, rather scholars began to focus on all aspects of the dramatic spectacle, including the staging of the text. Hispanists were challenged to look at modern-day adaptations of the plays and draw conclusions as to what they shared with the performances in early modern Spain. It was Louise and Peter Fothergill-Payne's *Prologue to Performance* that solidified the importance of performance within the context of Golden Age Spanish theater studies. This collection of essays recognized and initiated a dialogue that focused on the importance of performance

---

3. This negative attitude is well known because of Lope's comments in the *Arte nuevo*.

4. The website for the Association of Hispanic Classical Theater (www.comedias.org) is an invaluable resource for scholars and teachers alike. With regard to the *corrales*, the site includes some of John Jay Allen's inexhaustible work on the early modern performance spaces.

in response to what Isaac Benabu called a "lack of performance tradition" (23) in his essay "Interpreting the *Comedia* in the Absence of a Performance Tradition: Gutierre in Calderón's *El médico de su honra*," found in the same collection. Performance Studies continued to complement other theoretical approaches to early modern Spanish theater—but especially the *comedia*—as seen in such collections as Charles Ganelin's and Howard Mancing's *The Golden Age* Comedia: *Text, Theory, and Performance*, and Barbara Mujica's and Anita K. Stoll's *El texto puesto en escena*, to name two notable examples. Scholarship dealing with performance still abounds, as a glance at the *Bulletin of the Comediantes* reveals; also, the journal *Comedia Performance* is dedicated solely to the topic. Most recently, Susan Paun de García and Donald Larson have edited *The Comedia in English: Translation and Performance*, a collection of essays that deals with the translation, adaptation, and performance of the Spanish *comedia* for the modern stage.

The primary intention of this work is the application of performance and reception theory to a consideration of the innovations made by several playwrights whose work spans the Spanish Golden Age. Instead of concentrating solely on the tangible clues provided by the script, I focus on the more subjective aspects of its performance and subsequent audience response in order to emphasize that practice impacts theory just as theory influences practice. The first chapter of the study offers a historical overview of the events and trends that precipitated the bold innovations of dramatic theory and practice during the sixteenth and seventeenth centuries. It also revisits some important contemporary critical responses to this changing dramatic landscape and synthesizes performance and reception theories as the primary theoretical bases of the study. I utilize research in the area of performance theory by writers such as Elin Diamond, Herbert Blau, Marvin Carlson and Amalia Gladhart, and I incorporate the work of Hans Robert Jauss on the aesthetics of reception as well as Eli Rozik's views on the spectator's vital role in the interpretation of a work. By using as a point of departure recent theoretical approaches based on audience response and performance theories, the shift of textual authority to the representation of the script and its subsequent reception is emphasized, not only reiterating the vivacity of theater, but also broadening theater studies and further illustrating the interrelation between the dramatic spectacle, the message, its reception, and the resultant theory governing the theater of Golden Age Spain.

The remaining chapters of the study are divided chronologically and examine some of the technical innovations introduced by the following playwrights: Bartolomé de Torres Naharro, Juan de la Cueva, Félix Lope de Vega, Tirso de Molina, Pedro Calderón de la Barca, and Francisco Antonio de Bances Candamo, which stem from their sensitivity to the importance of performance and reception. In addition, each chapter examines the dramatic theory of each playwright based on their successes and failures on the boards, citing specific influences on the poet's dramaturgy, as well as his theoretical leanings, and the treatise itself. Furthermore, a representative play is explored from the perspective of performance and reception theories in order to demonstrate how, in each case, theatrical practice anticipated and affected dramatic theory. By using the works of Torres Naharro and Bances as bookends, this study encapsulates some major dramatic trends common to early modern Spanish theater, including the commercial, religious, and court traditions.[5] It also illustrates the steady progression and recognition of the importance of performance and reception throughout the Spanish Golden Age. While some playwrights took inspiration in the classics, they ultimately failed, leaving those that looked to the contemporary needs and desires of the public to reap the rewards of a more appealing dramatic spectacle. Finally, the incorporation of a variety of dramatic genres over an extended period demonstrates the universal nature of the study, establishing the fundamental role played by performance and reception not only when writing a play, but also when studying drama in general.

Chapter two explores the nascent and dynamic dramatic landscape of sixteenth-century Spain. On the cusp between the

---

5. For an examination of the effects of performance and audience reception on the dramatic genre of the interlude, see my article "Major Change in 'Minor' Theater: Luis Quiñones de Benavente's Dramatization of Dramatic Theory and its Effects on the Interlude in Early Modern Spain."

Middle Ages and the Renaissance, several playwrights abandoned Spain for the more profitable—both economically and artistically speaking—lands of Italy where a dramatic tradition had been flourishing for years. This exposure to Italian theater styles and theories, as well as a more modern theater-going public, compelled playwrights to rethink and restructure dramatic trends in Spain, combining the innovation of Italian style with the simple wholesomeness of Spanish drama. This newly introduced theory emphasized the importance of maintaining decorum within the plays and mentioned the practical aspects of performance, suggestions garnered from the performances of their plays, which served as a guide for future generations of playwrights.

Torres Naharro not only introduced a new sensibility to the Spanish dramatic landscape with regard to staging and playwriting, but he also pioneered an interest in dramatic theory. These innovations gained traction as plays began to be produced not only within the milieu of religious, street, and courtly festivities but also within the commercial realm. This new dramatic context also signified the establishment of a new audience with different values and whose primary intent for visiting the theater was entertainment. By emphasizing and synthesizing imagination and imitation into the creative process of producing dramatic works, Torres Naharro created fictitious but believable storylines that opened up the possibility for new, original works. He contributed in transforming the face of playwriting, since many subsequent dramatic poets enhanced history, making a possibly unoriginal story more entertaining, while encoding a didactic message within the play. By embracing Italian dramatic trends, Torres Naharro not only began to establish the importance of theory, but also to introduce new models to the secular stage, an initiative that was quickly adopted and expanded upon by the Iberian dramatic poets.

By bridging a gap between the more classically inspired plays of the Renaissance and the more period-based *comedia,* Cueva, too, proved an important player in the evolution of Spanish theater. Both his theory and his dramatic work mapped out the transition: early in his career, he started writing both comedies and tragedies but stopped producing the latter form, since his audience did not enthusiastically accept its somber tone and subject matter, a clear illustration of Cueva's recognition that it was important to consider the public's desires. Regarding his dramatic precepts, although his earlier treatises were primarily shaped by Renaissance traditions, Cueva proved to be a visionary regarding numerous aspects of the *comedia* that would soon emerge, and though his actual influence on the form will continue to be debated, the *Ejemplar poético* established his position as a contributor to the formation of the genre by his introduction of new techniques, keeping theater fresh and attractive to the public. He personified the change in the dramatic landscape at the turn of the sixteenth century, as he anticipated new trends while attempting to evoke the importance of old traditions. Having many of his plays staged in Seville, Cueva's career as a playwright reflected the successes enjoyed by few, but he also embodies the frustration of being overshadowed by the "Monstruo de Ingenios," Lope de Vega, whose literary production and success eclipsed all others.

In Chapter three, I concentrate on two *comedias,* and, by looking at the metatheatrical aspects of the two plays and their relation to their authors' dramatic treatises, it is clear that both Lope and Tirso understood the importance of performance and reception. Their treatment of both aspects of the theatrical spectacle illustrated their desire to present their ideas not only to the Spanish literary circles and academies, but also to the common theatergoer, whose grasp of such concepts may not have been as well developed. Audience reception acquired singular importance, since they sought the support of the public for the new style and innovations. True, both men judged differently the degree of public influence, but both agreed on and recognized the audience's impact on drama, and the reciprocal influence of the drama on the audience, forming a symbiosis in which each one benefits from the other.

Lope made a shrewd assessment of the desires regarding the theater-going public of early modern Spain: he realized that it was necessary to play to their needs and expectations. His work underlined the tension that arises from the processes of writing, performing, and interpreting a play. Though his *Arte nuevo* is full of irony, we must look at its target audience, the Madrid Academy, and consider that he would obviously play to their expectations and prejudices—yet another example of how reception affects production. Nevertheless, his plays reveal another story regarding the catalyst for the creation of his dramatic poetry: he gave the public what they wanted; this is clearly demonstrated by his use of ballads and common, well-known stories that he adapted for the stage. By looking at *Lo fingido verdadero* as a dramatic manifestation of his theory, we see how Lope reached out to the democratized public, explaining and developing the concepts that drove his creation. Further proof lies in the fact that he really did not need to explain his motivations to anybody, but he did so by choice.

Similarly, Tirso's creation of a dramatic world in the *Cigarrales de Toledo* makes the reader more conscious of all the players in the creative process, allowing us to reflect on each member's role. The ideas of reception become clearer as various reactions are manifested in the characters and the invented audience of the *Cigarrales*—perhaps even offering a model of conduct that the reader should follow. Tirso does not celebrate the audience, and though never eager to empower the public with the decision-making involved in the playwriting process, clearly the bad reviews of *El vergonzoso en palacio* caused quite a reaction in the playwright. This criticism compelled him include the play in the *Cigarrales* along with a comprehensive defense of not only the work itself, but also of the *comedia* in general. It is impossible to deny the importance of reception and performance in a study of Tirso's drama because it is an integral consideration for not only the scholar, but also the playwright.

Corresponding with the dramatic trends of late seventeenth-century Spain, Chapter four deals with two theater forms that arguably overshadowed the popular *comedia*: the *auto sacramental* and the court play. These genres shared as a predominant characteristic the grandiose nature of the staged spectacle, underlining the entertainment value inherent to the forms, but the didactic nature of both theatrical styles cannot be forgotten. Although the audience was more specific and homogeneous than that typical of the *corrales*, and though their message was often distinct from that of the more popular *comedia*, both types of plays were still affected by performance in the desire to facilitate the reception of the work, which often meant making the abstract notion more tangible and comprehensible.

Calderón specifically mentioned that representation was instrumental to the understanding of the *auto sacramental* because the performative aspects were easily lost during a simple reading, a notion essentially true of all dramatic genres. Its performance offered a religious lesson in an accessible manner, making the allegory come to life as the audience members were able to visualize its meaning, contemplate their own situation, and make their own decisions about the correct path to follow. Ritual relies on performance and its representation allows the spectator to enjoy the work on a superficial level while absorbing the message—either consciously or not—on a deeper level. Most certainly, ritual and performance are positively linked and mutually affected by the other. Calderón and others understood this relationship and took advantage of the overt and explicit artifice on stage often presenting a sort of "shock and awe" spectacle, driving home the religious dogma.

Bances Candamo faced special circumstances and different challenges as the court dramatist of Charles II. His elaborate staging and intricate storylines targeted a specific audience whose demands were different from those of the democratic theater-going public of the *corrales*. Considering himself a teacher who offered guidance and counsel by means of his works, he paid special attention to his public and recognized that his plays depended greatly on the court's reception. Like his predecessors, Bances strictly followed the rules of decorum, since it was his goal to produce a perfectly decorous play that taught and reinforced courtly values. His adornment of history not only made the tales more palatable for the audience, but it also added emphasis to the intrinsic message of the work.

Clearly, the six dramatist-theorists were cognizant of and driven by the needs and desires of their audience, which in turn influenced their dramatic works; in like manner, their playwriting would have an impact on the dramatic theory that they wrote toward the end of their careers. We see in their treatises that each playwright is concerned with the issues of decorum and of pleasing the public. Performance also comes to the forefront as the early modern Spanish dramatist-theorist begins to take into account its practical aspects as well as its power to transmit a message; as Diana Taylor posits, performance distills a truer truth than life

(46), supporting the self-referential nature of theater in that it reflects the theatricality of real life. These dramatists justify their innovation in two ways: first, they assert that change is normal and that they are in fact following the logical progression of nature, which constantly changes as time passes; second, they state that they are appealing to their audience, and that their public insists on a vibrant and ever-changing theater. However, the theater also influenced the public differently as audience response became conditioned to the "new" techniques and the desire for novelty and familiarity became intertwined: the play needed to be recognizable within a common generic mold, but at the same time variations could add vigor and increase the satisfaction of the public.

In art, both the artist and the spectator actively collaborate, and much of the value of the work is in this reciprocal interaction. It is important to keep the audience both receptive and perceptive because the play is dead, using the terminology of Peter Brook, without interaction between the two parties. Indeed, as Rozik suggests, both director and spectator are equal partners in the creation of a work: the director's creative interpretation affects—and is affected by—the spectator's response. All forms of art are certainly personal and unique expressions of the artists who create them. Nonetheless, these six Golden Age writers remind us that theater is the most public and revealing of all the arts since an active and interactive audience is a dynamic requisite element of its conception, making the public a lively player of a fundamental role in the theater.

This study's originality lies in its approach to examining some of the innovations on the early modern Spanish stage by focusing solely on the playwrights who also wrote dramatic theory. This detail demonstrates and records a sensitivity to the performance and reception of the work that was shared by successful playwrights. I do not pretend to document and explain all of the innovations of these six playwrights, but rather to discuss the effects of strategies that characterized their dramatic works with the hopes of initiating further dialogue about the theater of Spain's Golden Age. By applying recent theoretical approaches within the historical context of the extant treatises and dramatic texts, this study offers further entrée into the entire process of the dramatic spectacle: composition, performance, and reception of a play. Although I diverge from the popular and useful research on modern adaptations of classical Spanish theater, the goal of this study is the same: to bridge the past and the present in an attempt to better understand both eras.

CHAPTER 1: THE DYNAMIC LANDSCAPE OF EARLY MODERN SPANISH THEATER AND THEORY AS SEEN FROM A MODERN PERSPECTIVE

It is certain that theater, written in both Latin and the vernacular, existed in many European countries during the Middle Ages, but a firmly established Spanish tradition is an anomaly due to the paucity of extant dramatic and theoretical manuscripts dating between the twelfth and fifteenth centuries. This lack of tangible evidence can be attributed to numerous physical, social, and religious factors: the delicate nature of the folios on which treatises may have been written (Donovan 73), a prejudice against letters (Surtz 23), and the popularity of lyric poetry. Additionally, Moorish influence over all aspects of Spanish culture coupled with the constant struggle of the Reconquest of the Iberian Peninsula also provide unique factors that may have contributed to the seeming lack of theater.

I. A brief overview of the evolutionary trajectory of theater in early Spain up to 1700

The uncertain existence of Spanish medieval theater has continued to stimulate a polemic for Hispanists and dramatic historians alike. The earliest known manuscript of a Spanish dramatic work is *Auto de los Reyes Magos* (c. 1150), with the next extant manuscript, *Representación del nacimiento de Nuestro Señor* (c.1468) by Gómez Manrique, dating more than 300 years later. This could suggest that Spain lacked a dramatic tradition during the Middle Ages, a notion that many scholars are reluctant to admit. In fact, Ronald Surtz notes that previous Hispanists believed that Spain had enjoyed a liturgical dramatic tradition in both Latin and the vernacular that was analogous to the rest of Europe, and this scarcity of dramas is the result of the texts being destroyed or lost (15). This is a logical conclusion due to thriving theatrical traditions in neighboring regions such as France and Catalonia.

Other scholars challenge the existence of a Spanish liturgical dramatic tradition in Latin. In the landmark study, *The Liturgical Drama in Medieval Spain*, Richard Donovan investigated 135 manuscripts of liturgical plays from countries other than Spain and found no evidence of any native (Castilian) plays (51-57); there was evidence of a Catalonian tradition but Catalonia was not allied with Castile at the time. Donovan also examined other purported Spanish plays to find that they had originated in France, Catalonia, or Italy (57-63). He suggests three factors that contributed to the dearth of a Latin liturgical dramatic tradition in Spain: first, the use of the Latin liturgical drama was unknown in the Spanish Mozarabic mass, and with the introduction of the Roman-French rites in 1080, reformers viewed these dramatic representations as superfluous, choosing not to introduce them (69); second, the reforming monks were primarily from Cluny, and no liturgical plays have been found in their liturgical manuscripts (69); and finally, the delay of Castilian liturgical reform in comparison to the remainder of Europe, and the fact that a copy of *Auto de los Reyes Magos* does exist, suggest that a vernacular tradition was already in place and that a Latin tradition would have been unnecessary (70).

Surtz concurs, stating that liturgical drama in Latin was not necessary in Castile due to socio-religious factors. He cites a fifteenth-century Hieronymite monk, Fray Juan de Serrano, who saw his contemporaries manifesting their faith in battle against the Moors instead of attending mass:

> Es la gente (como todos saben) de su natural belicosa, y ocupada en continuas guerras con los Moros que viuen juntos con ellos, estua en esta parte como Barbara, desaficionada a esta blandura, y regalo diuno, tan importante para las almas [...]. (21)

The Spanish considered the Reconquest a religious rite in itself, much like the earlier crusades. They felt no need, therefore, to confirm their religious beliefs either by attending mass or by seeing dramatic representations; it seems that fighting the Moors was enough to reaffirm their faith in Christianity. It was not until the conclusion of the Reconquest in 1492 that Juan del Encina and his contemporaries began to write and present their first religious plays with some regularity, suggesting that the intrinsic need for spiritual reinforcement marched off the battlefield and set foot on the stage.

There exists concrete evidence of religious plays in the vernacular in Castile during the Middle Ages. One section of *Las siete partidas del Rey Don Alfonso el Sabio*, mandates that monks should not act in dramas of *escarnio* because of the irreverent nature of the plays. They were, however, permitted to perform in decorous plays that reinforced church doctrine (172).[7] The importance of this thirteenth-century treatise lies in the textual confirmation of a dramatic tradition and also in the acknowledgement of theater's influence over the audience.

Another example is the *auto sacramental*, an allegorical play originally performed in conjunction with the celebration of Corpus Christi, though later represented during other religious festivals, such as Easter. It is impossible to pinpoint the date of the first performance of an *auto* but they are documented as being performed in Spain during the fifteenth century.[8] The play was normally staged on a cart (*carro*) that was part of the religious procession, a dramatic representation itself due to the costuming and role-playing of the participants. As time passed, the *carros* became quite elaborate, consisting of various levels, extravagant decoration, and numerous stage properties; some productions called for such complex staging that numerous carts were used. The *auto* was a bold presentation of religious doctrine that wielded the power of performed allegory in concert with an awe-inspiring

---

7. The doctrine reads: "Los clérigos...nin deber ser facedores de juegos por escarnio porque los vengan a ver las gentes como los facen,...Pero representaciones hi ha que pueden los clérigos facer, asi como de la nascencia de nuestro señor Iesu Cristo que demuestra como el ángel vino a los pastores et díxoles como era nacido, et otro si de su aparecimiento como le venieron los tres reyes adorar, et de la resurreccion que demuestra como fue crucificado et resurgió al tercer dia. Tales cosas como estas que mueven a los homes a facer bien et haber devocion en la fe facerlas pueden: et demas porque los homes hayan remembranza que segunt aquello fueron fechas de verdat; mas esto deben facer apuestamiente et con grant devocion et en las cibdades grandes do hobiere arzobispos o obispos..."

8. See Josep Romeu Figueras and Hermengildo Corbató for ample information about the evolution of the *auto sacramental* in Catalonia.

performance space, serving to convert or reaffirm the faith of the public.

Besides religious theater, other paratheatrical manifestations of religious doctrine were also vital to the early development of theater in Spain. The sermon, for example, demonstrated theatrical characteristics simultaneously with the delivery of its message. In "Drama in Sermons: Quotation, Performativity, and Conversion in a Middle English Sermon on the Prodigal Son in a *Tretise of Miraclis Pleyinge,*" Erick Kelemen affirms the dramatic nature of the sermon by highlighting the specific roles played by the preacher and the worshippers, noting that the ultimate goal was to convert the listener and sustain a belief (1). In addition to the obvious, Kelemen astutely mentions that the sermon and the drama also occupied the same stage (4), that is, that the performance of both events was presented in the church and presumably near or in front of the altar.[9] I would add that the likely need to rehearse a sermon further exemplifies its dramatic nature because such practice acknowledges a subsequent performance. Keleman continues by suggesting that the act of citation and quotation of characters in the Bible was actually a mimetic function (10), as the priest played the role of that person, and the act of giving a sermon was a form of speech act because the priest intended to convert the faithful. Though the study focuses on English medieval sermons, its relevance lies in illustrating how the sermon was a didactic instrument used by all religions to propagate faith.

Dramatic representations were not limited to the religious stage, as secular society also enjoyed various types of performances. Dialogued poetry was essentially dramatic as two interlocutors presumably read (i.e., performed) their assigned part of the poem. The troubadour tradition exhibited dramatic characteristics since the works were recited—or read aloud—to an audience. Street theater was also popular at the time. In fact, Bruce Burningham's book, *Radical Theatricality: Jongleuresque*

---

9. This is also true in Spain, although the performance of the *autos* was eventually moved out of the church because of space limitations; it was necessary to accommodate the growing public and provide an adequate performance space.

Performance on the Early Spanish Stage, argues that it was the popular performance tradition that helped to fill the gap and influence the theatrical conventions of early modern Spain. The fifteenth-century courtly festivals were also precursors to theater, displaying many dramatic characteristics: masquerade balls took on dramatic form as the participants arrived in disguise, while humorous one-act interludes, or *entremeses*, utilized actors and costuming, and tournaments brought together several theatrical aspects in magnificent spectacles. Alan Deyermond states that, starting around 1461, participants began to prepare and perform representations of historic battles during tournaments (367), which imply rehearsal, costuming, and role-playing. These examples, both religious and secular, ushered in a noticeable transformation in a nascent theatrical tradition

At the beginning of the sixteenth century, McKendrick suggests that most Spanish dramatists dabbled in two overlapping types of drama: the medieval-inspired one-act plays in the style of Juan del Encina's early works, and the humanistic plays made famous by Bartolomé de Torres Naharro (38-39). Normally, the church or municipal authorities commissioned the plays to celebrate religious holidays, but a secular variety, inspired by classical as well as mythological sources and usually patronized by nobles, also existed. These one-act works, didactic in nature, included singing and dancing, but provided little progression of the dramatic action. They were primitive and ritualistic in nature, reflecting their medieval roots. They consisted mostly of simple dialogues between rustic characters or biblical figures. They took advantage of the comic potential of language by interspersing wordplay and local dialects, especially Sayagués, a local dialect common to northeastern Spain.[10] Like the secular one-act plays, the multiple-act humanistic plays were didactic and drew inspiration from classical, Renaissance, and biblical sources. These were characterized by a more developed argument and intrigue was often a defining characteristic. Both models served as a strong

10. Charlotte Stern examines the veracity of the Sayagués and the characterization of the Sayago shepherd in her article "Sayago and Sayagués in Spanish History and Literature."

foundation for the behemoth that was to become the Spanish dramatic tradition.

Due to his influence and contributions to the popularity of the art form at the end of the fifteenth century, Encina (1469-1529) is often recognized as the father of Spanish theater. He wrote at least fourteen and perhaps fifteen eclogues modeled after those of Virgil, a form that was familiar and intelligible to his courtly audience. Encina's work displays a shift from religious to secular theater: medieval themes inspired his early works while the literary humanism of Rome influenced his later plays. Not only was Encina influenced by his visits to Italy, but Joseph E. Gillet suggests that he also was influenced by his contemporary—and rival—Bartolomé de Torres Naharro ("Torres and the Sixteenth Century" 466). A later, humanistic play, *Égloga de Plácida y Vitoriano* (1493) emulated Torres Naharro's style by presenting an introit related to the play and introducing more modern subject matter. Encina's experimental later works, however, were not as well received by the court as his enormously popular earlier plays, but now scholars recognize them as his best pieces. In addition to offering a dramatic model for subsequent playwrights to follow, Encina influenced later dramatic traditions by presenting a variety of characters from all social classes. He elevated the artistic level of the courtly and religious dramas, bringing life to a previously dull and stagnant genre. By tracking his progression as a playwright, one clearly sees how the drama was growing out of the Middle Ages into the Renaissance, and Encina's work serves as the basis for all Spanish theater that would follow. Encina's imitators became plentiful during the first half of the sixteenth century; they included Pedro Manuel de Urrea (a.k.a. Ximénez de Urrea), Fernán López de Yanguas, Sebastián Horozco, and Diego Sánchez de Badajoz, all of whom helped to develop a strong dramatic tradition in Spain by writing numerous plays.

Two other important dramatists at the turn of the fifteenth century are Lucas Fernández (1474-1542) and Gil Vicente (1465-1537?). Fernández's work was characterized by its display of powerful theatricality, especially in *Auto de la pasión*, a play that anticipated the *comedia de santo* (Suárez-Galbán 15) and was the first play to deal with the theme of religious conversion (Wilson and Moir 31). Fernández was also the first to introduce the role of the *barba*, or comic old man, to Castilian theater in *Comedia de Bras-Gil y Berenguello* (Wilson and Moir 30). Vicente wrote for the royal court of Portugal and was arguably the most brilliant poet of the time. He wrote theater in Portuguese, Castilian, or a combination of both. Vicente's work gave a glimpse into the future, demonstrating the grandeur of the later Spanish theater. Like many of his contemporaries, Vicente dabbled with original themes and a novel use of language, as he wrote several types of comedy: rustic, moral, farcical, allegoric fantasy, and sentimental. McKendrick admires Vicente's genius, noting that he had great technical skills as a poet and dramatist (26) and wrote virtually *ex nihilo* (20), but she also suggests that his work lacked profound dramatic sensibility since he was tethered by the whims of his patron (26). His contributions included the dramatization of narrative materials (e.g., Tragicomedia de *don Duardos)* and the use of high lyric in a country setting, both of which previewed the *comedia nueva.*

One more dramatist guiding Spanish theater out of the Middle Ages was Torres Naharro (c.1485-1520), who wrote much of his work during his extended stay in Italy. Heavily influenced by the Italians' well-established theater and fixation on theory, Torres Naharro attempted to import Italian dramatic precepts to Spain. In addition, he showed a keen sense of the needs of the public and developed a relationship between the performance and the audience. He was a man before his time in that Spain was not ready for his modern dramatic stylings—the same holds true for Encina, whose later works were not well received by the Spanish public—evidenced by the fact that his plays were not performed there; nonetheless, he did gain exposure and his popularity in Spain was manifested by numerous printed editions of his complete works, the *Propalladia*, which will be discussed in Chapter 2.

The arrival of Italian popular theater to Spain and its welcoming public further provoked change in all theatrical aspects, both on and offstage. At first, the audiences were comprised largely of Spaniards who had lived in Italy, but as dramatic texts, adaptations, and translations arrived with more frequency, Italian style became more commonplace and the public itself diversified. The Italian playwrights were good dramatic craftsmen who had a mixed repertoire, from the religious *autos* to the schematized *Commedia dell'Arte*. On the boards, the Italians introduced trapdoors and machines as standard properties, and they imitated the convention of dressing actresses up as men. Their economic influence, however, was even greater than that of their stage innovations, because it was at the box office where the Italians had the greatest impact. It was common practice in Italy to charge admission to see the shows, which essentially democratized the theater by opening it to whoever could pay the price of a ticket. Spanish entrepreneurs recognized this market potential and began to build permanent theaters, bringing in roving troupes to perform. The financial possibilities were recognized not only by businessmen but also by *cofradias*, which began to emerge in the middle of the sixteenth century. These charitable brotherhoods funded poor hospitals from the profits of the theaters that they owned, a practice endorsed by the municipalities too, since they did not have to foot the bill for the productions.

As the sixteenth century progressed, Spanish theater encountered new influences and challenges as it became a commercialized art form. Drama had been primarily reserved for private consumption in the courts or for ritualistic purposes in the Church, but it was soon liberated from such confining spaces and began to emerge as a public form of entertainment. Playhouses were constructed to accommodate the increasingly growing public, as admission was granted to anyone who could pay. This new era opened the curtains for further experimentation as the theater reflected the need to appease the new and different public.

Lope de Rueda (c.1509-c.1565) was an actor and playwright, whose entrepreneurial spirit as a theater manager also influenced early modern theater (McKendrick 43). One of the first theater owners in Spain, he grasped the importance of offering theater to a diverse public. Rueda's theaters not only staged his own plays but also those of others. In an attempt to fulfill the entertainment needs of the public, he experimented with previously untried styles and exploited any subject matter to produce works that often combined base humor and stylish Italian elements. The theater of Lope de Rueda was not stilted and therefore held great appeal for the public because of its familiar topics and language. Although he wrote all sorts of plays, his *pasos* won the admiration of the general public and, most notably, of Miguel de Cervantes as they clearly influenced his *entremeses*. The *pasos* were humorous short sketches that mixed a vast range of comic elements and everyday language into an appealing dramatic form that was simple, yet simultaneously vigorous. The physical humor and clever word play of the *pasos* offered great comic potential despite their relatively simple plots and undeveloped characters.

Another popular form was the school drama. The Jesuits used these didactic plays for moral and rhetorical instruction. Due to the vast wealth of the church, no expense was spared in the costuming and staging of these performances. Neighboring schools even held competitions that were reminiscent of the drama contests in classical times. These allegorical plays celebrated Jesuit ideology but also demonstrated flexibility within a closed dramatic genre because the plays had to appeal to the public's desire to be popular. It may also be surprising that school dramas typically utilized tragicomic form, since one would expect that the classical tragic models would better stir the audience. McKendrick points out that the effect of the school drama on the theater-going public presents an interesting paradox: while it prepared the public for the religious and doctrinal theater of the *comedia*, at the same time it created and educated an audience for commercial theater (52). The irony is clear since it was often the Jesuits who censored the *comedia* in later years, though they helped to create the form.

In response to the popularity of the new, commercialized theater and its earthy humor, a movement to revitalize and cultivate the classical tragic mode was initiated during the 1570s. Though these Neo-tragedians did not strictly adhere to classical precepts, they did find inspiration in the moralizing and terror-evoking theater of Seneca, and the more contemporary Giovanni Battista Giraldi. Their plays presented contemporary themes in a Neoclassical style. Their lasting contribution to Spanish theater was establishing dramas that were written in verse. The works exuded a sense of respectability due to their historical and legendary subject matter, but the genre was not too popular because the playwrights had difficulty balancing art and entertainment. Furthermore, the Neo-tragedians tended to write for an all but nonexistent audience as much of the public did not support the stilted, somber form. This movement was based in

Valencia and was represented by Andrés Rey de Artieda and Cristóbal de Virués, for example, but other Neo-tragedians were found throughout the Iberian Peninsula, including the Galician Dominican monk, Jerónimo Bermúdez, and Cervantes from Madrid. Lope visited Valencia a number of times, and the result is that his contact with the Valencian Neo-tragedians impacted his theater.

Cervantes had always been influenced by the theater and yearned to be a serious playwright. He championed the classical tragic precepts and wrote the stunning *El cerco de Numancia* (1580s), one of the finest Spanish tragedies ever written. Cervantes's attempts at writing *comedias* were not, however, successful and he finally acknowledged in the prologue to *Ocho comedias y ocho entremeses* that he had not enjoyed great success as a playwright and ceded the proverbial crown to Lope: "[d]exé la pluma y las comedias, y entró luego el monstruo de naturaleza, el gran Lope de Vega, y alzóse con la monarquía cómica" (III r). Cervantes does not, however, cede all of the laurels to Lope, taking credit for introducing the three-act play, the personification of abstract concepts, and the use of national themes (III r); claims that may be justified on the commercial stage, but are misguided within the history of Spanish theater

On the cusp of Renaissance and Baroque theater is Juan de la Cueva (1550-1611), a dramatist torn between a strong humanist education and a desire to produce popular theater. This ambitious playwright wrote the dramatic treatise *Ejemplar poético* to document his achievements in the introduction and evolution of the *comedia nueva.* He was an important figure in the theater at the end of the sixteenth century and though overshadowed by Lope, his contributions are nonetheless significant. Cueva's innovations and dramatic theory will be discussed in detail in the next chapter.

The Baroque period of the Spanish Golden Age began towards the end of the sixteenth century when Lope de Vega (1562-1635) began to produce poetry, prose, and theater. In *Versions of Baroque: European Literature in the Seventeenth Century*, Frank Warnke defines the Baroque as a literary period "in which underlying, shared spiritual preoccupations find expression in a variety of stylistic and thematic emphases" (9). The *comedia* characterized Baroque artistic sensibilities and offered a means of escape from the confusion of everyday life, while at the same time reinforcing the conservative social climate of sixteenth- and seventeenth-century Spain. Duncan Moir, in *The Golden Age: Drama 1492-1700, A Literary History of Spain,* posits:

> The Spanish *Comedia* of the seventeenth century, a neat and satisfying art-form which could be the vehicle for many different kinds of plays, was the ultimate result of technical and poetic experimentation carried out by many dramatists in the late sixteenth. But the basic characteristics ... were fixed and established as norms because they became the practice of one prodigiously successful dramatist, Lope de Vega Carpio. (53)

While in the past, many scholars attributed the invention of the *comedia* to Lope, a brief exploration of the history of early modern Spanish theater demonstrates that there were numerous other precursors that also helped mold the dramatic form. Without a doubt, it is Lope who made the *comedia* the national theater of Spain, a fact substantiated from extant, contemporary statements by both supporters and detractors alike, but Lope did not, however, invent the *comedia*; rather, he reintegrated art into the form. In a 1624 letter to Antonio Hurtado de Mendoza, he readily admits that the form existed before he started writing, but it was without style and talent:

> Necesidad y yo partiendo a medias
> El estado de versos mercantiles,
> Pusimos en estilo las *comedia*s.
> Yo las saqué de sus principios viles,
> Engendrando en España más poetas
> que hay en los aires átomos sutiles. (401)

A prolific writer, Lope produced masterpieces in all literary genres at an extraordinary pace, and although attacked by many critics, he was adored by even more admirers of his work. Lope de Vega's influence on Spanish theater will be discussed in Chapter 3.

The followers of Lope, aptly named *Lopistas*, numbered among some of the most famous playwrights of the Spanish Golden Age. Tirso de Molina (1584-1648) was a monk whose moral and religious plays dominated the stage along with those of

Lope in the early 1620s. His works were intellectual and psychological, with a certain hard-hitting directness that inflamed critics. Tirso was a strong supporter of the *comedia nueva* and in the *Cigarrales de Toledo* he staunchly defends the style and innovation of the new form. Tirso's contributions and works will be explored in Chapter 3 along with Lope de Vega's. Other well-known *Lopistas* include Guillén de Castro (1569-1631), a playwright famous for his elegant, albeit often misogynistic, historical *comedias*; Antonio Mira de Amescua (1574-1644), whose plays often questioned the social codes of contemporary times; Luis Vélez de Guevara (1579-1644), a courtier and *converso* best known for his frequent use of stage machinery in his plays; and Juan Ruiz de Alarcón (1580-1639), a Mexican dramatist, scorned by his contemporaries primarily because of his roots in the Spanish colonies and a physical handicap, who manifested his reciprocal contempt in his plays by sharply criticizing the social pretensions of the Spanish noble class.

Women also wrote dramas during the seventeenth century, but their production and success were constrained by the patriarchal society of Spain and its colonies. The female playwrights can be divided into two categories: the affluent women that occupied the courts (María de Zayas y Sotomayor, Ana Caro de Mallén Soto, Leonora de la Cueva, for example), and the nuns that wrote from the convent (Sor Marcela de San Félix and Sor Juana de la Cruz). Their works seemed to follow established conventions—both theatrical and societal—but at the same time were often subversive. They questioned the boundaries imposed upon women in terms of intellectual creativity and interrogated the patriarchal structure of society. They commonly put the female characters at the forefront of the argument and inverted gender roles. Their theater was unique. In *Dramas of Distinction*, Teresa S. Soufas demonstrates how it should be considered on its own terms and not compared to the works of their male contemporaries. Though its influence was miniscule compared to that of their male counterparts, the importance of woman-authored literature is apparent.[11]

---

11. Scholarship dealing with the women playwrights of Spain—and Mexico, in the case of Sor Juana—is plentiful and the subject continues to interest

The theater of Pedro Calderón de la Barca (1600-1681) marked the pinnacle of early modern Spanish theater. Calderón not only reelaborated, reinvented, and revised earlier plays, but he also wrote some of the greatest works in Spanish literary history. His plays were intellectual and metaphysical and his characterizations set him apart from his contemporaries, who mainly concentrated on the dramatic action. A careful craftsman, he utilized flawless versification to explore such topics as free will and honor. Many of Calderón's plays had open endings since he chose to explore life's dilemmas, but he did not attempt to solve them; his plays inspired contemplation about one's situation in the world. Like Lope, Calderón inspired a school of dramatists who attempted to emulate his style and artistic ability. Calderón's most famous disciples included the unconventional and dramatically daring Francisco de Rojas Zorrilla (1607-1648), the witty and stylish Agustín Moreto y Cabaña (1618-1669), though the majority of these playwrights could not approximate Calderón's greatness.

Dramatic trends changed drastically in the 1640s. The state sporadically shuttered the *corrales* for long periods of times due to military action or periods of royal mourning; the court performances were also limited greatly. This closure, which ended in 1651, essentially signaled the end of the heyday of the *comedia*. That same year, Calderón took religious vows and dedicated himself to writing only *autos* and court drama. Many other playwrights also abandoned writing scripts for the *corrales* since composing court plays promised bigger paydays and more creative freedom. Indeed, theater was still an important factor in Spanish

---

Hispanists. Critical articles abound in several excellent collections of essays that dedicate at least a section to these women writers. For example, part two, "Taking the Woman's Part", of Anita K. Stoll's and Dawn L. Smith's *The Perception of Women in the Spanish* Comedia, contains three articles by Teresa S. Soufas, Constance Wilkins, and Daniel Heiple that deal with Ana Caro and María de Zayas. The same editors' *Gender, Identity, and Representation in Spain's Golden Age*, also includes a section, "Women Representing Women," with articles by Soufas, Catherine Larson, Sharon D. Voros, Yvonne Jehenson, and Marcia L. Welles. Joan Cammarata's *Women in the Discourse of Early Modern Spain* includes studies by Fredrick A. de Armas and Monica Leoni, as well as a section titled "Transforming Literary Conventions: Feminine Aesthetics and Gender Norms," with articles by Deborah Compte, Susan Paun de García, and Lisa Vollendorf.

society, but the new plays performed in the *corrales* were generally lower quality than those staged during the first half of the century.

One notable exception was Francisco Antonio Bances de Candamo (1662-1704), another disciple of Calderón and the last notable playwright of the seventeenth century. As the court dramatist for Charles II, Bances closed the curtain on the theater of the Spanish Golden Age as the last of its important playwright-theorists. Although the *comedia* had already been established as the dramatic form of choice, it was, nevertheless, the subject of controversy—especially by the Jesuit priests Ignacio Camargo and Gonzalo Navarro Castellanos, who mainly challenged the morality of the theater. In an attempt to legitimize and defend modern *comedias*, Bances wrote his dramatic treatise, *Theatro de los theatros*, which is examined in detail in Chapter 4.

The attacks on the theater that Bances faced were nothing new; dramatists and theorists alike had maintained a passionate and arguably abusive dialogue criticizing and defending innovations on the stage. Such volatile and vehement commentary, however, was not unexpected since the dramatic tradition had changed so drastically and become so important to the Spanish culture. The next section gives an overview of the tension between the supporters of innovation and the defenders of tradition, as well as of those who took a neutral stance.

II. The changing nature of theater criticism and dramatic theory during the sixteenth and seventeenth centuries.

Clear references to dramatic conventions in Medieval Spain revealed that dramatic theory was not non-existent. These allusions to theater and performance appear in a variety of texts, both obscure and well-known, including royal edicts, dictionaries, liturgical writings, letters, and prologues to other literary works. The search for examples of dramatic theory from the Spanish Middle Ages can prove challenging: although theatrical conventions are mentioned in some medieval treatises, it is clear that the drama was not a dominant art form. In fact, some scholars contend it was not even considered art at all, and others treat the Middle Ages as a transitory period between the narrative and dramatic traditions, with the troubadour tradition, so prominent in Castile, serving to sate the public appetite for dramatic representation.[12]

As theater gained momentum during the sixteenth century with the works of Encina and his contemporaries, concrete dramatic criticism began to surface. Acceptance of the evolving art form was mixed, and interestingly enough, both positive support and negative criticism stemmed from essentially the same source: while enthusiasts of the evolving form applauded the innovation and divergence from classical forms and formulas, its detractors scorned those very same changes.

The first clear example of Spanish dramatic theory is found at the beginning of the Spanish Renaissance. The *Prohemio*, or prologue, to Torres Naharro's *Propalladia*, published in 1517, clearly inspired by Italian models, revisited and rewrote established classical precepts while simultaneously offering new ideas to a nascent Spanish dramatic tradition. Torres Naharro saw drama as an art form distinct from lyric or epic poetry and offered the *Prohemio* as both a descriptive and prescriptive treatise of his new dramatic theory. He laid a foundation of dramatic theory that was to be expanded and dramatically changed a century later by Lope and others.

Cueva also supported a reinvention of what the theater did, and he wrote various treatises dealing with the form. The poem *El viaje de Sannio* (1585) suggests six types of poetry and specifically contrasts comedy and tragedy; the former was characterized by life and harmony as opposed to the death, and the latter exemplified discord (107-08). Three years later, in "Epístola dedicatoria a Momo," found in the *Primera parte de las comedias y las tragedias* (1588), Cueva claimed that comedy deserves as much praise as tragedy because of its imitation of real life. He continued with a spiteful, but soon to be common, notion that critics of the new form were simply ignorant (6-8). Cueva's *Ejemplar poético* (1606) is arguably the first original statement of literary precepts written in Spanish. A contemporary of Lope, he was not as well-

12. Bruce Burningham addresses the anomaly of the apparent lack of secular theater in Spain during the Middle Ages. He convincingly argues that it was the popular performance tradition that helped to fill this gap.

known as his counterpart; nevertheless, his innovative theater and dramatic theory also impacted the dramatic landscape of the sixteenth and seventeenth centuries. Since Cueva wrote the *Ejemplar poético* late in his career and during the heyday of Lope's *comedia*, many have speculated that he composed the treatise to take credit for some of the innovations instituted on the stage at the time. He also wrote *Los cuatro libros de los inventores de las cosas* in 1608, which detailed the history of the *comedia*, describing its origins, its practices, and the importance of decorum across time.

Other proponents of the *comedia* fervently defended the new dramatic art form, praising its innovative nature, criticizing its detractors, and highlighting its imitative tendencies. Nearly all of its supporters mentioned how playwrights had recognized the need for change to accommodate the desires of Spanish contemporary audiences. The public's expectations had transformed; audiences tended to prefer more modern theatrical pieces since classical works did not appeal to their seventeenth-century sensibilities.

Starting with Cueva, supporters of the *comedia* rebutted the attacks of detractors by suggesting that these critics were uninformed regarding theatrical trends and unwilling to accept change. Protectors of the new form espoused the ideas that since no aesthetic principle possessed absolute authority, contemporary poets were not bound by them that change was inevitable, and that it was impossible to hold on to the past, especially when referring to such a dynamic art form as the theater.

Many critics and playwrights praised the imitative character of the *comedia* and its integration of contemporary situations, which produced a more enjoyable theater. Since the public demanded change from classical models, it was necessary to introduce familiar subject matter. Juan Rufo was a strong supporter of the comedy and *pasos* of Lope de Rueda and admired his ability to move obstinate audiences. In the prologue to *Comedia de Sepúlveda* (1597), Lorenzo de Sepúlveda commented that most detractors of the comedy were "gente de tan bajo entendimiento" and unwilling to accept change, though it was inevitable because "en esta profesión no puedan ganar premios con las extrañas conteniendo en semejante materia con ellos" (15). He noted that comedy was esteemed in the past, and asked why it was disparaged during the sixteenth century (15-16).

Luis Alfonso de Carvallo's play *Cisne de Apolo* (1602) praised drama as the most noble manifestation that could be written by a poet (qtd. in Sánchez Escribano 115), and exalted the *comedia* for its realistic imitation of life: [...] la comedia es una imitación de la vida, espejo de costumbres, imagen de verdad, [...] (qtd. in Sánchez Escribano 115). Various forms of drama are explained in this example of metatheater. Such self-referentiality is not the only innovation adopted by *Cisne*, but the play followed new trends including a three-*jornada* structure, and a *loa* that was unrelated to the play, indicating confidence in the public as knowledgeable theatergoers. Agustín de Rojas's laudatory *Loa de la comedia* (1603) praised the didactic nature of the *comedia*, suggesting that the introduction of noble characters to the form was an honor instead of a disgrace (qtd. in Sánchez Escribano 120). In *Segunda parte de la vida del pícaro Guzmán de Alfarache* (1604), by Juan Martí, the power of laughter was said to "Limpiar el ánimo de las pasiones por medio del deleite de la risa" (208). Following decorum was also suggested to avoid ridiculous plays, and there was also mention of the *gracioso* as separating the Spanish *comedia* from their Greek and Latin predecessors (45).

Another supporter, Cristóbal de Mesa, wrote in "A Juan de Velasco, Condestable de Castilla" in *Rimas* (1611) that though ancient poets produced great works, the contemporary audience did not desire past forms because they were not appropriate for the modern man, who was simple and easily confused: "[a]gora ya la simple gente moza /de Aristóteles hace poco caso, / y todo lo confunde y lo destroza" (qtd. in Sánchez Escribano 167). His was not an uncommon stance, as many playwrights and critics expounded upon the ignorance of the *vulgo* but also recognized the importance of pleasing those who buy the tickets. Mesa goes one step further by grouping many critics with the common man, calling them all ignorant (a notion repeated by Lope in numerous letters) (qtd. in Sánchez Escribano 167).

The most famous treatise defending the *comedia* is the *Arte nuevo de hacer comedias* by Lope, who was vocal in his support for the emerging dramatic form. Written during the years 1604-08, and published in 1609, it remains one of the most important documents in Spanish literary history. The piece authorized the *comedia* in its response to questions posed by the Madrid Academy concerning the legitimacy of the dramatic art form. A detailed examination of Lope's influence on the theater and the public's sway over the artist will be discussed in Chapter 3 along with a study of Tirso, a strong proponent of the *comedia* and of Lope. A great playwright in his own right, he staunchly defended the *comedia* in *Cigarrales de Toledo* and *El vergonzoso en palacio*.

By recasting traditional models and adding modern twists, successful dramatists produced, according to the seventeenth-century dramatic poet Ricardo de Turia, a noble dramatic genre (177). Ricardo de Turia espoused the *comedia* in *Apologético de las comedias españolas* (1616) where he constructed a convincing defense of the new theatrical form calling it a noble genre and noting that the controversial practice of mixing classes has always been present in theater: "[y] los españoles no han sido inventores deste mixto poema… que muy antiguo es, […]" (qtd. in Sánchez Escribano 149), and mentioning works by Sophocles and Aristophanes. He also stated that the playwright should aim to please the contemporary audience, not the ancient one since "estas comedias no se han de representar en Grecia ni en Italia, sino en España, […]" (qtd. in Sánchez Escribano 151). At the end of the treatise, Turia recognized the importance of performance and how it was a separate notion that is not necessarily included in the script:

> Con todo no se las aseguro feliz, por ver que no es un mismo contraste el que quilata en el teatro y el que califica en la impresión; no todo lo representable tiene esplendor impreso, ni todo lo impreso ilustra al que lo recita. (qtd. in Sánchez Escribano 153)

Guillén de Castro offers similar support in *El curioso impertinente* (1618) applauding the *comedia* for its novelty, innovation, and the importance that it gave to the audience (205). Esteban Manuel de Villegas' satirical "Elegía VIII" from *Las eróticas o amatorias* (1617), personified the spirit of the *comedia nueva*, praised the *Propalladia* for initiating a change in theater (qtd. in Sanchez Escribano 159) and urged young playwrights to write *comedias* because it was the new, important art form that appeals to the masses:

> Juventud castellana, ya ¿qué temes?
> Yo te prometo honor: suda y escribe,
> que Apolos hay acá con quien te extremes.
> Deja el latinizar, que ya no vive
> sino sólo en la pluma del germano,
> por ser su idioma bárbaro y caribe. (qtd. in Sánchez Escribano160).

These rousing verses exemplify that the dramatic poet should no longer model his creation on classical traditions but rather the contemporary norms.

In 1617, the *comedia* and Lope were subject to a vicious attack by Pedro de Torres Rámila in *Spongia.* No copies of the treatise exist as it is believed that Lope and his supporters destroyed them all. This attack prompted a rebuttal entitled *Expostulatio Spongiae* (1618) by Alfonso Sánchez de Moratalla. He adopted a similar perspective as that in the *Arte nuevo* asserting that nature dictates change and a static world is unthinkable. He praised Lope, stating that he had surpassed the greatness of his predecessors and is the founder, creator, and master of the *comedia* (qtd. in "Ideas" Menéndez y Pelayo 307).

The ambitious and scholarly *Invectiva a las comedias que prohibió Trajano y apología por las nuestras* (1622), written by Francisco de Barrera, maintained that the *comedia* was the perfect synthesis of ancient forms and contemporary styles and a fitting response to the new appetites of the public. He cited classical theater by noting that Terence and Plautus were innovators in their time, so it was to be expected that there was originality in the contemporary theater. Furthermore, he stated:

> [N]o basta para su duración el nombre de leyes o preceptos, pues no ha ninguno a quien haya dado privilegios de eternidad de tiempo…. (qtd. in Sánchez Escribano 225)

So, no system of precepts was permanent. Similarly, the *Nueva idea de la tragedia antigua* (1633) presented the opinions of Jusepe Antonio González de Salas that as tastes and styles changed with the times, no aesthetic principle possessed absolute authority and contemporary poets were not bound by them (5-6). Success guided the art form, though the ability to move the public depended on clear and intelligible enunciation of content and emotion (176). González praised Cueva's fusion of the new with the old. Bances, too, was often attacked by critics, and though the *comedia* had already enjoyed a long and successful run as the national theater of Spain, it was still assaulted—and insulted—by numerous detractors, especially the clergy. He wrote his dramatic treatise, *Theatro de los theatros* (1689-94) from a defensive posture in response to these criticisms.

Support for the *comedia* came from the religious sector, too, and the laudatory treatises written by priests at the end of the seventeenth century merit special attention. The 1682 document *Aprobación del reverendo Padre Fray Manuel Guerra y Ribera a la verdadera quinta parte de Calderón* applauded the dramatic form in general and especially acclaimed Pedro Calderón de la Barca. Guerra suggested that the dramatic form not be judged in sweeping and general terms, because there was no accounting for the taste of the critics nor of the playwrights. Guerra, referring to Calderón, affirmed that this "monstruo de ingenio," perfected the *comedia* because all of his works were good and virtuous (qtd. in Sánchez Escribano 324-25) and propagated the notion that the *comedia* was not bad if the rules were followed and if it revealed a doctrine that amazed and entertained an audience. Calderón, noted Guerra, was a genius who imitated nobody, who paved new roads without treading on old ones, but when he did revisit familiar subject matter, he improved on it. Guerra concluded by adding that even though Calderón produced a perfect art form in the *comedia*, his *autos sacramentales* were even more admirable, overshadowing their secular counterpart.

Padre José Alcázar included an elegy to Lope and Tirso in his *Ortografía castellana* (c. 1690), stating that since art is infinite, the classical playwrights only preceded contemporary poets chronologically, not intellectually or artistically. His work includes precepts on how to write a *comedia*, strong praise for the pioneering spirit of Lope and Tirso, and stronger criticism for the Spanish theater-going public, especially the *mosqueteros* (108-18).

José Pellicer de Tovar's *Idea de la comedia de Castilla* (1635) is another important treatise that served a dual purpose in the study of the *comedia*. This essay not only offered high praise for the art form but it meticulously examined the formation of the *comedia* and prescribed twenty precepts that should govern its creation.[13] Pellicer insisted that the *comedia* was one of the great contributions of Spain, noting that the worst Castilian poet was nonetheless a notable artist with regard to originality, style, and method (qtd. in Sánchez Escribano 265). His admiration extended even further towards Lope, who, he stated, had perfected the form (qtd. in Sánchez Escribano 264).

Although it was often an illiterate, impressionable, and uncontrollable mob, the public's ever-increasing influence on the direction that drama would follow in the future was recognized by playwrights and critics alike. Embittered opponents of this transformation complained that since the *vulgo* could not grasp a literary theater, the art form had to be tempered to their level of comprehension. Conversely, others were concerned about the theater's effect on the gullible and impressionable public. Luis de Crespí de Borja exemplifed both concerns in his *Respuesta a una consulta sobre si son lícitas las comedias que se usan en España* (1649),[14] presenting the conflict faced by playwrights, who were obliged to write for an audience they did not particularly like. Numerous critics, such as Cristóbal de Suárez de Figueroa, centered their criticism on the fickle, rambunctious, and volatile behavior of the Spanish audiences (217). The playwright found himself stuck in the undesirable position of being dependent on the

---

13. The treatise has gained much attention from Sánchez Escribano and Porqueras-Mayo in *Preceptiva Dramática Española del Renacimiento y el Barroco* because it is "...una teoría detallada, sistemática y completa, de validez general" (364).

14. The text, which is preserved only in a seventeenth-century manuscript, is reproduced in Cotarelo y Mori's *Bibliografía de las controversias sobre la licitud del teatro de España*. The following citation is of particular interest because it summarizes Crespí de Borja's opinions with regard to the *comedia*:

> Qué es ver deshacerse un hombre en afectos de melancolía, ira y sentimiento por una muger, como si real y verderamente reinaran semejantes pasiones en los que las fingen á los ojos del vulgo, que miserablemente como incautas avecillas apetitosas de estos livianos fingimientos caen en la red sutil y engañosa que se teje de tantos vicios como se representan á sus ojos? (197)

unpredictable—and often hostile—entity that was the Spanish theater-going public.

At the end of the sixteenth century the departure from classical precepts preoccupied many classically influenced playwrights and critics, who found inspiration in traditional models and subject matter and were hesitant to accept and to promote new forms. Lupercio Leonardo de Argensola, for example, disapproved of the new trends seen in the theater and warned of their possible negative effect on the gullible public (71), insisting that classically modeled tragedy offered limitless didactic possibilities regarding the fragility of life (69). All critics did not share the opinions of Argensola and finally accepted the *comedia* as a valid art form.

The more moderate Alonso López Pinciano, also a backer of classical precepts, offered a flexible literary system in an attempt to harmonize and synthesize classical and contemporary literary theory.[15] His treatise, *Philosophia antigua* (1596), consisted of a series of humanist letters and dialogues, summarizing classical and modern (Italian Renaissance) literary theory as well as introducing Aristotle's *Poetics* to Spain for the first time. López Pinciano took a syncretic approach, stressing the moral teaching aspect of literature, and in relation to the theater, he suggested that a play should not risk boring the public in order to maintain rigid rules (49). He warned against copying the classical playwrights, suggesting in *Respuesta de don Gabriel a la epístola octava* that the storyline be changed so as not to copy classical drama (Fragment IV). He also recognized the impact of performance and the performers in the *Respuesta de don Gabriel a la epístola décimotercera*, noting how performance and gesture manifest drama (Fragment I). Though inspired by classical teachings, López Pinciano did understand the importance of adapting old standards to contemporary times. His work is not only commendable because of its erudition but also because of his sensible and judicious posture towards change.

---

15. Menéndez y Pelayo suggests that López Pinciano is the only humanist of the sixteenth century who presented a complete literary system, and, as one of the most influential literary theorists of early modern Spain, his contributions to dramatic theory are nevertheless–and undeservedly–overshadowed by those of Lope de Vega.

Cervantes was inspired by classical dramatic traditions and his literature revealed a skeptical attitude toward the changes to theater produced by the popularity of the *comedia*. Though he later retracted much of his criticism, hesitantly acknowledging the inevitable supremacy of the new dramatic form, Cervantes's stance regarding the innovative theatrical form was presented, often ironically, in his literature. A most ardent attack appeared in Book I, Chapter 48 of *Don Quijote*, whose commentaries by the *canónigo* are famous for their antagonistic views of the *comedia*. Referring to tragedies, the *canónigo* deftly noted that it was better to be praised by a few wise men than by the confused vulgate, whose members are lascivious and dense. He added that economic self-interest was to be blamed for the shift away from the classics: the culpable theater owners would rather earn money than present good drama, so the playwrights were not obliged to write high-quality drama. The *canónigo* also endorsed censorship of the plays before being presented to the public and he praised Rey de Artieda and Cervantes for remaining faithful to classical precepts. Such a tone of strong opposition changed to hesitant acceptance in *El rufián dichoso*, which acknowledged the inevitable transformation of all things across time and admitted that comedy was not bad, simply different (2.1.1229-32). In the play, the character *Comedia* admits that familiar tragic forms have been displaced by the *comedia*, a new style of theater that was unique in its combination of new and old styles (2.1.1241-51). Also, in the prologue to the same collection of plays, Cervantes withdraws from his anti-*comedia* campaign by accepting the preeminence of the dramatic form.

Suárez de Figueroa's criticism echoes that of Cervantes in his early years. It is in the *Plaza universal de todas ciencias y artes* (1615) that he deemed the new theater undesirable because it ignores "*arte*," referring to traditional style (189), and the rules of decorum. Similar negative commentaries were seen in Carlos Boyl's poem *A un licenciado que deseaba hacer comedias* (1617), Jacinto Polo de Medina's essay *Academias de jardín* (1630), and Álvaro Cubillo de Aragón's epistle *El enano de las musas* (1654). These works share a common preoccupation with the contemporary playwrights' conscious disregard for classical motifs and style.

Cascales offered a contradictory case, as he appeared at first to be an ardent critic of the *comedia* but later tempered his opinion, supporting Lope de Vega's *comedia*. His first treatise, *Tablas poéticas* (1617), was steadfast in its scorn for the *comedia*, offering no room for reworking or reconsidering the topic. The work, according to Sanford Shepard, represented an inflexible posture that only permitted opposition to the new dramatic form (158); but Epistle III, entitled "*Al Apolo de España, Lope de Vega. En defensa de las comedias y representaciones de ellas,*" written between 1613-17 (Barceló 232), and later published in *Cartas filológicas* (1639), reveals another side of the man: he emerged not as an enemy of the *comedia* but as a defender of Lope's national theater. In fact, the friendship between Cascales and Lope is well-documented; Lope praises his friend on two occasions, in *Laurel de Apolo* (1630), and in a sonnet in *Fama póstuma* (1636). Cascales's reversal brings into question the sincerity of his early attacks. Shepard suggests that his exaggerated and unyielding stance in *Tablas* regarding the *comedia* was a rhetorical strategy used to illustrate the unconventionality of the new form but it was not an indication of his tastes (181).

The subjective judgment of moral propriety was another obstacle that playwrights confronted in early modern Spain. Both the Church and the government controlled much of what the public saw, and the two institutions most often worked in unison. The theater was continually threatened by and subject to censorship and to closure by both the government and the church because, as Edward C. Wilson succinctly sums up: "the word spoken in public was always thought to be more scandalous than what might quite legitimately be read in private" ("Stage Censor" 170). Institutionalized censorship, enforced by the Spanish Inquisition, was a constant preoccupation of the playwrights in the sixteenth and seventeenth centuries. Claudio Sánchez Albornoz describes the Inquisition's chokehold on the culture as an uneasiness and fear caused by possible deviation from royal orthodoxy must have frustrated and stifled enthusiasm, fossilizing the intellectual spirit of the country (561). Miguel de la Pinta Llorente concurs, stating that the Inquisition cannot be defended because it asphyxiated intellectual growth (18). Besides the obvious result of prohibiting some works, this suppression further affected literary texts: the censors ordered changes to the original manuscripts; they would alter the scripts themselves; and they also controlled the premieres of a play. In conjunction with the Church, the government was instrumental in mandating norms of theater. Numerous decrees of the Council of Castile dictated theatrical practice, one example being the prohibition of women on stage in 1586.[16] In 1615, it was decreed that all public performances were subject to censorship; furthermore, all theaters were closed by the State at the time of royal deaths, most notably from 1646-49 to mourn the death of Prince Baltasar Carlos.

Impassioned resistance from the religious sector of Spanish society was common, although it is interesting that some major figures of the *comedia* themselves were clergy (Tirso and Mira de Amescua), or took vows later in life (Lope and Calderón). The opponents came from all orders, but many were Jesuits, which is surprising since the Jesuit school play was so influential during the sixteenth century in conditioning the public to subsequent theatrical trends. Camargo strongly opposed the *comedia*, questioning its morality but not its divergence from traditional precepts. His most scathing attack on the *comedia* was found in the *Discurso teológico sobre los teatros y comedias de este siglo* (1686), which included the following allegation regarding the *comedia*: "[l]os argumentos o asuntos de las comedias… son por la mayor parte impuros, llenos de lascivos amores, entretejidos de mil artificiosos enredos…" (qtd. in Sánchez Escribano 327). This extensive list of unfavorable characteristics continued, until he finally concluded by stating that the *comedia* was immoral despite its popularity .

The commentaries were not always so polemical by nature, often showing a more neutral stance. Not all commentators were adamant about taking one side or the other and many playwrights straddled the fence regarding their view of the *comedia,* integrating new trends into their works. Rey de Artieda, for example, found inspiration in the classics but also strayed from some of the rules. In the light-hearted tragedy *Los amantes* (1581), he includes comic

16. After this was repealed, women were allowed to act on stage under three conditions: they had to be married, they could not dress as men, and boys could no longer cross-dress.

aspects such as a *gracioso*-type character, as well as a hero of humble birth. Rey de Artieda defends his work in a letter addressed "Al ilustre señor don Tomás de Vilanova" (1581), stating that the play does retain some classical traits (e.g., everyone dies) and that although homage should be paid to the classics, it is important to introduce new ideas and concepts to entertain the public, also suggesting that the poet ought to look into the future as opposed to living in the past (67). A later work, *Discursos, epístolas y epigramas de Artemidoro* (1605), questioned the morality of actors and the liberties that they took both on and offstage but did not condemn the *comedia* as a genre because of the behavior of the actors who performed the plays. He did harbor some discontent towards Lope and the flexibility of the *comedia* in the *Epístola al Marqués de Cuéllar sobre la comedia* (1605).

Understanding that art is dynamic by nature, Virués also wrote tragedies following both classical and modern styles. His *Obras trágicas y líricas* (1609) was comprised of seven works: three classically inspired tragedies and four plays that combined classical and modern styles. In the prologue to the *Tragedia de la cruel Casandra* (1609), Virués acknowledged the inevitable evolution that promised to transform the theater as a whole (qtd. in Sánchez Escribano 153), but he remained faithful to the classical tragic form. Feliciana Enríquez de Guzmán also synthesized innovation with classical practice. Addressing the readers in the *Primera parte de los jardines y campos sabeos* (1627), she defends her use of tragicomedy in the classical sense as a solution to her attempts to intermingle innovation and tradition (250-51).

Another critical path taken by some of the more moderate and less polemical critics was to clearly (re)define the dramatic genres and to insist that they remain separate. In *Poética de Aristóteles traducida de latín* (1623), Juan Pablo Mártir Rizo offered an outline of classical comedy, noting its generic differences, in all respects, from other theatrical forms (qtd. in Sánchez Escribano 226-27). Similarly, Antonio López de Vega proposed in *Heráclito y Demócrito de nuestro siglo* (1641), a classical explanation of dramatic, lyric, and heroic poetry, describing comedy as using plebian language, having a variety of social classes, and disregarding set precepts (qtd. in Sánchez Escribano 277). Like Mártir Rizo, López strove to avoid the adulteration of the genres, seeing them as separate and incompatible forms.

These representative examples of critical response to the theater illustrate the variety of drama criticism seen in early modern Spain. Such different reactions should not be surprising because change is always answered with varying degrees of support or criticism. While many remained unyielding in their principles, it is intriguing to see how others were more malleable and at least acknowledged the importance of the transformation of the theater. It is also noteworthy to see that criticism stemmed from both inside and outside literary circles, which signals the enormous impact of theater on society. It was an accessible art form enjoyed by all classes, who participated in helping to mold a new literary tradition.

III. The historical reception of performance, or, examining the stage from a public perspective

Throughout much of the last half of the twentieth century, critics often performed close readings of the written text, concentrating on the inner workings of the plays as literature. Although these explications proved revealing, they tended to downplay the fact that theater was originally meant to be performed. A number of recent critical studies demonstrate a shifting of perspective in the exploration of the Spanish *comedia* and other styles, leading to the study of audience reception and an interest in its performance.

Various models inform my theoretical approach to this study, though response and reception theory lie at its base. I examine not only the playwrights' contributions to the theatrical representation but also the ways in which other participants, including, actors, critics, censors, and audience, also help to effect change in drama. I use an eclectic approach which draws from several areas, both familiar and more obscure, with the intention of providing a cohesive and viable theoretical model that offers insight into the possible factors that affected Spanish theater in the past. It is my goal to approach early modern Spanish theater from a position that concentrates on performance and its effects on reception, all of which is encompassed within a historical context.

In order to begin to approach the theater of sixteenth- and seventeenth-century Spain from this perspective, I examine the past in a systematic manner, combining concrete evidence, in the form of extant commentaries, with theoretical approximations of possible audience reception and response. Jauss offers a useful model for allowing the critic to discuss the historical consciousness of the time: the horizon of expectations. He explains that all literature reflects its pre-texts and antecedents, which presupposes that each reader or spectator uses knowledge of those pre-texts to create a set of expectations about new works encountered, based on his/her experience with past examples in the same genre. Thus, by looking at both antecedent and contemporary works, one can formulate a hypothetical attitude of the public since the later text is presumably a response to previous texts (79).

For the purpose of this study, I utilize the first five principles offered by Jauss in his construction of an aesthetic of reception. The first two explain that the historicity and analysis of a work are formulated by preconceived notions based on comparison with previous works that the audience has already read or seen performed (21-22). History establishes the addressees' experience in relation to the work and remains an indispensable factor in its reception (19). Literary production evolves as it confronts previously established horizons of expectations. This "horizontal change" is measured by the distance between the horizon of expectations and the work: the closer the distance, the more familiar the work is, because it adheres to prescribed standards of taste; on the other hand, if the distance is too great, the work may not be appreciated or it may be considered incomprehensible. A middle ground, therefore, must be found so that a work is not only new but also recognizable. This leads to the third concept, which explains how the horizon of expectations allows one to determine the artistic character of a work according to the degree of its influence on a presupposed audience (24); also known as poetic effect, it is at its greatest when a genre has been established by a horizon of expectations that is then systematically shattered. A clear example is Cervantes's *Don Quijote*, a novel in which numerous literary styles are presented and recognized by the audience, only to be subsequently satirized by the author. Jauss saw an undeniable relationship between the text and the expectations of the audience regarding the reception of the work, and though a new style may be rejected or attacked at first, it may then be accepted as a turning point, or a new form, as it slowly becomes part of the ever-evolving horizon of expectations (26). For example, although the Spanish public did not espouse Encina's Italian-inspired *Plácida y Vitoriano* and they did not even see the plays of Torres performed, the new dramatic style soon became fundamental to theatrical convention.

Jauss's fourth and fifth principles demonstrate the application of the horizon of expectations to past literatures. The fourth tenet explains how the horizon of expectations allows us to get a glimpse of possible perceptions of a work:

> The reconstruction of the horizon of expectations, in the face of which a work was created and received in the past, enables one...to pose questions that the text gave answers to, and thereby discover how the contemporary reader could have viewed and understood the work. (28)

By looking at a historical context, foregrounding it within those parameters, one can begin to theorize the affective qualities of the text on the reader within the belief system of that society. For example, since many *comedias* interrogated the rigorous honor code of Spain during the seventeenth century, it is plausible to consider such a play a response to societal concerns. The dramatic poets of the Golden Age often addressed polemical contemporary issues, though sometimes in a disguised manner, when writing plays.

In the fifth theorem, Jauss suggests that the critic must also pay close attention to the literary work's position within history and indicates a continuum produced by a reactive chain of texts:

> The theory of the aesthetic of reception not only allows one to conceive the meaning and form of a literary work in the historical unfolding of its understanding. It also demands that one insert the individual work into its literary series to recognize its historical position and significance in the context of the experience of literature. (32)

This implies that the placement of a work within an historical frame allows it to be judged against the background of other works, and of everyday life, recognizing the significance of its context. Furthermore, Jauss states that the next work in the series can solve formal and moral problems left behind by the last work, presenting new problems in turn (33). New literary works are always striving to fulfill an intrinsic need in the public for novelty; moreover, as time progresses, the values of a society change and are reflected in its art. Jauss's work suggests a useful method for bridging the chronological gap separating past critical practice from current perspectives on the theater.

An interest in reader-response theory has extended into other genres, including theater studies, where it confronts even more variables than ever as audience-response theory. The fundamentals of reader-response theory can aid in formulating an accessible and practical approach to audience reception. One of the initiators of reader-response theory, Wolfgang Iser, suggested that texts were constructed by an implied reader through the phenomenon of reader response (107). The literary text provided a foundation from which the reader must construe meaning since the act of reading is interpretive. This approach easily lends itself to the analysis of audience reception, as the reader transforms into the spectator, which is a notion not only implied but necessary, as Carlson affirms in *Performance: A Critical Introduction*: "[p]erformance is always performance for someone…that recognizes and validates it as performance" (7). As the public reacts to a play and creates meaning, the resulting interpretation is susceptible to constant alteration since no two performances—and no two audiences—are the same. Consequently, the text is not "pure" since it is subject to factors outside the control of the reader, including the director, actor, and censor, who themselves react and alter the text.

Stanley Fish addressed the question of public reception and the collective nature of the audience, explaining that because the text itself was empty, it was the job of what he called the interpretive community to find meaning based on the group's own established codes and protocols (171). Fish assumes that communities that share the same goals and ideals will interpret a literary work in a similar manner; consequently, collective interpretation takes precedence over individual. These notions are also useful because they recognize the cohesiveness of a community and the sets of beliefs that govern interpretation. Fish's ideas lead to a basic understanding of theater because they underscore the importance of the public in the interpretation of a literary work, illustrating how an assessment of a text's reception complements a scrupulous examination of the text.

Susan Bennett formulates her theory of audience reception on a cultural model, emphasizing the interrelation between culture and theater and focusing on the material, or on-stage, conditions for the production and reception of theater as it is construed as cultural practice. Theater cannot be alienated from culture, because the public must identify with cultural clues in order to gain insight into the art form. For example, the beauty and style of Japanese Kabuki theater is recognizable to any spectator but it takes a familiarity with Japanese culture to truly understand the subtleties of the art form. Cultural markers must be established in order to pre-activate the expectations, or in Jaussian terms, the horizon of expectations, of the audience. Perhaps inspired by Fish's notion of the cohesiveness of an interpretive community, Bennett adeptly proves that an aesthetic code is culturally determined by noting that an audience may share a collective reaction and usually concur on what is good and bad. Her theoretical perspective primarily deals with subversive twentieth-century drama, an approach useful for this study, since the theater in early modern Spain could also be deemed as subversive. Bennett posits that theater is not monolithic, since the audience fulfills a thinking and acting role in the dramatic production (87). She illustrates her perspective by offering a two-part frame model (139) that intersects at the point where the audience's cultural understanding and theatrical experience meet: the outer frame represents theater as a cultural constant, consisting of the event, the selection of material, and audience expectations; the inner frame is the particular event itself, which includes production strategies, ideological overcoding, the on-stage condition of performance, and the spectators' experience of the staged world. The theater is tied to the audience on various levels, economic and performative, so new directions depend on the audience.

In the 2002 study "Framing, Decoding, and Interpretation: On the Spectator's Vital Role in Creating Theatrical Meaning," Rozik examines the spectator's role in the dramatic process, arguing that interpretation is a creative progression that generates meaning through the spectator's reception of a work. This process starts with the most basic step of framing a situation, which occurs before reading the text–or in this case, before going to the theater; it continues by decoding the text, an activity constrained by cultural convention; and finally arrives at interpretation, when the spectators reach beyond decoding signs and provide associations that originate in their cultural knowledge of contextualized domains (11-14). Interpretation takes place on various textual levels: icon, motif, and whole fictional world; it is a set of mental operations of specific rules performed by an addressee on a text. Rozik notes that these functions are performed by both director and spectator, both of whom become equal partners in the creation of a dramatic piece, as one complements the other: the director's creative interpretation affects—and is affected by—the spectator's response. It is the spectator who must determine the impact and the nature of each fictitious world. This approach complements Jauss's because it recognizes the importance of cultural orientation in the examination of audience reception (14, 21).

In *New Directions in Audience Reception*, Willmar Sauter emphasizes the need to incorporate performance theory into audience reception theory. Sauter claims that the study of audience reception has gained popularity because of recent advances in the tabulation of various factors concerning the audience: demographics, attitudes, preferences, etc. (5). Any theory of reception, he suggests, must include the performance, a series of possible interpretations always in front of an audience, and the spectator. It is essential to look for the interplay between these elements and to describe such interaction in theoretical terms. Reception theory has led us to critically discuss the transfer of artistic responsibility to the receiver of the spectacle, forming a symbiotic relationship; this was sensed by several astute playwrights who began to focus on the bidirectional collaboration with the public.

Performance theory can aid the exploration of the Spanish theater as it illustrates the ways in which performance can encode a textual message in action. This perspective may diverge from more conventional criticism of early modern Spanish theater, though it is not in opposition to it, since performance theory also recognizes the need to reconcile the past and the present. Jauss's view that the audience is an "energy formed by history" highlights the need to investigate the constantly changing horizon of expectations and resultant reception by audiences from all periods. Indeed, Peter Brook states that "meaning never belongs to the past" (12), emphasizing the evolutionary and dynamic nature of theatre.

Diamond defines performance both as the act of doing and as a thing done, encompassing numerous cultural manifestations on and off the stage. Although each instance is seen as a unique process, traces of previous performances always remain embedded in later ones (2), creating a bridge between the present and the past. She observes: "It is impossible to write the pleasurable embodiments we call performance without tangling with the cultural stories, traditions, and political contestations that comprise our sense of history" (1). Performance may produce interpretations that only partially depend on past experience; nevertheless, echoing Bennett's study, Diamond posits that an *a priori* knowledge is needed for full comprehension. In successful performances, a bridge of shared meaning allows the audience to understand the message of the text; perhaps the context is different from that originally intended, but it is intelligible. Such mediation allows for, and even enlists, the modification of language, creating the dichotomy of appearing familiar to the audience but at the same time new.

In "Drama, Performativity, and Performance," published in 1998, W. B. Worthen searches for a relation between the dramatic text and performance, challenging previous conventions of the authority of text over performance. He proposes that a performance is not merely a "reading, interpretation, realization *of* the text," but by inverting the conventional ideal of priority of text over performance, the text is understood as a consequence of the performance, whose power reflects the transformative nature of cultural transmission of textual and cultural meanings (1100-01). The dramatic representation unveils the social and behavioral practices of a specific point in time. That is to say, a performance may invoke the past, textually or historically; however, it also characterizes the text in the present context. Worthen echoes Joseph Grigley's comment by stating that "the fixedness of a text is as illusory as the fixedness of an interpretation; neither is final, neither is authorial" (1101), nor, I would suggest, authoritative. Following the logic of Worthen's and Grigley's theories on performance, we can better see how representation emerges as a key element in the transmission and negotiation of theatrical art and examine the ways in which texts survive throughout time.

If we recognize that the theater was originally intended to be performed, we invert the traditional notion that the written text dictates performance. In this performance-driven approach, the text is remembered by merit of being a subtext; it is the performance that completes the written text. The actualization of the script gives it life and meaning. In his 2006 study, *Teoría del teatro*, Santiago Trancón defines performance as a complex process that relies upon individual as well as collective creativity, and, I would add, public reception. Performance is, by nature, a privileged space for the creation, transformation, and combination of codes and signs of all types, all of which constitute theater (248). Referring to Calderón's works, Manuel Delgado eloquently describes the relationship between the performance and message as body and soul respectively, to demonstrate how performance embodies the intended message of the playwright (18-19), and, in a more modern context, that of the director. I suggest a similar but distinct conceptualization in the following physiological model to illustrate the proposed relation between text and performance: it may be helpful to look at the text of a dramatic work as a skeleton and the performance as the surrounding flesh. The written text structures the performance as the skeleton frames the body; nevertheless, the body may take on numerous shapes and forms apart from the basic structure afforded by the skeleton, as is the case with performance. If we approach performance from the "outside in", we see how the body covering the skeleton can exhibit an infinite number of forms, although we may discover the same textual structure as their basis. It does not make sense to judge the performance based solely on the skeletal text. One may look at the body and be able to have a good idea of the skeletal structure, but in looking at the skeletal structure it is nearly impossible to get an exact impression of the surrounding body. Kirsten F. Nigro develops a similar view of interdependence between the written and the performed text, explaining that it is impossible to represent a drama without a script; similarly, the script cannot be read and assimilated without recognizing its effects as spectacle. Nigro asserts, as do most performance critics, that no script is complete unto itself, which underscores the originality of the actualizations of that written text on stage (121). She recognizes the importance of the written text, but concludes that the final dramatic spectacle is the result of the combination of many components that supplement that text.

An approach utilizing performance theory can offer fresh insight to the study and appreciation of the theater. The reevaluation of the hegemonic relationship between the performance and the written text initiates a shift of textual authority. By surrogating the written text, performance propagates new ideas derived from contemporary culture. Therefore, performance is not an adulteration, but rather a proliferation, of the text. Many critics are concerned with the potential changes to the original text that can arise in performance, an anxiety not unique to the study of Golden Age Spanish theater. Jonathan Miller points out that some scholars believe that Shakespeare should no longer be performed at all, but he adds that Shakespeare permitted his own plays to be performed; consequently "there must have been something in his mind which saw [performance] as a preferred state of his work" (31). Miller also affirms that it is in the act of "going through the risks of ravaging and depredation that the immortality [of a play] is guaranteed" (36). Consequently, performance perpetuates the dramatic work and mutation and change are inevitable, especially since theater is a dynamic art form. Miller's comments on Shakespeare also apply to the *comedia* and other Spanish forms, and the newly spawned interest in adaptation of the plays illustrates the inherent vivacity that early modern theater in Spain possesses. A performance-driven approach to a specific play text can allow for multiple interpretations of the text because it evaluates all components of the performance and is receptive to its intrinsic subjectivity and evolutionary energy.

The essential relationship between performance and audience reception is undeniable, and it is difficult to imagine one without the other: the fact that a performance is virtually always destined for an audience illustrates the interdependence that the two phenomena share. Gladhart states that "When performance as event is emphasized, the observer of the event becomes not only an objective recorder of data but the necessary shaper of the data observed" (19). So the public is both *a part* of and *apart* from the performance. Gladhart's observation helps us to understand the inseparability of performance and audience: the performance is for the audience, and the audience must record (i.e., remember) and analyze the performance. The goal of this study is to examine the ways in which performance and audience reception influenced change in early modern Spanish theater, looking at the dramatic treatises of six prominent playwright-theorists and discovering how experience on the boards inspired a change in dramatic trends.

The next chapter discusses the innovative practices of two theater pioneers in sixteenth-century Spain: Bartolomé Torres Naharro and Juan de la Cueva. Both playwrights wrote during times of great transition. During an era when religious and street theater were extremely popular and predominant, Torres Naharro essentially brought dramatic theory to Spain from Italy and styled his work after Italian models. Cueva, too, was writing during a time of transition as Spanish theater found itself abandoning classical conventions and combining them with popular theater, eventually resulting in the *comedia nueva*, which would be the dominant form of theater until the mid-1600s. Both men documented their innovations, which were based on previous experience and the staging of them earlier in their careers.

CHAPTER 2: THE BEGINNINGS OF SPANISH DRAMATIC THEORY OF RECEPTION AND PERFORMANCE

The Renaissance in Spain was a period of great intellectual and literary growth that blossomed out of a synthesis of established medieval practices and a resurgence of interest in classical models. The theater in Spain was no exception. On the cusp between the fifteenth and sixteenth centuries, Spanish dramatic convention was characterized by the liturgical drama and jongleuresque performance, a practice that "encompasses a performative aesthetic and set of praxes that underpin a wide range of performance traditions" (Burningham, *Radical* 4). Changes to Spanish theater arose as several playwrights abandoned Spain for Italy, and, after finding themselves immersed in its rich—both economically and artistically speaking—and distinct dramatic tradition, brought back remnants of Italian dramas and theatrical trends, which they modified to fit the Spanish public's expectations.

This chapter examines the innovations and dramatic theory of two important playwright-theorists of sixteenth-century Spain: Bartolomé de Torres Naharro and Juan de la Cueva. Although they wrote during different eras of the sixteenth century, both men produced their works at the beginning of periods of great change in Spanish drama. Also, both were almost forgotten, Torres Naharro's work and precepts were swallowed up in a dramatic vacuum, and Cueva was overshadowed by the reputation of Félix Lope de Vega. In recent years, Torres Naharro has not received as much critical attention as his contemporaries Juan del Encina and Gil Vicente,[1]

---

1. Important critical studies were undertaken in the nineteenth century, see Leandro Fernández de Moratín and Marcelino Menéndez y Pelayo. At the beginning of the twentieth century, Joseph E. Gillet's monumental edition of the *Propalladia* (The first three volumes were published between 1943-51 and edited by Gillet; the fourth was published after Gillet's death in 1961 and edited by Otis H. Green), the collection of Torres Naharro's complete works still serves as a fundamental point of departure for any examination of the poet because of its thoroughness and rigorous intellectual commentary. More recent studies by John Lihani and Edward Malinak also have helped to unravel various questions about the dramatic innovations of Torres Naharro. Stanislav Zimic's extensive

and it is my intention to reopen a dialogue about his work. I examine the ways in which theatrical practice was influenced by performance and audience reception, and in turn shaped theatrical theory in Torres Naharro's *Prohemio* to the *Propalladia* and his *Comedia Ymenea*, exploring the interrelationship of theory and practice in early modern Spanish theater. Juan de la Cueva, too, has been mostly ignored by many scholars, having been eclipsed by Lope ever since the end of the sixteenth century. His work, nonetheless, also merits special attention because of its contribution to Spanish theater. Cueva was torn between a strong humanist education and a desire to produce popular theater, a conflict he eventually resolved by combining the two styles in his dramatic pieces. Writing at a time of transition at the end of the sixteenth century, this ambitious playwright wrote the dramatic treatise *Ejemplar poético* to document his perceived achievements in the introduction and evolution of the *Comedia nueva.* His dramatic works reflected the changing trends of Golden Age Spanish theater as a general shift from the tragic to the tragicomic mode occurred. Indeed, his *Comedia del infamador* was a precursor to the *Comedia nueva* and demonstrated innovations that resulted from his sensitivity to the desires of the public, conventions he outlined in his final dramatic treatise.

I. Torres Naharro's *Prohemio* to the *Propalladia*: the first Spanish dramatic treatise

Italian models and Renaissance thought clearly influenced Torres Naharro, and such a foregrounding of theory and practice began to influence Spanish theatrical trends. Due to his experience both on and offstage in Italy, he recognized the need to formulate and introduce precepts that addressed modern-day needs and concerns. More importantly, he became cognizant of critical tendencies not yet seen in Spain, which would prove paramount in

---

two-part study, "El pensamiento histórico y satírico de Bartolomé de Torres Naharro," questions many of Gillet's conclusions about the work of Torres Naharro, and demonstrates how Erasmus greatly influenced the poet.

inspiring his own formulation of a treatise of dramatic precepts.[2] Torres Naharro's conception of the important role of the spectator within the general dynamic of a dramatic spectacle affected his theater greatly; he played to the public's desires in an attempt to entertain and delight by using such strategies as integrating numerous languages into the play for comic effect and including familiar characters and locations. Furthermore, Torres Naharro wrote specific plays directed at particular publics: nostalgic plays for the multitude of expatriated Spanish audiences, historical accounts of military victories for the visiting Portuguese court, or socially conscious and moralistic plays for the general audience. The reality of having his plays performed on Italian stages led to the evolution of Torres Naharro as a dramatist,[3] and he was compelled to invent a new style not familiar to his Spanish counterparts. On March 26, 1517, Torres Naharro published the first edition of the *Propalladia*, a collection of theater and poetry. The collection was enormously popular, with an unparalleled nine separate editions—three outside of Spain—published in its first fifty years.[4] Due to its fame, the work did not escape the scrutiny of the Inquisition, who, in 1559, banned the *Propalladia* in the *Index Expurgatorio*, apparently for controversial content and characterizations in the constituent *comedias*; John V. Falconieri

---

2. Much has been written on Torres Naharro's adoption and adaptation of popular Italian trends to his theater, but to what extent remains controversial. Gillet, Zimic, Lihani, Donald McGrady, Othon Arroníz, and Miguel Ángel Pérez Priego recognize that Torres Naharro borrowed from styles and tendencies commonly seen in contemporary Italian theater but his plays still remained Spanish by nature. Marcella Salvi and Raymond Grismer describe his theater as a hybrid cultural product caused by the encounter of Spanish and Italian cultural contexts. N. D. Shergold and John V. Falconieri assert that the Italian influence is so prevalent in Torres Naharro's theater that it is logical to situate his dramaturgy within a purely Italian context.

3. Because of the established theatrical tradition in Italy, the theater-going public was generally familiar with classical and humanistic dramatic forms—not just the primitive plays prevalent in Spain at the time.

4. According to Gillet, the editions are as follows: 1517 Naples, 1520 Seville, 1524 Naples, 1526 Seville, 1533 Seville, 1535 Toledo, 1545 Seville, 1546-49 Antwerp, 1572 Madrid; he then states that the 1563 Madrid, 1573 Antwerp, and 1590 Madrid editions did not exist (*Propalladia* IV 440).

suggests that Spain was not ready for such a work (37). An expurgated edition was later published in 1572 in Madrid.

The *Prohemio*—or prologue—to the *Propalladia* is the first example of dramatic theory in Spanish.[5] Torres Naharro divided the preface into three parts: an introduction, an evaluation of classical theory, and an explanation of his own dramatic precepts. From the beginning, the document demonstrates an egalitarian character in its recognition of the plurality of classes in society. The first lines set a fatalistic tone for the text in their description of the laborious plight of the working man: “El pobre labradorcillo, por su fatal estrella encaminado desde los pueriles años para el litigio y largo contraste de la dura tierra” (1-3).[6] Being of humble roots, Torres Naharro sympathizes—or at least, empathizes—with the lower classes and the daily hardships they suffer. One should not overlook the mention of the working class at the opening of the treatise because it emphasizes the importance—and existence—of the *vulgo*, a group that was largely ignored in the past. Torres Naharro alludes to the simple and rustic nature of his art, stating that his are the fruits of labor of a poor working man whose only intention is to please and satisfy his public (10-11). These words suggest that he considered himself one of them, creating a sense of solidarity since he, too, is at the service of others and toils in his labors (12). Furthermore, by referring to himself as "ipse semipaganus" (13), Torres Naharro reveals his feelings of mediocrity among so many great scholars in Rome, considering himself semi-cultured and unable to shake off his brutish Extremaduran roots (Gillet, *Propalladia* IV 407-08). It is impossible to know whether this was an ironic rhetorical strategy, an attempt to ingratiate himself with the lower classes, or even something in between, but the relevance of Torres Naharro’s recognition of the lower classes proves important in his apparent attempt to cater to the whole audience, a factor that certainly affected his playwriting. When producing his plays, he is guided

5. It is actually one of the first examples of a prologue from the Spanish Renaissance. See Alberto Porqueras Mayo’s work on the prologue in the Spanish Golden Age.
6. All citations are from Gillet’s edition and refer to verse numbers; the text is found on pages 141-43.

by his own instincts. In fact, he compares himself to an inexperienced traveler lost on a frightful journey, entreating the public to accept his humble work for what it is: "si vuestra cortesía piadosamente no adoba lo que mi ignorancia presuntuosamente gasta" (13-14). No matter what affiliation the poet feels with the lower classes, his noble audience is firmly embedded as the primary receivers of the work. He never ignores his patrons and recognizes the need to please the "soberuias mercedes de los altos principes" (8). He attempts to form a relationship with the public by means of his humble attitude and direct address to the audience. He recognizes their station and his subservience to them, but at the same time he forms a relationship with them based on these differences. This introductory section concludes with another plea that the work be received well, although it may not be acceptable to his noble audience:

> Menos mal me ha parescido hazeros yo por mis manos este presente de cosa conoscidamente no buena, que esperar que por sus pies incorrectas y viciosamente a vuestra notice veniesse; mayormente que la más d'estas obrillas andauan y afuera de mi obediencia y voluntad. (20-24)

Torres Naharro suggests that weaknesses of the text are not his fault since the collection's composition was out of his control, presumably referring to the need to please the audience at all costs. This insecure attitude is a ruse. Indeed, it seems reasonable to believe that Torres Naharro is cleverly manipulating the reader by instilling in them a sense of superiority, his humility also appears contrived and a mere rhetorical device that was to become more popular in the early modern introit in which an actor (often the poet himself) sought to laud the virtue of the public. The suggestion of such false praise is corroborated by his habit of insulting the audience during the same prologue to the play.

Because he wrote and staged plays for a mixed audience, Torres Naharro demonstrated a sensibility not seen in earlier Spanish dramatists, one that emphasized the importance of audience reception in the success of a performance. His work had a more widespread character and its moralistic message targeted all classes. In "Play-Audience Relationship in Bartolomé de Torres Naharro," John E. Lihani, noting that a mixed audience attended the performances, divides them into two categories: the popular public, who was entertained by jokes at the expense of their patrons and moved by patriotic subject matter; and the distinctive, elite audiences, who were more interested in fantastic stories and faraway locations (95). Devoting attention to all members of the audience helped to democratize the theater and expanded the scope of the play's message.

Torres Naharro's erudition surfaces in the second section of the *Prohemio*, which contrasts with his humble demeanor at the beginning of the document. He begins the section by recalling the classical roots of theater and explaining the meaning of the title, *Propalladia*, chosen to honor Pallas Diana.[7] By dedicating the work to the goddess, he draws attention to the urbane aspect of the treatise since she not only represented wisdom, righteousness, and war, but also the civilized aspect of life.[8] He then describes the contents of the compilation as "pasto espiritual" (28), an interesting use of the word *pasto*, which normally refers to animal feed. Nonetheless, according to the *DRAE, pasto* can refer to an impetus that encourages a certain result or desire, and in this case, it pertains to the education of the public. This clever choice of words suggests a predilection for moralizing, which is also seen in the introits to his plays, and his perception of the rustic and unrefined character of the common classes; the analogy to the animal world should not be discounted. Such an attitude becomes commonplace in dramatic treatises of the sixteenth and seventeenth centuries. He continues the food metaphor by comparing each division of the *Propalladia* with different courses of the meal: *antepasto* and *pospasto*, in the middle is the "*principal cibo*," or the main course, which are his comedies (29-33). This assertion emphasizes the esteem that he gave to his theatrical works.[9] Like food, theater gives pleasure and life to those that partake in it. The popularity of prototheatrical works and primitive dramas in Spain

---

7. "Intitulélas *Propalladia*, a prothon, quod est primum, *et* Pallade; id est, prime res Palladis, a differencia de las que secundariamente y con más maduro estudio podrían suceder" (28).
8. For a detailed explanation, see Lihani, *Bartolomé* 25-27.
9. Lihani deems the quality of the *Propalladia* uneven due to the writer's less-than-spectacular command of sentimental vocabulary in his lyric verse (*Bartolomé* 22-23).

is undeniable, but Torres Naharro recognized the importance of a more formal theatre tradition and its ability to spread a message in a wider context than lyric poetry, for example.

At this point, Torres Naharro adopts the role of observer and downplays his expertise of literature, noting that experience has been his teacher: "pienso que deuo daros cuenta de lo que cerca d'ellas me paresce; no con presunción de maestro, mas solamente para seruiros con mi parescer, tanto que venga otro major" (33-36). He briefly mentions the dramatic conventions of Cicero, Acron, and Horace, all of which he later adopts and modifies.[10] In fact, instead of explaining in detail what elements of classical theater he was treating, a disdainful tone toward the classics surfaces, underscored by his use of "et cetera" (44). This, according to Gillet, demonstrates a certain condescending attitude, which is reiterated in the lines "Todo lo cual me paresce más largo de contar y necessario de oýr" (45-46). This opinion of the classics did not surprise Gillet, who commented that Torres Naharro's perception "is typically Spanish, compounded of deliberate disinterest and niceties of scholarship and an honest desire to vitally absorb and renew, rather than imitate, the ancient heritage" (*Propalladia* IV 430). In this document, Torres Naharro demonstrates his familiarity of classical theory and how this knowledge in conjunction with practical experience is used to formulate a revolutionary dramatic poetics; Lope uses a similar strategy in his *Arte nuevo* almost 100 years later. Indeed, Torres Naharro invoked classical poetics as a point of departure in the development of his own poetics, which was a case of renovation and not repetition of past principles. Indeed, he formulated the new literary system by paying heed to the needs of the modern public instead of emulating past traditions.

Torres Naharro boldly opens the elaboration of his dramatic precepts with the line "Quiero ora dezir yo mi paresce pues el de

---

10. Torres Naharro was most certainly exposed to classic dramatic principles in Italy, though most likely not the primary sources. According to Gillet, Torres Naharro's references to the precepts of Tullius Cicero, Acron Helenius, and Horace are probably borrowed from the *Familiaria Prenotamenta* of the Belgian humanist-printer Jodocus Badius. These commentaries were found in the editions of Terence's comedies as early as 1500 and most certainly by 1502 (III, 22).

los otros he dicho" (46). His authoritative tone continues throughout the rest of the document, a confidence resulting from his experience of actually having staged productions in a secular context. Torres Naharro's awareness of the importance of public reception and performance to the success of the play is demonstrated in his definition of comedy: "comedia no es otra cosa sino un artificio ingenioso de notables y finalmente alegres acontecimientos, por personas disputado" (47-49). Gillet points to the performative implications of "por personas disputado." This phrasing is key and not a "supererogation, for, in 1517, the awareness that a play was meant to be performed and not merely declaimed or read was not yet general." Gillet also underlines Torres Naharro's awareness of the importance of performance by pointing out that the poet uses the often-misinterpreted word *recitar,* which does not mean "to recite;" rather, it is either an Italianism from *recitare,* meaning to act or to perform, or a Latinism meaning to act, both implying the poet's awakening dramatic consciousness (*Propalladia* IV 430). Similar uses of *recitar* are found in other works, including at the end of the introit to the *Comedia Trophea*: "que una comedia a de ser / que os vernán a rescitar" (213-14), and in the preface to the earliest *suelta* of the *Tinellaria*, prove improbable the words were arbitrary lexical choices. Overlooked is the rest of the sentence, especially "un artificio ingenioso." This choice of words points to the necessity of creativity in the artist's attempts to please the audience. It suggests new rules in the composition of dramatic works, and introduces us to the notion of the fictitious, yet believable, storylines characteristic of the *comedias a fantasia.* Imagination is brought to the forefront in the composition of a play and it displaces or adorns well-known subject matter.

Torres Naharro contemplates practical performance issues in the treatise, including play structure and number of characters. He endorses a five-part division of plays, which allows for better performance by the actors and improved comprehension by the public. He states, "La diuisión d'ella en cinco actos, no solamente me paresce buena, pero mucho necessaria; avunque yo les llamo jornadas, porque más me parescen descansaderos que otra cosa, de donde la comedia queda mejor entendida y rescitada" (49-53). Gillet assumes that Torres Naharro's use of the term *jornada* in this sentence actually refers to *descanso*, meaning the natural interval provided by the structure.[11] Lihani goes one step further, resolving that a missing sentence, which explains how the breaks between the *jornadas* constitute the intermissions, is the source of confusion (*Bartolomé* 2). Also notable is the use of the Latinism *acto*, a first in Spanish (Gillet, *Propalladia* III 23). Horatian theater clearly influenced his decision, as Torres invokes the poet earlier in the text: "y como Oratio quiere, cinco actos" (44); Zimic suggests that Terence and Plautus also served as models for the division ("Pensamiento II" 119). He utilizes the natural breaks to benefit all participants in the dramatic event: they gave the actors a chance to rest, and the public a chance to rest and contemplate the action. Furthermore, he often included recapitulations at the beginning of each act to remind the audience of past action, a strategy clearly aimed at facilitating the reception of the work. The number of characters and its influence on the reception of the play did not escape Torres Naharro either. His experience with stagecraft taught him that the ideal number of characters in a play is between six and twelve (59-60); too few could lead to boredom and too many could be confusing: "es mi voto que no deuen ser tan pocas que parezca la fiesta sorda, ni tantas que engendren confusion" (53-55). Possible confusion could arise from too many characters and compounded by so many exits and entrances. His intention to prescribe a set number of acts and characters demonstrates his practical orientation to the playwriting process. These decisions seem driven by the desire for a favorable reception of the works, an impetus that influenced not only his structural aspects of the plays he wrote, but also many other factors: behaviors on stage, choice of subject matter, and sources of inspiration, that were derived from real life events or the imagination.

Torres Naharro states that the rules of decorum form the foundation of a play, steering a comedy as a rudder does a ship, and he contends that they must always take precedent in the mind of the playwright:

---

11. See Gillet, *Propalladia* IV 436, note 2, referring to the introit of the *Comedia Serafina.*

> Es decoro vna justa y decente continuación de la materia, conuiene a saber: dando a cada uno lo suyo, euitar las cosas inpropias, vsar de todas las legítimas, de manera que'el sieruo no diga ni haga actos del señor, et e conuerso; y el lugar triste entristecello, y el alegre alegrallo, con toda la aduertentia, diligentia y modo possibles, etc. (60-66).

This statement echoes Horace's advice in the *Ars poetica*: "be your subject what you will, only let it be simple and consistent" (42). Choice of subject matter also falls into the realm of decorous decision-making and plays an important role in determining the popularity of a play. Torres Naharro's use of contemporary topics in his works held much appeal for his audiences. Different themes and contexts entertained the public according to daily preoccupations. As such, it becomes clear how his theater reflected current problems since it was a reaction to them. Gillet marvels at Torres Naharro's ability to recognize the desires of his public, noting that he "remained completely Spanish: in his satire without subtlety or malice, healthily and simply disgusted, but also in dramatic types and situations, which are simple, strong, clear, made to satisfy himself and the Spanish public" (*Propalladia* IV 565). Torres Naharro, however, did not limit his subject matter to Spanish and Italian themes. The *Trophea,* for example, was written to celebrate a Portuguese delegation's visit to the Pope, and, by taking inspiration from Lusitanian history and myth, the dramatist showered the guests with a spectacle honoring the greatness of their country. Torres Naharro understood that the rules of decorum encompassed both social and intellectual spheres, grasping the necessity to maintain them in order not to anger the audience and consequently spoil the theatrical illusion of the play, and, on a more practical level, his patronage. Most of his dramas succeeded in staying within the boundaries of decorum and of proper behavior, but he did allow himself to portray indecorous behavior onstage in his introits and in the *costumbrista* trappings of the *comedia a noticia* as a vehicle to convey a message.[12]

---

12. Zimic recognizes the realistic nature of the *comedia a noticia* but he is hesitant to call the works *costumbristas*. The playwright's *costumbrismo* was used to illustrate pedantry, grotesqueness, and human ignorance; he suggests

While Torres Naharro's use of different languages and registers was not unique at the time, Vicente, for example, wrote in Portuguese, Spanish, or a combination of the two, his works benefitted from his ability to carefully craft dialogue and integrate different languages for a pleasing dramatic effect. Writing for the more international public of Rome, he composed a polyglot theater and developed a relationship between the public and the play. He notes: "Ansí mesmo hallarán en parte de la obra algunos vocablos ytalianos, especialmente en las comedias, de los quales conuino vsar, hauiendo respecto al lugar y a las personas a quien se recitaron" (76-79). Of course, this does not suggest that his characters spoke perfect Castilian, Italian, etc., but rather that the inclusion of variants made for funny plays, two prime examples being the *Soldadesca* and the *Tinellaria*. In these *costumbrista* works, the playwright reproduced the different languages and their variations, imitating those common to contemporary times and familiar to the audience. Realistic language strengthened the characterizations in the plays, added an often sardonic edge to the work, and strengthened the characterizations of the figures on stage. The use of Sayagués, for example, was instrumental to the success of the introit as the language conjured in the minds of the international audience a fascinating picture of a foreign, yet recognizable character, the country bumpkin.[13] Torres Naharro had to be cautious and prudent, however, when writing polyglot plays, since the presence not only could produce a comic effect, but also could alienate certain members of the audience who did not understand the language being used. In fact, Lihani notes that both he and Gillet struggled to pick up all of the linguistic nuances in the plays, and suggests that similar miscomprehension would have occurred with Torres Naharro's "melting pot audience" (*Bartolomé* 43). Indeed, the *Serafina* exemplifies how the overuse of the different languages can hinder the comprehension and enjoyment of a play; Torres Naharro apparently learned from this experience

---

that the characterization is a means to an end not the end itself ("Pensamiento I" 70).

13. For this study, let it suffice to say that accurate or not, the image invoked by the use of the rustic character is important because of it appealed to the audience and offered a recognizable figure.

since it is the only play where the mix of languages proves challenging.

Register was another linguistic factor that fell within the bounds of decorum. The playwright's utilization of language also raised his comedy to a higher, more cultured level. The language did more than entertain; it also solidified the relationship between the public and the players. In "Torres Naharro's Comic Speakers," Nina Cox Davis observes that by interspersing courtly language with the rustic dialects, he placed the comic players on the same level as the powerful spectators, reinforcing the link between the public and the poetic representation that is crucial to the continued patronage of the work (143). There was complicity amongst the play and the public that developed from the otherness of the onstage speakers. In other instances, he strove to maintain a formal manner of speaking, which should have appealed to the public since it was familiar to them. Torres Naharro was sensitive to the desire of maintaining a certain fidelity to Castilian: "Algunos d'ellos he quitado, otros he dexado andar, que nos son para menoscabar nuestra lengua castellana, antes la hacen más copiosa" (79-81). Torres Naharro did not overuse stilted or erudite vocabulary; in fact, Juan de Valdés described his work as being "muy llano y sin afectación ninguna" in *Diálogo de la lengua* (241).

Torres Naharro's use of the *introito,* or introit, and the *argumento,* plot summary, at the start of each play set up the performance by calming the crowd and drawing them into the theatrical context. The references to the work reminded the public that they were going to see a play, and that play would have some didactic function. The prologuist, normally dressed as a rustic shepherd and usually played by Torres Naharro, addressed the public, recounting racy stories of boastful adventures and sexual forays to pique the audience's attention. The bawdy stories contained didactic lessons and the narrator often scolded the audience for their moral improprieties, but in general, this sermonizing was veiled by dramatic performance, permitting Torres Naharro to preach without offending. Unlike later playwrights, who typically begged for forgiveness for any shortcomings of the production at the end of the play, Torres Naharro closed the introit with such an appeal. Next came the *argumento,* which commonly offered practical advice about the work. Although neither the introit nor the *argumento* were new devices, their use by Torres Naharro highlights the importance of recognizing the needs of the audience by facilitating an understanding of the work. This would have been especially useful for the inexperienced Spanish audience—had his works been performed in Spain—since they would presumable benefit more from his guidance than the audiences in Italy, who were accustomed to classic theatrical conventions. Furthermore, the introit that he staged was independent from the primary dramatic work, which seems to be a precursor to the varied dramatic spectacle common a few decades later, which integrated different forms of drama: *loas, entremeses, bailes, mojigongas* etc., into the day's performance.

The concluding part of the *Prohemio* is Torres Naharro's most important contribution to Spanish theater: the division of comedy into two categories: the documentary *comedia a noticia*, and the fictional *comedia a fantasia*, both of which would affect subsequent theater traditions for centuries. The two styles differed in the source of inspiration for the subject matter and the extent to which imagination was used, but both opened new doors of possibilities on the Spanish stage. The *comedia a noticia* was realistic and *costumbrista*, focusing on historic and real life events. Of course, the poet embellished some of the events for dramatic purposes. Green calls the *comedia a noticia* a remarkable innovation (211). The realistic treatment of real-life subject matter provided a canvas onto which a critical portrait of society was painted in a dramatic fashion. Torres Naharro tackled such topics of questionable army recruiting (*Soldadesca*) and papal corruption (*Tinellaria*). He daringly staged sordid details in these interrogations of society.

Recognizing the inevitable need for change, Torres Naharro stood apart from other Spanish playwrights of the times and introduced a new, more relevant dramatic art form to his country. His *comedia a fantasia*, which described imagined events that nevertheless appear true (69-71), resulted in an attractive and innovative style that appealed to audiences. Torres Naharro demonstrated a sensibility not common to earlier Spanish dramatists, one that emphasized the importance of audience reception in the success of a performance. His work had a more widespread character and its moralistic message targeted all classes. By foregrounding the imagination, Torres Naharro's theater moved away from previous theatrical traditions based primarily on history and the Bible. Finding inspiration in the imagination added limitless possibilities to the stage. He was able to cater to the desires of the public and to offer original works. This recognition and use of the imagination moved theater into the Renaissance. He offered different situations and offer new dramatic models. His works were characterized by more dramatic action and an actual storyline, which, for example, were much less prevalent in the eclogues of Encina. Torres Naharro's designation of the imaginative comedy would survive until the end of the seventeenth century, as Bances utilized similar terminology, and its influence on the creative process still exists today.

The combination of a strong dramatic tradition in Italy and a nascent tradition in Spain inspired Torres Naharro to write plays in an innovative manner. In the *Prohemio,* Torres Naharro acknowledged the power of the drama and the importance of the audiences. The *Prohemio* prescribed directives to make a play both entertaining and didactic, including comments about the text as spectacle and observations concerning extra-textual factors. His suggestions also imply that the dramatic text contains an inherent mutability, a quality that the written text simply cannot communicate. Experience was his most useful guide when composing dramas and dramatic theory. As a professional playwright in many royal houses in Italy, Torres Naharro understood the complexity of audiences and the necessity to please the public. His exposure to Italian dramatic theory and practice was instrumental in his adaptation of Spanish theater. His dramatic musings in the *Prohemio* clearly remind the reader of Horace's *Ars poetica* in topic and even structure, but he was not tied down to the classic precepts, rather, he took them and modified them according to his experiences, formulating dramatic concepts that had never been seen in the Iberian.

Torres Naharro introduced many innovations to the Spanish stage. Some of his innovations include the romantic comedy, the first cloak and dagger (*capa y espada*) comedy, the introduction of the *gracioso*, the independent introit, the development of heroic and novelesque themes, including *pundonor*, and psychologically intense characterizations. These innovations were the result of imagination and his sense of creativity. Many of these examples are seen in the *Comedia Ymenea*, arguably his best play, in which the entire dramatic spectacle is foregrounded, not just the message of the play, which was more common on the medieval stage.

II. The innovative *Comedia Ymenea*

Though all of Torres Naharro's dramatic works incorporate the dramatic conventions that he later recorded in his *Prohemio*, none better illustrates these principles than the *Comedia Ymenea,* a prototype of the Spanish cloak and dagger play.[14] By mixing traditional and innovative practices, Torres Naharro introduces a new and fresh dramatic form to the Spanish stage. Besides adding to the entertainment value of the work—the work was written for performance for a courtly crowd in Italy—this drama interrogates contemporary culture, demonstrating a suspicion of societal norms and a celebration of love. The plot is simple: Ymeneo falls in love with Phebea, much to the dismay of her brother, the Marqués, who attempts to preserve the family honor. The play ends in marriage but not until after we see much tension, some violence, and plenty of emotion. By addressing such themes as freedom of choice in marriage and the honor code—a first for the Spanish stage—this urbane comedy shows a shift in sensibility from that of previous generations of Spanish playwrights, whether secular or religious. The *Ymenea's* numerous innovations appear on various levels: structural, character, thematic, and generic, which makes for a modern drama. For these reasons the play distinguishes itself from the more ritualistic and less dramatic medieval theater, and it is clear that both the didactic and entertainment functions of the work are deemed important.

---

14. Some critics search for connections between Torres Naharro and Lope, especially in terms of the *Ymenea* as a forerunner to the *comedia.* Gillet goes so far as to say that if he had lived during the time of Lope de Rueda, Torres Naharro would have been not only a prophet, but also the originator of the *comedia* (IV 206).

The way that Torres Naharro structured the spectacles: *introito*, *argumento*, and *comedia*, reveals a sensitivity to public reception of the work and initiates a shift in dramatic trends underway at the time. He combines innovative and traditional dramatic practices to produce a form that is both new and familiar. The introit reminds one of classical and medieval style, but it is followed by the *argumento*, a new concept, and then the *comedia*, the principal work, which he has reinvented. This structure, common to all of his plays, demonstrates the transition and transformation of conventional forms to a more modern practice. All parts of the spectacle, moreover, reveal a cognizance of the importance of performance and reception. Indeed, the introit takes advantage of primitive styles and conventions, but is, in fact, used in a modern manner. The coarse digressions of the brutish yokel draw the public into the spectacle. He begins it by banishing ill will and bad feelings and setting a jovial tone: "¡Ahuera, ahuera pesares! ¡ Sús d'aquí, tirrias amargas!"(7-8). His colorful language and brusque demeanor are meant to capture the attention of the noble audience as he praises their nobility and, at the same time, discretely admonishes their idleness while watching the play:

> Vengan prazeres a cargas
> y regozijos a pares;
> qu'el plazer
> más engorda qu'el comer.
> Y ah qu' esta noche garrida,
> de los hombres y mujeres
> quien menos huelga, más yerra. (9-15)

The prologuist's irony is subtle as he hurls an underhanded insult at the members of the audience about their idle lives. He continues with humorous stories about his misadventures with women of questionable morals. His stories are racy and misogynistic, immediately invoking the spirit of the *Libro de buen amor*, and other medieval styles. He then returns his attention to the audience and begs for forgiveness for his brusque manner, again acknowledging the nobility of his public and reiterating his esteem for them:

> Vuestra grandeza me llama;

no puedo menos hazer
de venir
do deuo y quiero seruir. (153-56)

These acquiescent words, reminiscent of those in the *Prohemio*, reflect the prologuist's attitude throughout the rest of the introit. He cleverly manipulates the public and reinforces the relationship that has been formed between the actor and the audience, seemingly appealing to their egos. Of course, these words do hold many truths, since it is the playwright's job to serve his patron. This introit distracts the audience by couching the introduction of new innovations within a familiar and humorous context. From the beginning of the work, Torres Naharro builds tension to maintain the attention of the audience; this unrest continues throughout the play. The prologuist establishes a comfortable tone in the house and forms a relationship with the public, makes them laugh, and comforts them, so anything new will be acceptable and even welcomed. Furthermore, by using the familiar and simple figure of the shepherd, ubiquitous in the medieval eclogues, he minimizes the impending unease possibly caused by innovation, since he is a simple, innocuous figure. The recognizable character placates the audience as they are introduced to something new.

The clearest indication of the importance of audience reception occurs at the end of the introit when he offers advice regarding the reception of the play, informing the audience of its five-act structure and that the play is not a humorous comedy: "No es comedia de risadas" (175). This statement segues to the *argumento.* The *argumento* that follows is a novel technique that tells the plot to the public to ensure their understanding of the play and, in the case of the *Ymenea,* to assure them that it will end well, although tensions will build. The *argumento* became necessary as plots became more complex; they were present in all of Torres Naharro's plays, demonstrating his acute understanding of the nuances of providing an accessible work to his public. Furthermore, these two components of the dramatic work served to break the dramatic illusion of the play. His use of direct address and metatheatrical strategies, reminded the public that they were seeing a dramatic piece, from which a lesson could be learned.

Besides including the *argumento*, Torres Naharro employed other strategies to ensure that the public could follow his plays. As such, public reception began to play an even more important role as storylines became more developed and audiences became more heterogeneous. The five-act structure of the principal work divides the action into manageable chunks easily processed by the audience. Since the play begins *in medias res*, the use of recapitulation serves to inform the public of what has previously transpired. Along the same lines, Torres Naharro utilizes brief summaries of presumably confusing situations, for example, in the fourth *jornada* as Ymeneo visits his beloved Phebea, leaving his servants outside to stand watch, the two men recount past events in their discussion, presumably for the audience's sake. This use of summary suggests a self-consciousness of the dramatic process. The same strategy is seen in the final act when virtually all of the characters recap previous events, which permits a better understanding of the play and allows the audience to formulate their own interpretation of the poet's message. As with the introduction of the *argumento,* this new style of drama with its well-developed plot and the action dictated the need for recapitulation. Furthermore, the length and complexity of the play dictated the need for summary.

The script also orients the public by means of extra-textual and visual signs. For example, at the beginning of the play, the costumes of the characters inform that it is nighttime since the men are dressed in clothes suitable for their nocturnal forays. Stern notes that costuming in plays gained importance during the Renaissance as the textile industry grew and a general preoccupation for clothing blossomed (221). As a further guide for his audiences, Torres Naharro provided a number of clues that supplied necessary information, enriching the theatrical experience: his use of familiar geography, for example, "la Casa de Valencia" (I, 66) and "la Sillería" (I, 272) would have served as familiar touchstones for much of his audience. The familiarity of the different aspects of the work makes the play more amenable to the public. In the *Prohemio*, Torres Naharro notes that the *comedia a fantasia* should seem real although it is fictional. His plays maintained a local flavor recognizable to his public; whether it consists of Italian nobles, expatriate Spanish, or Portuguese diplomats visiting the Pope.

Torres Naharro also used music and songs to orient the public as to the trajectory of the storyline in his works. In the *Ymenea*, the presence of songs not only adds entertainment value to the spectacle but also reflects the tone of the play. In the second act, for example, Ymeneo hires a group of musicians to sing to Phebea with the hopes that the serenade will advance his courtship, an example of the heartfelt verses include:

> La pena con que fatigo
> es de mí tan fauorida,
> que, de envidiosa, la vida
> ya no quiere star comigo.
> Ella se quiere perder;
> vuestra merced lo meresce
> y el coraçón se enloquece
> de placer
> con tan justo padescer. (II, 42-50)

Following the song, the musicians sing a *villancico* that describes the bittersweet feelings of love that he has for her. The pain that she causes in him is refreshing: "Es más preciosa ventura / vuestra pena / que qualquiera gloria ajena" (I, 50-53). Remnants of the medieval notions of courtly love are clearly heard in these words, where any contact with his beloved is judged better than none at all. At the end of the play, the case is different and the words of the song become triumphant and jubilant, praising the power of love to conquer all: "Victoria, victoria, / los mis vencedores / victoria en amores…¡Victoria, victoria! (V, 361-63, 371). Songs and music are a fundamental part of any culture and their inclusion in Torres Naharro's dramas is not surprising. They not only serve to entertain, but also to measure and record the emotions and tone of the play. Oftentimes, they also transformed the role of the public in the spectacle. In fact, in other plays, such as the *Trophea*, Torres Naharro supplied the lyrics of the songs to the audience members, who then would sing along with the musicians and actually become performers within the work.

In his plays, Torres Naharro presents original characters, and the *Ymenea* is no exception. Although some are clearly inspired by past literary pieces or social conditions, they are effectively reworked so that they are new but recognizable. These fictional characters add depth to the plays and make the stories more interesting to the public. In the case of the *Ymenea*, the play not only relies on the progress of action, but also on the development of the characters. This is a new innovation on the stage, and one that promotes audience involvement because of the mimetic portrayal of the characters. In presenting fallible and, therefore, believable characters, the dramatic work is more convincing and draws the public into the fictional world. Furthermore, Torres Naharro takes advantage of the horizons of expectations of the public in his introduction of new characters that serve to portray societal norms and preoccupations of the times. Along with the innovative characters presented on stage by his plays, Torres Naharro also took contemporary themes and represented them in a new manner, which would have appeal because of their novelty and also because they reflected issues of the times.

With the possible exception of the anonymous composer of the *Auto de los Reyes Magos*, Torres Naharro was one of the first playwrights to develop his characters in the modern sense, and to not rely solely on stereotypes. The purposeful development of the psychological aspects of the characters gets the attention of the public since the character becomes either more relatable or more different to them; no matter the case, this characterization evokes a greater response in the audience members. Torres used asides to inform the public of the inner thoughts and opinions of the characters, and while this is not a new technique—it is found in classical Greek theater—it reveals, nonetheless, his recognition of the public's role in the dramatic spectacle as participants (i.e., receivers of the text). These asides are not explicitly delineated as stage directions but rather pointed out in the dialogue between characters; one particular example is at the beginning of the first act when Ymeneo describes his love for Phebea while his uninterested and incredulous manservant, Boreas, gives his take of the situation under his breath:

YMENEO. Guarde Dios, señora mía,
Vuestra graciosa presencia,

mi sola felicidad,
....
pues yo vos guardo en mi pecho,
vos me dexáis en la calle.
Bien me viene
que sin culpa muera y pene.

BOREAS. ¿Aun agora començamos,
Y tantos duelos tenemos?

YMENEO. ¿Qué hablas allá, villano?

BOREAS. Digo, señor, que nos vamos,
que mañana tornaremos,
y quiçá con mejor mano. (I, 1-30)

Boreas's aside is important because it reveals much about his character and that of his master. It may build a sense of complicity between the public and the servant since the audience learns of the contempt that he has for his master. It also allows the public to judge Ymeneo for themselves. This particular scene, for example, brings into question if his love afflicted him to such an extent that he lost his sanity, which was the case with Calisto in *Celestina*,[15] or, on the contrary, if he is a young man with a crush, whose actions are affected but not dictated by his love; this latter option seems more reasonable. In fact, such a conclusion pushes the public away from collusion with Boreas since his master seems to be friendly. The case differs from Rojas's work, where the public would have laughed at and scorned the exaggerated reactions of Calisto. This scene demonstrates the complexity of the story and the interactions between the characters. Of course, the work was written for the upper classes, although servant-classes would have been present, so the message is directed toward them and may serve as a warning to the dubious intentions of their servants. At the same time, the servants present at the performance may see another message, that of the capricious nature of the noble class. The opening of the *Prohemio* corroborates such an idea since the poet acknowledges and may even relate to the servant classes. Torres Naharro uses these strategies to make the public interpret the works, things are not just laid out in black and white, rather the audience must make its own conclusions. In terms of love, the

---

15. Many have made comparisons between the two works. See Gillet, for starters.

same holds true for the character of Phebea, in her heartfelt confession of love for Ymeneo, the public empathizes with her. She wants to be married to her lover but is willing to comply with the norms of society—by dying—if this is not a possibility. It is a familiar stance taken by Melibea, but with more optimistic results.

In terms of the introduction of new characters and their development, the *Ymenea* is unique. Indeed, Torres Naharro introduced to the stage characters inspired from past works, especially *Celestina*,[16] but Torres Naharro's great dramatic instinct shines through in his innovative use of characters in the play, especially in the *gracioso,* Boreas, Ymeneo's servant, and his female counterpart, Dorotea, Phebea's servant. These characters serve as distorted counterparts to their masters, guide the plot, and become involved in a love affair parallel to that of their respective masters, a common technique later used in the *comedia.* In the comical third *jornada*, Boreas attempts to court Dorotea and only succeeds after much begging and pleading (3.151-62), mirroring his master's earlier behavior while seducing Phebea. Dorotea, however, does not succumb as easily as her mistress, imparting an implicit jab at the questionable morality of the noble class. Later, Turpedio, the Marqués's servant, also attempts to court Dorotea and fails miserably, further demonstrating her ability to see through false compliments and dishonorable intentions (3.241-98). She belittles him because of his young age and the scene is ridiculous and hysterical. In the play, besides offering comic relief, Turpedio faithfully serves the Marqués and attempts to temper his master's behavior with a witty voice of moderation. The servants play a greater role in the play, perhaps pointing to their greater role in society.

The noble class also receives a reworking in the play. Gillet notes that Torres Naharro invented the character of the Marqués as a "young and spirited brother, clothed by Arabic and Hispano-

---

16. Gillet points out that the *Ymenea* contains trappings of *Celestina*: night scenes, less-than-faithful servants, to name a few, but Torres Naharro's play stands apart from Rojas's work due to several modifications: Torres Naharro introduced the notion of honor, invented the character the Marqués, effectively replacing the useless Pleberio in *Celestina*, and he replaced the suicide of Melibea with the threat of death of Phebea and the oral consummation of marriage, devices commonly seen in the Comedia (*Propalladia* IV 519-20).

Gothic law, with all of the power of a father over his daughter" (*Propalladia* IV 519). He also suggests that this character was developed in order to differ from Pleberio, Melibea's father, since the outcome of the play and its explicit message is distinct from *Celestina* (*Propalladia* IV 520). The Marqués is a gallivanting young man, who enjoys the nocturnal forays typical of his class and his status as a bachelor. He symbolizes traditional norms, but at the same time, demonstrates their hypocrisy since he will strip women of their honor but will protect his own at all costs. This medieval, antiquated character serves as a contrast to Ymeneo. The protagonist is charismatic because of the devotion he shows to his beloved, Phebea, and to his servants, who he considers more brothers than lackeys. In the play, Ymeneo offers his friendship and fraternal love to his servants as a reward for their faithfulness (1.112-18), a move that undoubtedly pleases the servants and simultaneously instructed the nobles who are watching the play to treat them fairly, as all men are equal. The personalities of the two men form a strong contrast and also symbolize the changing times: the Marqués represents traditional, medieval values and Ymeneo is more liberal and steady headed, indicative of Renaissance ideals. For example, his love for Phebea is genuine, and though it is passionate, it is not uncontrollable. His character is one that is equally controlled by his heart and his head. Following the same line, the contrast of the characters' tenets and beliefs reflect the change in dramatic trends at the time. The acceptance of Ymeneo's more modern viewpoint and behavior reflects the same type of transition from the medieval dramatic trends to the Renaissance theatrical stylings developed by Torres Naharro.

Characterization is directly affected by performance. Indeed, Phebea's plucky, independent character is not fully revealed in a reading of the script, and the same is true with the development of other characters; the text is not sufficient by itself and clearly requires performance. Furthermore, performance embodies cultural norms, making them accessible to the spectators. The behavior of the *graciosos* would have much more impact as their language, actions, and stereotypical cowardice come to life. The same holds true for Phebea's comments in the fifth act, when she admits her love for Ymeneo and defies her brother, stating that she will marry whom she pleases. The words enunciated by the actors are vital but require accompanying gestures and interaction among the characters they impersonate. In the *Ymenea* performance supplements the play script by strengthening characterization and portraying cultural ideals. Miguel Romera Navarro underscores the importance of performance to convey the passion between Phebea and Ymeneo. Stating that the dialogue is not enough, he insists that actions (i.e., performance) speak louder than words and are imperative to convey and to comprehend the play's embedded messages (52-53). By foregrounding performance, its fundamental role in the whole dramatic spectacle becomes even clearer. Performance fills in the gaps of the dramatic text, they are interesting on the page, but when performed by the actors they interest the public more. These characters stick with the public because of the creativity of Torres Naharro.

On the thematic level, Torres Naharro addresses two major themes in the *Ymenea*: honor and love. Moving away from the common medieval representations of love as an uncontrollable force that overwhelms a person's physical, mental, and emotional being, the *Ymenea* presents love as a strong force that impels men—and women—to act in an extreme manner, but they are not irrational. This equilibrium reflects the more stable conception of man common to the Renaissance. Man has taken control of his life and his world, and though he may lose control briefly due to his emotions, reason returns. So, it is not the abstract notion of love that necessarily changes, rather it is the way man is able to deal with the emotion. In the play, both Ymeneo and Phebea take great, life-threatening risks in the name of love. The ending of the play is different from earlier works because the two are married, an ending that becomes convention in the *Comedia nueva* of the seventeenth century. Where in the past, righteous behavior was taught by counterexample, culminating in the *loco amor* in *Celestina*, in Torres Naharro's play this is not the case, and the positive power of love comes to light. No one dies, though the threat certainly existed, and things end positively. This change in perspective reveals a more optimistic viewpoint of the Renaissance.

The importance of honor in society is at the base of this play and it is another factor that distinguishes *Ymenea* from *Celestina* (*Propalladia* IV, 519). Torres Naharro does criticize its jurisdiction and drastic consequences. The Marqués is determined to maintain his family honor at all costs, Ymeneo also desires to protect his honor and that of his lover; Phebea accepts the consequences of losing her honor, and the servants poke fun at the exaggerated honor code of the time. The honor theme is ubiquitous in early modern Spanish theater and varied opinions about its prevalence in society have been the topic of countless studies. Recently, scholars have pointed to the idea that although there was an honor code in Spain, it has been much overblown on the stage, resulting in an exaggerated conception of the cultural convention.[17] Honor and its recuperation has always been a topic common to Spanish letters. Whether it is the El Cid's complaint against the González brothers, the *Infantes* of Carrión, or the case in *Cárcel de Amor*, which gives an exaggerated version of honor in which the woman is condemned to death just or simply having been accused of taking a lover, the honor code is always portrayed as extreme and merciless. Rojas satirizes this cultural obsession after Elicia vows revenge for the murder of Celestina.

Torres Naharo treats honor seriously, reiterating its importance in Spanish society. The convention would have been recognizable to the public. Of course, Torres Naharro's penchant for social criticism is well documented, especially in the *comedias a noticia*, but it also comes through in this play. The hypocritical attitude of the Marqués reflects honor code practices of the times since he is guilty of the same crimes of which he accuses Ymeneo. Phebea also sheds a negative light on the honor code and on society as a whole since she submits herself to her brother for punishment. The public would see and hear her heartfelt confession of her love and consequently question the values of society. Ymeneo is the new manifestation of honor, still brash but taking responsibility for his actions in order to marry. In fact, plays dealing with honor sell seats, and Lope mentions as much in the *Arte nuevo,* Torres Naharro obviously recognized this several

---

17. See Matthew Stroud's *Fatal Union*. He also touches upon how this was a convention that universally pleased the public but it was not universally practiced in society. More recently, see his article "Defining the *Comedia*, On Generalizations Once Widely Accepted That Are No Longer Accepted So Widely."

decades before. It is difficult to know exactly how accurately the dramatic representations of the honor code portrayed actual cultural practice, but even in an exaggerated state, we clearly see that this aspect of society did exist or it would not have been staged. Torres Naharro was well aware of the problems that plagued contemporary life and his interrogations of them on stage also reminded the public of moral shortcomings both personal and societal. His examination of the honor code, for example, was particularly appropriate to his noble public, since it would have been them that would have fallen under its constraints and consequences—no matter how extreme—since the lower classes were not governed by such strictures. In the case of the *Ymenea*, Torres Naharro offered an ending that gave a reasonable and decorous solution to what was perceived as an unreasonable part of society.

In fact, decorum is followed throughout the play, making for a well-balanced work. On a linguistic level, the characters' speech is appropriate to their social station. On a social level, they also follow the expected norms of conduct. The Marqués actions are expected from someone of his position, the head of a household with a single sister. His change of opinion may be unexpected but it is not unreasonable. After the dramatic monologue and confession of his sister, and the proclamation of love by the noble Ymeneo, he allows for their marriage and pardons her past actions. This decision would have to be applauded by the audience and accepted as rational, allowing for the happy ending. Even if the couple's secret affair is viewed as seditious at first, it is justified because of their feelings of mutual love; it does not have the dubious characteristics of the young, irrational love seen in *Celestina*, for example. Phebea also acts decorously throughout the play. At the end, she treats her brother with the respect he deserves but she is not completely submissive. She accepts her death sentence but will not renounce her love for Ymeneo. Ymeneo shows much of the same behavior since he treats her with respect, and defends her life before the sword of her brother. Torres Naharro has taken the honor code, demonstrated its shortcomings and offered a suitable ending for the play in which the cultural standards are modified but in a way that the honor code remains intact and becomes more flexible. The play is a comedy and needs to end as such.

In the *Ymenea*, Torres Naharro takes recognizable and contemporary themes and dramatizes them for the enjoyment of the public. He is aware of their impact and, as a result, takes great care when crafting the play. As theater is constantly changing, so are the treatments of such topics as love and honor. Here, both are introduced in their familiar, albeit exaggerated, manifestations, which are then tempered to more accurately reflect the more rational temperament of the Renaissance society. Like Calderón and other playwrights in later years, Torres Naharro did not present the themes as black and white issues, rather, they were left open—although one can certainly see the playwright's attitude—for interpretation, again underlining the important role of the public in the generic spectacle. This focus on the public is also seen on the generic level of the play, the *comedia a fantasia*, where a fictional storyline is produced in a realistic context. The *Ymenea*'s innovation is clearly guided by considerations of reception and performance. Due to the ever-increasing popularity of fictional prose, most prominently the novels of chivalry, it is not a surprise that the romantic comedy was introduced to the stage. This, in combination with the increasing influence of Italian dramatic styles, and a more optimistic psyche, influenced Torres Naharro's playwriting. His romantic comedies were filled with action, intrigue, and romance. He offered a different form of entertainment from the primitive styles common to Spanish *jongleuresque* theater and the proto-theatrical practices.

Of course, all artistic production is creative and imaginative; nevertheless, Torres Naharro was the first to recognize the role played by the imagination in the playwriting process. As mentioned earlier, the use of imagination opened the door to an infinite number topics and variations. It allowed for theater to progress as new ideas and concepts could be dramatized in order to appeal to the public. This is not to say that the earlier styles were forgotten, on the contrary, they were revived and given new life; remnants of the eclogues are seen in the introits, for example. Imagination, however, brings much more to the plays than more interesting storylines. As Green points out, many works at the beginning of the sixteenth century had what he calls "imaginative authority." Imaginative authority refers to imaginative power of literature to impose itself on the receiver of the text; it is a power that moves the characters in the text, the receivers of the text, and which follows them after finishing the work. He points to Rojas's *Celestina,* Torres Naharro's *Comedia Serafina, Lazarillo de Tormes,* Tirso's *El confiado por desconfiado*, and *Don Quijote*, which is the unquestionable example of this concept (209).

Similar to the *Serafina,* imaginative authority is seen in the *Ymenea*. According to Green, the imaginative authority of the *Serafina* occurs when Torres Naharro modifies the folkloric account that inspires the play and does not allow the protagonist to kill his wife in order to run off with another woman; rather, the man is struck with confusion caused by a guilty conscience for having such thoughts (211). He concludes the following:

> The replacing of death by confusion and loss of identity will have a fruitful development in Spain's classic drama of the seventeenth century. Its appearance here, before 1520, constitutes a noteworthy landmark. The poet has made a convincing psychological analysis, and has found authoritative words with which to express it. (211)

In the *Ymenea*, the concept of imaginative authority also manifests itself. The remarkable characters of the play when paired with the imaginative storyline reach out to the public. The final act holds great impact as tension builds and emotions grow on stage: Ymeneo's quick exit, seemingly leaving his beloved at the mercy of her brother, causes unease and apprehension of what will occur next. Phebea's heartfelt confession and steadfast proclamation of love evokes sympathy and pride at the same time. The Marqués' resolute attitude toward the honor code suggests a sense of doom, which is alleviated when he accepts the marriage of the couple. In a short time, the playwright has given a psychological analysis of the characters. The emotions and psyche of the love-struck couple had been seen in earlier works, but it is Phebea's brother's change of attitude that carries the most weight. The actions and words of the lovers convince him to spare both of them, and to allow their marriage. Essentially, the Marqués goes against the societal norms that he represents. By reworking the honor code on the stage,

Torres Naharro's play stays with the spectator as it reveals other options than blindly following traditional norms. The originality and strength of the characters manifest the idea of progress and change, reflecting the transition that was occurring in society at the time and continued to be in effect. His innovative work was forward oriented in terms of style, composition, and message. Using past experience and classical traditions a point of departure, Torres Naharro took risks in his dramas and yielded theatrical works and sets of dramatic precepts that affected subsequent theater in Spain. Writing theater in Italy gave Torres Naharro the opportunity to step out of the Middle Ages and into the Renaissance by offering new models, ideas, and concepts, while taking advantage of the rich source of subject matter of his native Spain, making both countries integral to the production of his works. Of course, we cannot say that he was completely Italianized; rather, he learned to combine an earthy, Spanish sensibility with the humanistic Italian norms, anticipating and producing a new form that would later evolve into the comedia.

In recent years, Torres Naharro has not received as much critical attention as his contemporaries Juan del Encina and Gil Vicente,[18] but his work deserves to be revisited, especially since several literary theories and methodologies of the last fifty years offer new ways to approach theater and its driving precepts and, ultimately, to more clearly understand the development of early modern theater in Spain. It is worthwhile, therefore, to examine the ways in which theatrical practice was influenced by performance and audience reception, and in turn shaped theatrical theory in Torres Naharro's *Prohemio* to the *Propalladia* and his *Comedia Ymenea*, exploring the interrelationship of theory and practice in early modern Spanish theater.

Torres Naharro's dramaturgy unquestionably influenced future generations of playwrights. If we follow Gillet's gauge of

---

18. Both playwrights have attracted the attention of scholars throughout the twentieth century. In 2009, a group of theater scholars and members of the AHCT, Susan Paun de García, Benjamin Gunter, Yuri Porras, Kerri Wilks, and Benjamin Nelson, have undertaken a project that explores new approaches to Encina's ecglogues by exploring the adaptation. Regarding research on Vicente, Zimic is one of the leading experts.

how to determine the success of a dramatist, we see that Torres Naharro stands out in all categories: the number of performances; the number of printed editions; the frequency, volume, and quality of the criticism; and the extent to which his ideas and methods are accepted and imitated (*Propalladia* IV 467); although his works were not performed in Spain, the printed texts clearly had an influence on the future of Spanish theater.

Documented evidence of Torres Naharro's performances does, however, exist in Italy, including a letter written by Isabella d'Este praising his work (Lihani, *Bartolomé* Ch. 7 note 3). Also, Francisco Delicado wrote in *La lozana andaluza* that his work was still being enjoyed in Italy eleven years after his death: "Mi señor, no sé mañana ni el sábado, que terné priesa, pero sea el domingo a cena, y todo el lunes, porque quiero que me leáis, vos que tenéis gracia, las coplas de Fajardo y la comedia de *Tinellaria* y a *Celestina*" (190).

In Spain, Torres Naharro's influence may have been chiefly felt through the printed editions of *Propalladia* (439). Besides the remarks provided by Valdés and Juan de Timoneda, numerous commentaries took various literary forms: Fernando Merino wrote poems praising Torres Naharro that appear in the *Propalladia*, and further praise is seen in the letter written by Barberius and addressed to Bocius describing the poet, also found at the beginning of the work. Cristóbal de Villalón stated "nunca alguno mostró en verso tanta agudeza como en las [comedias] que Torres Naharro trovó: y no ovo en la antigüedad quien con tanta facilidad metrificase" (178). The number of editions of his *Propalladia* indicates that the readership of Torres Naharro was widespread, although his direct influence on Spanish dramaturgy is less noticeable. Gillet opines that it was Torres Naharro's misfortune to not have gifted followers and suggests that if his principles had been understood and his examples followed with any success, a solid tradition might have been established ("Torres II" 206). His work, nonetheless, made waves and initiated change on the early modern Spanish stage.

Torres Naharro wrote his plays with their performance in mind, and though the texts were not performed in Spain because this particular theatrical tradition had not yet matured, Timoneda recognized in the prologue to his *Obras completas de Juan de*

Timoneda (c.1583) that the works were performable (3). Gillet notes that "it is hard to believe that the dramatic output of the earliest years of the sixteenth century was not destined to be performed" (*Propalladia* IV 639). Torres Naharro exhibits concern for his audience's reception of the text throughout the play, from his choice of subject matter to his use of certain key performance strategies. The inclusion of the audience in the performance became standard for Torres Naharro, as he transformed the public into active players, whether they were being addressed in the introit or singing at the end of the play. Torres Naharro motivated a critical attitude in the audience, who found themselves challenged to question issues that the plays addressed. Clearly basing his system of dramatic precepts on his own successes and failures on the stage, Torres Naharro included them in the *Prohemio,* prescribing tried and proven dramatic techniques that would serve as a guide for subsequent playwrights and moving Spanish theater towards the techniques that would emerge in the *comedia* of the seventeenth century.

III. Juan de la Cueva's *Ejemplar poético*: Spain's first original dramatic treatise

Writing on the threshold separating the Renaissance and the Baroque, Juan de la Cueva proved to be an important figure in the transition of Spanish theater before Lope because of his experimental tendencies and innovative ideas. Toward the end of the sixteenth century, he reinterpreted and dramatized familiar legends and historical events, staging popular culture for the Sevillian public. Cueva understood the importance of satisfying his audiences, and he accomplished this by fusing classical styles with popular trends, causing McKendrick to assert that Cueva's theater was a compromise between his formal literary formation and his theatrical instinct to write his works for public performance (53). In addition to being a prolific poet and balladist, Cueva wrote three dramatic treatises that documented the transformation of Spanish theater: the first two, *Viaje de Sannio* (1585) and "Epístola dedicatoria a Momo" (1588), were written contemporaneously with his plays and foresaw the direction in which drama was heading; they documented a transition from Neoclassical tragedy to the modern *comedia nueva*. The third, the *Ejemplar poético* (1606), was written at the end of his career, years after he stopped writing plays. It served as a retrospective of past literary trends and their relation to the current conventions. His explanation of theater found in the *Ejemplar poético* and its relation to performance and reception will be examined shortly.

The first two treatises exhibit a more personal tone than the *Ejemplar poético*, although all three works demonstrate an understanding of the literary trends of the times and a penchant for innovation. The poem *Viaje de Sannio* versifies Cueva's discontent with the lack of recognition he has received from his peers. The work recounts the search of an archetypal buffoon, Sannio, for the god Jupiter in order to solicit the fame he feels that his literary achievements deserve. During his forays, Sannio converses with various mythological characters, including Apollo, with whom he discusses the tenets of poetry. Sannio's discourse follows Aristotelian lines, stating that poetry imitates nature and can have a variety of topics, which determine the tone of the work (47). He then describes six types of poetry, of which the epic is the oldest, clearest, and most esteemed because of its depiction of heroic feats and use of varied versification; comic poetry is most popular because of its portrayal of ordinary human life; and tragic poetry is most common with its stories of kings and nobles (55). Sannio distinguishes between tragedy and comedy by their endings: the inevitability of death in tragedy is not necessarily seen in comedy (56). Commenting on the poet's responsibility to satisfy the needs of the public, Sannio states, "Al poeta l'es dado hablar de cosas o sean verdaderas o fingidas en metro, i porque al gusto sean gustosas que de ficiones vayan rebestidas" (66-67); this gives the poet license to alter the historical events within the literary work for aesthetic purposes, making them more appealing. Sannio also mentions how both the historian and the poet are expected to tell the truth, but the latter should be expected to do so in an engaging manner. In *Viaje de Sannio*, Cueva explains the basic principles behind the decisions he has made while producing his plays and poetry. He does not go so far as to say that imagination should alter history, but that art can embellish historical accounts, making them more entertaining. This reworking of history into literature is both innovative and unique, and will serve as a prototype for the *comedia.* Cueva's moderate attitude conforms to the changing literary trends of the time. He still seems dedicated to Neoclassical tenets but recognizes how styles change in response to public tastes. The "Epístola dedicatoria a Momo" was included in the 1588 reprint of *Comedias y tragedias* and directed to the Greek god of Comedy. This work details Cueva's early conception of theater. He describes comedy as a useful and didactic tool that imitates human life and exemplifies contemporary cultural practices. In his time, Cueva states, educated playwrights were writing—and a heterogeneous audience was enjoying—both comedy and tragedy, so it was unnecessary to qualify one form as superior to the other (6-7). Noting that the tendency for change is powerful, Cueva is steered by the inherently dynamic nature of theater and chooses to break from the established and rigid dramatic precepts of the era. He does not, however, lose sight of the importance of classical models, though his work does suggest that they be revisited and revised in accordance to the times, instead of merely reproduced.

Cueva's *Ejemplar poético* is arguably the first original statement of literary precepts written in Spanish, and his most important theoretical work. Cueva divided the treatise into three epistles. The work outlines precepts that direct the composition of several genres of poetry, both lyric and dramatic. Cueva's attention to detail stands out in all three parts, revealing an extremely well-trained poet. His humanistic training clearly influenced his literary production and theoretical leanings, though he was not entirely bound to classical precepts. Both experience and intuition guide his doctrine and he staunchly defends his writing throughout the text. In the *Ejemplar poético*, Cueva highlights the importance of clarity, decorum, and simplicity. He suggests that aesthetic conventions and creative energies must counterbalance one another, resulting in innovation. New rules inevitably replace outdated one. Furthermore, the renegade Spanish creative spirit and the unrefined tastes of the general public help to define poetic composition.

The *Ejemplar poético* offers a comprehensive description of poetry and it presumably served as documentation of his literary production as a whole. A constant in all three epistles is Cueva's insistence on the importance of clarity, consistency, and propriety, especially in terms of versification, language, and decorum. These factors are especially relevant to dramatic poetry—the most public of poetic art forms—since the heterogeneous audience of the late 1500s were dismayed by the inconsistencies of poorly written plays. Also, Cueva is clearly preoccupied with the *vulgo*, which he described throughout the work and always in negative terms. Many of his observations toward the *vulgo* parallel those of his contemporaries, and most notably, of Lope de Vega in his *Arte nuevo.* Cueva expresses dismay with the changing tastes of public; for example, his earlier works are not as appreciated by the public, which bothers the poet:

> Así, el que hurta del ajeno escrito,
> aunque luego le agrada y le recrea,
> le ofende al noble honor tan vil delito.
> Hace que el vulgo libremente vea
> su cortedad de ingenio, y manifieste
> por suya aquella obcenidad tan fea.
> Y justamente hace que le cueste
> las plumas que le quiten y la fama,
> sin que remedio a reparalle preste. (II, 409-17)

Classical conventions are left behind as the new taste of the public dictates the ways in which all forms of poetry are to proceed. Cueva recognizes how the receivers of the text impact its production and innovation, demonstrating a forward-thinking stance. His predilection for innovation is also driven by the understanding that the public is not solely responsible for the changing trends in Spanish literature; the artist, too, is involved in this evolution. The *Ejemplar poético* served as a guide for any poet that was compelled to follow new poetic trends.

The *Ejemplar poético* is a combination of specific dicta and general advice regarding the composition of poetry. In the first epistle, Cueva notes how the combination of *arte* and *ingenio*—the former facilitates and the latter inspires—affects his poetry. He states that his work diverges from the vulgar path taken by other poets as "llegaré al punto en que veréis cantado / lo que el Arte al ingenio perfecciona, / y de quien es, si ha de acertar, guiado" (I, 16-18). Restraint is important to the composition of good poetry. Versification needs to be clean, easy, and formal (I, 49-54) and a carefully chosen vocabulary should not be weakened by overstatement: “La elevación de voces y oraciones / sublimes, muchas veces son viciosas / y enflaquecen a la fuerza a las razones” (I, 55-57). Cueva maintains that judiciousness needs to be maintained so that art does not appear too lofty or lowly. Experience taught him that appropriate language choice is imperative to good poetry. Castilian words are preferred though a small smattering of neologisms is acceptable as long as they are not overdone (I, 130). Latinisms are discouraged (I, 80), presumably because of a possible pedantic impact on a text; the use of any foreign words demands good judgment (I, 330). Discretion in selecting subject matter is also necessary. To illustrate his point, Cueva compares prudence to a warhorse, of which one can lose control very easily (I, 339-41). One notable contradiction in the first epistle reveals a conflicted Cueva in relation to following rules and conventions. At first he notes that “Ningún preceto hace ser forzoso / el escribir verdad en la poesía, / mas tenido en algunos por vicioso” (I, 235-37) but forty lines later offers a different opinion: “Así el que escribe al modo que le aplace / sin sujetarse a reglas ni precetos, / de estimación carece lo que hace” (I, 274-76). This ambivalence suggests that poets should diverge from convention, but not so much that the work loses its esteem.

In the second epistle, Cueva continues his lengthy discourse on Spanish poetry. His nationalistic pride is evidenced by his assertion that only Castilian poetry is comparable to that of the ancient Greeks and Romans, and he lists numerous Spanish poets that measure up to their classical predecessors (II, 82-100). He then focuses on the attribution of certain meters to specific situations, hendecasyllable verses, for example, are appropriate for praise and advice (II, 153-55). These ideas transcend to the stage, where he, too, wrote in polymetric verse. In terms of poetic composition, he mentions that mixing comedy and tragedy makes for successful poetry (II, 310-12), perhaps with the intention of taking some of the credit for the popularity of the tragicomedy that was so popular at the time. He also continues his ranting against the vulgar public: “Hace que el vulgo libremente vea / su cortedad de ingenio, y manifieste / por suya aquella obcenidad tan fea” (II, 412-15), yet another admission—and admonition—of the public’s influence on the arts. Clearly, mixing versification helped to compose a variety of original poetic works.

The *Ejemplar poético* was an outlet used by Cueva to assert his contributions to poetry—and especially to theater, since his he feared that his legacy would be swallowed up by the success of Lope and the *comedia nueva*. It is in second half of the third epistle where Cueva explains his observations concerning theater. From the beginning, he distances his art, which is pure, chaste, and proper, from the "vulgo ávaro" (III, 24-25). The tone of the treatise has produced differing critical responses: Edward C. Riley called it outspoken (186), while more recently McKendrick described it as timid and ambivalent (53), but despite these assessments, Cueva's *Ejemplar poético* is significant as it creates dramatic possibilities and emphasizes the shifting nature of the theater. The document as a whole—and especially the section on theater—is defiant. True, some contradictions exist in the three epistles, but it must be noted that Cueva was a frustrated and proud artist, who most likely wanted to get credit for what he perceived as his contributions to Spanish literature. By writing this later in his career, during the reign of Lope de Vega, the document cannot be seen as a timid gesture. In it, he tries to come out from the shadow of Lope.

Cueva stakes many claims, both true and false, regarding his contributions to the early modern Spanish stage. McKendrick points out that Cueva mistakenly takes credit for some innovations that are not his own: the introduction of the king to the comedy and a four-act structure (54-55). Nevertheless, Cueva's early claims of innovation on the stage demonstrate a cognizance of the impact of reception on the playwriting process, though his perception of these innovations may have been misguided. While his assertion of instituting the four-act play structure is not accurate, it does reveal that reception was important to him since he saw the structure of the play as important. Like his contemporaries, he called each act a *jornada*, which reminds of Torres Naharro's designation. The placement of a king or gods on the comic stage demonstrates his understanding of the dramatic potential of mixing classes, causing tension that would be interesting and less stilted than the classical tragic play. It opens the doors for new situations and communication between different characters. McKendrick also notes that Cueva does not recognize two of his actual lasting contributions to the Spanish stage: the introduction of polymetry and the emphasis on the divine authority of the king (54). Cueva, however, did recognize the impact of introducing familiar subject matter, especially national history, and contemporary social issues to the theater, an obvious result of the transformation of the theater-going public's expectations. Most certainly, these are not new ideas but they are effective ones. The treatise also shows how experience dictates practice and theory: Cueva wrote plays in one manner, but, especially later in life, his theories of the theater did not necessarily pertain to his own works, but rather to the hugely successful *comedia*.

This part of the *Ejemplar poético* reveals a bold Cueva in which he explains how many of his own precepts serve to guide the new form of dramatic poetry called the *comedia*.[19] Calling this new manifestation of comedy a "fabula ingeniosa," Cueva notes that the drama fills a void and satisfies the public (III, 484-92). Imagination is fundamental in the composition of plays—a concept that Torres Naharro introduced almost a century earlier—and his plays combine history with imagination, making them new but familiar. The only solution for success is to follow the momentum of innovation. Cueva refuses to accept any blame for breaking from already-established paradigms; he jokingly states, it is the perpetual vice of Spaniards to disobey rules (III, 499-501). Clearly frustrated with the unsuccessful results of Neoclassical theater, Cueva expresses sympathy for fellow Sevillian playwrights who never achieved greatness because they restricted themselves to following outdated precepts (III, 538-40). He remarks that drama has always conformed to the concerns of contemporary times and that innovation continues to be a part of the theatrical experience, so changes should not be judged as bad, but normal (III, 523-25).

Cueva mentions the public at this point, arguing that modern theatergoers demand much more than their predecessors, much to the detriment of theater. He laments the increasingly unsophisticated audiences that populate theaters. Clearly demonstrating a negative attitude toward the contemporary

---

19. Cueva boldly states his feelings of disgust toward its critics in verses 1455-57.

theatergoer, he asserts the difficulty of presenting classical theater to the Spanish public because of their unpolished nature, contrasting them with the Greek audiences: "O por ser más tratable o menos fiera / la gente, [era] de más gusto o mejor trato / de más sinceridad que en nuestra era" (III, 547-59). The new works needed to be short, clear, and simple, without adornment and artifice, which permits the audience to maintain their concentration (III, 550-52). Diverging from these past conventions is not all bad, in fact, it is to be expected since theater reflects contemporary culture and appetites. Earlier conventions would have been seen as obsolete for the modern audience:

> Si del sujeto comenzando gustas
> y a él se inclina tu afición dichosa
> y con el mío el modo tuyo ajustas,
> confesarás que fue cansada cosa
> cualquier comedia de la edad pasada,
> menos trabada y menos ingeniosa. (III, 580-85)

His confidence in the new styles is as noteworthy as the distaste he demonstrates toward classical works. Cueva claims that dramatic poets of the past, however, still deserve praise for their works, ideas, and teachings, but he boasts that although originality, grace, and resourcefulness are inherent in all Spanish writing, the new playwrights surpass their predecessors in the production of precisely composed dramatic art (III, 589-612). He maintains that originality is fundamental to the new comedy, saying that themes and arguments should always be new or never repeated in the same language (III, 616-21), which explains how these works' virtues outshine those of their predecessors.

Having clearly modeled the *Ejemplar poético* after Horace's *Ars poética*, Cueva emphasizes the importance of following the rules of decorum that are learned from experience as a playwright. This knowledge comes from practice and familiarity with the artform and the public. Of course, a certain amount of tension needs to be formed between the play and the audience in order to maintain interest, but there is a fine line and it is experience that teaches the playwright where such a boundary lies. The direction of costuming and acting must also be dictated by rules of decorum. His explicit instructions concerning costuming, where he mentions *estrañeza*, meaning admiration or novelty, suggests the characters' costumes added to the spectacle of the performance. Cueva then discusses speech, noting that language must correspond to the time and to the state of affairs of the action (III, 622-24). Regarding typical characters and their behavior on stage, he lists several stock roles and suggests how they should be performed, each one corresponding to the social status and age of the character (III, 629-36). The public does not expect and would not accept a character presented outside of context. The novelty of a work must carefully balance with convention, so it is clear that theater embodies the delicate balance of imagination (*el ingenio*) and convention (*el arte*) described at the beginning of the first epistle.

With regard to choosing and presenting subject matter on the stage, the playwright needs to practice equal judiciousness. Cueva elaborates on the care one must take when dealing with true subject matter, especially history. He recommends that the playwright not introduce jokes and humor unless intending to establish a lighthearted tone (III, 638-42), which is incongruent with a historically based story. He distinguishes between comic and tragic plays, and insists that the former still remains within the bounds of decorum with regard to style and verse (III, 640-57). So, the reaction of the audience should be on the mind of any playwright, and Cueva's suggestion to stay within cultural boundaries is not surprising. Novelty on stage is appreciated, but unfamiliarity is not tolerated, especially by the boisterous public so common to the times.

According to Cueva, a comedy is an active and happy work that consoles and entertains the public, and, although it may begin with unhappy circumstances, the play must end well (III, 661-65). He praises humanist thinker Juan de Mal Lara's contributions to the advancement of drama, claiming that his understanding of the necessity to conform to contemporary needs added vigor to stiff classical verse (III, 697-99, 703-05). Also, to avoid confusion in a comedy, Cueva warns against the inclusion of historical and tragic subject matter (III, 709-11). Following the notions first introduced to Spanish drama theory by Torres Naharro, Cueva confirms the notion of the semi-fictional nature of the comedy and, like his predecessor, espouses use of imagination (III, 715-17). Reiterating his opinions concerning the unsophisticated nature of the public, he concludes that the successful poet must recognize that the audience speaks a different language: "hállete el vulgo siempre diferente / en lenguaje, pues hablan los poetas / en otra lengua que la ruda gente" (III, 724-26). He also advises aspiring writers to play to the desires of the crowd and to avoid classical influences (III, 751) because they may not be appreciated or understood.

Though he wrote plays that did not necessarily fit the mold described in his last treatise, Cueva did successfully meld Neoclassical traditions and modern sensibilities, opening the door for a new style of theater that conformed to the needs of a public accustomed to a commercial dramatic tradition established by such playwrights as Lope de Rueda and the popular Jesuit School Dramas. In an attempt to elevate Spanish drama to a new level, and following the lead of Mal Lara, Cueva suggested that by relaxing the stiff Neo-Aristotelian canons imposed on drama, the overall quality of drama would be improved. Both on the Sevillian stage and on the pages of his theoretical treatises, Cueva continued to hold classical models in high esteem, but altered their style to a form more acceptable to modern sensibilities, though never changing them so much as to make them unrecognizable.

Senecan tragedy, for example, held great sway over Cueva, who was the first to introduce the style to the Spanish stage (Morby 384). These plays, which often included sensational, grotesque, and magical characteristics intermingled with rhetorical devices such as monologues and commonly dealing with vengeance, were exploited by the playwright in an attempt to evoke an emotional response in the public. His tragedies revealed shocking scenes, such as the seven heads of seven princes placed on stakes and the mention of bodies being burned alive in *Los siete infantes de Lara*, as well as examples of suicide in *Ajax Telamon, La muerte de Virginia y Appio Claudio*. Many of his comedies, for example the *Viejo enamorado*, included magic, omens, and dreams to impress the audience. In his plays, Cueva commonly borrowed a Senecan framework, beginning with an exposition, either a monologue or a dialogue that introduced the situation, and the characters, followed by the momentary victory of the antagonist, the resolution of the catastrophe (where a *deus ex machina* restores the advantage to the protagonist), the climax, and the ending.

Cognizant of the persuasive potential of language, Cueva utilized various rhetorical strategies in his plays with the intention of coercing and enlightening the audience. Monologues informed the audience of past events or actions that occurred off stage, including the emotional account of the murder of the brothers in *Siete infantes*, as well as the monologues in *Ajax, Virginia,* and *La constancia de Arcelina*, all of which introduced the plot. Cueva wrote with a clear vocabulary, interspersed with word play, and created a comic effect by means of the scatological humor of the characters. Rhythmic and alliterative repetition of the same or similar words was used to keep the audience entertained: in *La muerte del Rey don Sancho*, Cueva mixed *gusto* and *justo* in an amusing exchange between characters, and other examples abound in the debates of *Virginia* and *Ajax*. Furthermore, Cueva's diverse integration of mixed versification, for example, the combination of Spanish *redondillas,* with various Italian meters formed a polymetric drama that benefited both actors and public: the actors could remember lines and perform them more easily, and the audience understood the works better because the type of verse corresponded to the nature of the event on stage. The introduction of ballad fragments formed another point of contact between the spectators and the plays, allowing for the public to participate through its recognition of antecedent texts. All of these strategies specifically point to the importance of performance and reception of the text.

An examination of Cueva's theater as a whole reveals other, more specific characteristics that further explain the motives behind his dramaturgy. For example, the structure of the plays consists of an introit and four acts. In contrast to past traditions, the introit was thematically independent of the play, demonstrating his faith in the audience to follow the story. This also implies that the play was able to stand on its own, utilizing textual clues within the script and extra-textual performance clues to facilitate comprehension. Cueva's use of leitmotifs further confirms his confidence that the public could recognize references to common mythological stories, i.e., hubris in *Ajax* with the conflict between

Ajax and Ulysses.[20] Furthermore, Cueva's plays were recognizable to most audience members because of the familiar character that each possessed. His choice of subject matter commonly embodied universal themes and he drew inspiration from history and familiar Spanish legend, remembering the feats of famous heroes, kings, events, and literary works: El Cid was seen in *Sancho*, *Celestina* was mentioned in *Siete infantes*, and in the *Comedia de la libertad de España por Bernardo del Carpio,* the defeat of Charlemagne was recounted. Cueva also took inspiration from other sources such as Italian theater, utilizing some common devices: false accusation in *Siete infantes* and the stereotype of the braggart soldier common in the *commedia dell'arte.* Finally, he even included political allegory in his plays about the Spanish intervention in the struggle for the Portuguese throne.[21] Clear examples include *Bernardo del Carpio*, where we see a conflict between personal freedom and moral obligation, and *Virginia,* in which he anticipated the controversial honor code.

The incorporation of ballads became trademark to Cueva's plays. Having published two volumes of ballads, he facilitated their adaptation to theater, giving his works a unique feel as they were grounded in an artistic form that was inherently familiar to the public. Francisco E. Porrata describes two degrees of incorporation of ballads into the theater of the sixteenth century: primary incorporation of the *romance* with all formal aspects, constituting part of the speech of the character to advance the dramatic action, as well as those that appear within a monologue; and secondary incorporation, which did not integrate all the characteristics of the poetic form, that is, the title was mentioned, or the ballad was incorporated into the work as part of the dialogue, with the verses being inspired by ballads but not written in balladic form (193-94). Cueva's formal and thematic incorporation pertained to the former category.

---

20. Cueva's faith in the audience's familiarity with history proved detrimental in *Tragedia de los siete infantes de Lara*. Cueva, assuming that the public was familiar with the treacherous circumstances surrounding the brutal deaths of the princes, omitted the scene and consequently did not create the strong dramatic effect that their inclusion could have added.

21. See AnthonyWatson, *Juan de la Cueva and the Portuguese Succession*.

Cueva's situation differs from that of the other playwrights examined in this study because his *Ejemplar poético* is not a defense of his own plays but rather of the *comedia.* We must, therefore, look at his earlier work with the intention of pointing out the ways in which his plays predicted the new dramatic trends made popular by Lope and how they inspired him to compose his last treatise of dramatic precepts. By looking at the *Comedia del infamador* as an antecedent to the *comedia*, we can see how it fit into the trajectory of the changing scope of Spanish theater. The play exhibits traits described later in the *Ejemplar poético*, and these characteristics are clearly linked to enhancing audience reception and comprehension of the work, demonstrating Cueva's intuitions regarding the text's performance on stage. Although Cueva almost fanatically emphasizes regard for decorum in the *Ejemplar poético*, this fascination began much earlier in his plays. The playwright clearly believed that following the rules of decorum would please audiences, since any divergence could upset the public and ruin the theatrical experience for them. Also, *El infamador* contained several characters later mentioned in the *Ejemplar poético*, suggesting that these character types, along with others, were well received during Cueva's stage productions. We see that the play also ended well, but not in a wedding, foreseeing the later suggestion found in *Ejemplar poético* that poetic justice must be served, presumably pleasing the public's sense of fairness.

IV. A precursor to the *comedia nueva*: the *Comedia del infamador*

Premiering in 1581 in Seville's Corral de Elvira and arguably Cueva's best play, the *Comedia del infamador* anticipated the *comedia nueva* that soon followed, illustrating a keen intuition on the part of the playwright. This mythological and didactic work dealt with contemporary issues and presented familiar characters, offering many clues with regard to the importance of audience reception and performance to the success of the dramatic spectacle. It also, according to James P Wickersham Crawford, presented a rudimentary model of a cloak and dagger play (169). The tragicomedy opens with Leucino, the protagonist, exalting the power of his money and boasting of his amorous conquests, although we soon learn that the maiden Eliodora has refused all of Leucino's advances. In desperation, he attempts to force himself upon her but is unsuccessful because of the interruption of Nemesis, the god of vengeance, who comes to her aid. Venus, representing pagan love, promises to facilitate Leucino's conquest of Eliodora and disguises herself as Feliciana, Eliodora's servant, to assure the consummation of Leucino's passions. Meanwhile, Leucino, with the help of one of Eliodora's servants and the brutish mercenary, Farandón, makes plans to break into Eliodora's house, and, to reassure himself of his success, has the go-betweens, who also practice witchcraft, read his future, but they misinterpret the negative auguries as positive. They enter the house, Eliodora puts up a struggle, and chaos ensues, resulting in Eliodora inadvertently killing an attacker in self-defense. She is summarily detained after Leucino lies, saying that the death was a crime of passion brought about by Eliodora's jealousy, a story corroborated by Farandón. Concerned with the honor of their families, the fathers of Eliodora and of Leucino each blame their own child and demand their deaths. Her father decides that he must poison his daughter instead of having her executed publicly, but the poison sent to her via Feliciana suddenly turns into a bouquet of flowers. The goddess Diana appears and resolves the problem of the false testimony of Leucino and Farandón. Leucino confesses and is sentenced to be drowned in the river Betis, while Farandón is to be burnt at the stake, but the god Betis appears and begs that such a man not spoil his pristine waters; Diana agrees and orders that he be buried alive.

As to be later described in the *Ejemplar poético*, the rules of decorum take center stage in *El infamador*. The carefully crafted drama reflects the meticulous process of playwriting that Cueva followed in his career. Decorum shapes innovation in the playwriting process by regulating the use of popular culture, language, theme, structure, and characterization. In the *Ejemplar poético*, Cueva frequently repeats that change is a powerful and necessary force, a notion that *El infamador* materialized on the stage much earlier, demonstrating how to combine a classically inspired theater style and a more popular dramatic form. The play's hybrid character introduced innovative aspects dictated by contemporary tastes but is also contained by the rules of decorum, which are typical to the classical theater and its governing precepts. Indeed, it is the propriety of the play that stands out most, which foresees Cueva's emphasis in the *Ejemplar poético* of maintaining control when composing poetry, as well as his classical background. He highlights the ability of the Spanish playwright to offer a new dramatic form dictated by decorum but one that is still entertaining:

> Finalmente los sabios i prudentes
> dan a nuestra comedias la ecelencia
> en artificio i passos diferentes.
> Esto sabido, importa l'advertencia
> del modo qu'an de ser i a qué te obliga
> el decoro qu'enseña la experiencia. (III, 613-18)

In *El infamador*, Cueva adheres to the rules of decorum, which is no easy task because he introduces potentially scandalous characters and situations. The Roman gods and monsters, for example, appeal to the imagination of the public and their actions—especially those of Venus—build tension in the play. Clearly cognizant of what his public wants, the playwright integrates innovative dramatic strategies and revisits accepted practices and subject matter when composing his plays, but he does so in a controlled manner and the resulting work does not overwhelm the public with indecorous materials. As a result, Cueva's treatment of the thematic, structural, and artistic levels of the play highlights the importance of performance and reception in the entire dramatic spectacle.

Cueva combines popular culture and classical references in *El infamador*, resulting in an appealing and imaginative play. Its popularity is documented and corroborated by the fact that it was actually performed in Seville, one of Spain's liveliest theater-scenes at the time.[22] In a recent study, John Storey offers six different notions of what the popular culture entails, three of which

22. In sixteenth century Seville, several *corrales de comedias* were constructed, underlining the popularity of the commercial theater in the Andalusian capital. They include the *Corral de Don Juan*, the *Corral de la Atarazanas*, the *Corral de la Huerta de la Alcoba*, the *Corral de San Pedro*, and *Corral de Doña Elvira*, arguably the most famous. Two other theaters were built at the beginning of the seventeenth, the *Corral de la Montería* and the *Corral del Coliseo*. See Hugo Rennert for a detailed description of the theaters in early modern Spain.

apply to Cueva's play and theater in general in sixteenth-century Spain.[23] He mentions that popular culture is that which is widely favored by the public, a commercial and mass culture, and one that originates from the people. *El infamador* exemplifies the notion of popular culture in the modern sense of the word. It is a play that perpetuates societal and cultural norms and represents the preoccupations of a society in the arena of mass culture, which would be the theater of early modern Spain; there was no other medium that reached so many people of so many different social stations. Furthermore, the story includes folklore, or in this case, local mythology. Cueva's *El infamador* introduced gods to the stage, not an innovation in the history of theater, since court plays often included mythological figures, but quite possibly a first for the commercial stage. The personification of vices and virtues in the form of recognizable gods may have inspired awe in the public and most certainly extended the didactic purpose of the play. The presence of Venus and Diana represented a clear contrast between uncontrollable lust and rational comportment. Cueva underscores deviousness in the play by including Venus as a personification of the dangers of a capricious and pagan love. He counterbalances Venus's imprudence with the wisdom of Diana, who overcomes all iniquity. The integration of classical figures within a contemporary context produced an effect that was identifiable and novel. Cueva managed to write a play in which stilted references were understandable to most. For example, when a lesser-known Roman god was introduced, another character would describe and introduce them in the dialogue. A clear example is Morfeo (Morpheus in English), the god of dreams. In this scene Venus describes to the *Dios del Sueño* how she would like to transform herself into the Eliodora's servant, Felicina, to facilitate the noblewoman's rape, and the god responds:

> Tu mando será presto obedecido,
> y así para cumplirse tu deseo,

---

23. Storey suggests the following: widely favored culture, the culture left over from what is decidedly high culture, mass culture, culture originating from the people, a tool used by hegemonic powers to win consent of subordinate groups, and as postmodern culture, where there is no difference between high and popular culture. (5-14)

el sueño enviaré luego que has pedido.
  No será Iceladón, aunque dél creo
que hará lo que mandas, ni a Fantaso,
mas el que allá enviaré será Morfeo.
  Este es tan diestro cual conviene el caso,
....
  Conviene que dejando el perezoso
sueño, a Híspalis vayas con presteza,
los vientos precediendo presuroso;
  allí has de tenerla así sin que señora
has de aquejarle con graveza
a Felicina, moza de Eliodora,
con sueño profundísimo y pereza;
  has de tenerla así sin que señora
sea de sí, sin que se mueva o sienta,
hasta que a Venus le parezca hora. (2.2.61-67, 2.2.78-87)

Those audience members not familiar with Morfeo are informed of his powers; those who know who he is, are reminded of the same. In addition to the obvious result of informing the audience, such a strategy builds tension as the audience learns of the imminent action. Also in the play, Cueva had the gods introduce themselves, one especially dramatic example is when Nemesis interrupts Leucino's first attack of Eliodora:

  Quién soy yo lo dire. ¡Vete, Eliodora,
con quien la excelsa Híspalis se honora!
  Y porque entiendas la deidad que tengo
y que soy de los dioses celestiales,
yo que soy la diosa Némesis, que vengo
a dar castigo a semejantes males;
los bienes premio y los males vengo,
y véngolos de suerte en los mortales
que con aquesta mano poderosa
doy la vida o la muerte rigurosa. (1.9.473-82)

In both cases, the role of the character becomes evident, which is important for an understanding of the work. Cueva did not only rely on the background knowledge of his public when writing his plays, but also filled in informational gaps where he saw it necessary. Of course, there were those spectators that were already familiar with the pantheon of gods, but many were not and, therefore, benefited from the extra information. This strategy was necessary so that the public could follow the story. This was not done for every reference, of course, but only for those that were most important to the story in the eyes of the playwright. The comprehension of an obscure allusion may have imbued a feeling of superiority for those spectators who had captured the gist. By tying these gods to the storyline, he helped the reception of the message by presenting it in a new way but within a familiar context.

Other commonalities are seen in the references made to other, well-known literary works. The intertextuality of the play reminds its public of the collective nature of the work because of the shared cultural references. In addition, these references break down the dramatic illusion of the play and the public is then able to consider the message embedded in the text and on the stage. The familiarity afforded by the metaliterary character of the work, especially the references to Fernando de Rojas's *Celestina*,[24] adds another dimension of popular appeal to the work. While, traces of *Celestina* are frequent in the play,[25] Cueva's attention to decorum results in a distinct vision of the Rojas's fictitious world. Leucino never has the chance to assault Eliodora, who refuses him outright and concretely, which is different from the relationship and emotions shared by Calisto and Melibea. In the end of both works, the suitors die, but the death of Leucino is an explicit example of *deus ex machina*, not clumsiness, which characterized Calisto as a lover, suitor, and nobleman. Cueva presents Leucino's actions as inexcusable and swift justice is done. In *El infamador*, the go-betweens are also failures and there are three of them, questioning

---

24. Few scholars who talk about *El infamador* fail to mention its obvious inspiration in *Celestina*. See James Pyle Wickersham Crawford's *Spanish Drama before Lope*, Miguel Ángel Pérez Priego's *Cuatro comedias celestinescas*, Mario N. Pavia's *Drama of the Siglo de Oro: A Study of Magic, Witchraft, and Other Occult Beliefs*, Jonathan Thacker's description in *A Companion to Golden Age Theater*, Gillet, Edwin S. Morby, and Richard Glenn, to name a few.

25. The echoes of the *Celestina* resonate throughout the play: the go-betweens, as well as in Teodora's walking monologue in the first act, are clearly reminiscent of Rojas's work. The conjuration of Pluto is also common to both works. Cueva's characterization of Leucino as an irrational, passionate boob and of Farandón as a brutish mercenary, remind us of Calisto and Centurio. Also, the lament of Hircano offers another version of Pleberio's *planctus*.

the effectiveness—and propriety—of their trade and ultimately making their attempts laughable. Cueva pokes fun at the conjuration since two of them misread the auguries that foresee the assault of Eliodora. So, Cueva gives them a different voice and meaning, one that corresponds to his times and manner of composing poetry. He reins in the *Celestina*'s chaotic world. While Rojas's work clearly had enormous influence on the play's storyline, other works also pervade the text. Eliodora and Felicina (or Venus disguised as Felicina) discuss their current reading. As Jauss points out, contemporary literature responds to questions posed by past literature, and this play is not an exception. *El infamador* takes these works, revisits them, and revises their stories to make them contemporary. The references to the *Libro de buen amor* and *El Corbacho* found in the play also illustrate the metaliterary bridge that Cueva constructs between his work and others, adding yet another familiar context to the play. The two women complain of the misogynistic nature of the works, an example of metacriticism since their words parallel a similar message in *El infamador*. Indeed, Cueva successfully orients his play as a response to these medieval works as it is in constant dialogue with them. In this play, the women dominate the men, and their strong characters offer a strong contrast to the contents of the medieval tomes that the two women have just finished reading.

Although the play was novel in many respects, certain parts would have been familiar to the Sevillian public. The inclusion of familiar geographical and cultural references, for example, lends a sense of ownership to a work. Seeing familiar geography in a play also affects the reception of a work. Recognizable landmarks give a sense of ownership to the population and makes the play that much more enjoyable to them. By using local references, the playwright paints a picture immediately recognizable to the public, adding meaning to the play. This phenomenon still holds true today. For example, the residents of New York City most certainly saw the late-eighties and early-nineties sitcom "Seinfeld" in a different manner than someone from Columbus, Ohio, or Los Angeles, California. The show, nonetheless, acquired a heterogeneous audience. It is precisely this appeal that makes a work a hit and not just an esoteric or local phenomenon. In *El infamador*, Cueva utilized this strategy in terms of geographical and cultural references and makes it very Sevillian in character. The imagery provided by references to "la Vega" (1.7.352) and "el Prado" (1.7.358) do not need explanation for the Sevillian audience. These parks in the city were fertile and lush green areas meant to evoke emotions and memories of the local population. The introduction of specific characters, for example, induces different reactions in different people: it would be refreshing to those familiar with the person and intriguing to those who were not. This strategy differs from a convention common of the *comedia nueva* that situated dramatic works in exotic locales, both to appeal to the public's taste for something different and to mask local criticism. This play follows Torres Naharro's tendency to specify the location of the action, which was seen in his critical *comedias a noticia.* Another familiar reference, Betis, the Roman god of what is now the Guadalquivir River, is a somber yet strong character that refuses to allow Leucino to be drowned in his waters. The river is a point of pride in Seville, and Betis's demands reflect the admiration of the population's desire to preserve the river's pristine waters. Leucino's body would blemish the sanctity of the river, as he did with the honor of Eliodora. Due to such admonition, his crime rises to a new level of seriousness since the river god rejects him. This rebuff reflects the seriousness of his transgressions, which go against the grain of Sevillian society, represented in the form of Betis. His misbehavior warrants swift punishment and a symbolic exile from the city, in the form of death. Cueva's inclusion of other Roman deities augmented the sense of familiarity, since, according to legend, Seville was founded by Hercules, further underlining the influence of classical mythology on the culture.

In addition to including Betis, Cueva's play anticipates, if not introduces, another Sevillian literary figure, that is, Don Juan. It has been suggested by Fernández de Moratín that Leucino is a prototype of the Don Juan figure made popular by Tirso de Molina and that has remained a mainstay in literature, both Spanish and otherwise, into the twenty-first century. Scholars have discussed this polemic for years. The argument arises because of the difficulty to pin down the roots of the character. Some argue that Don Juan was invented by Tirso as a counterexample of good comportment during the sixteenth and seventeenth centuries.

Others, including Menéndez Pidal, propose that there are traces of the Don Juan figure in ancient ballads that were inspired by a real person (qtd. in Weinstein 10). Taking into account Cueva's knowledge and love for ballads, it is quite possible that he, too, was inspired by such a reference to the character. Another possibility remains, that the Don Juan figure was based on a contemporary figure in Seville at the time. Though no specific sixteenth-century figure has been cited,[26] the city was the gateway to the Americas and flush with newly found riches and old fortunes, so libertines were most certainly roaming the streets. The most reasonable conclusion is that of Gillet: Leucino was indeed a rebellious character and, while not necessarily a prototype of Don Juan, he is definitely a precursor.

The introduction of these characters to the Sevillian stage was an innovative way to emphasize common values of the culture. They left an impression on the audience—or the reader, in our case—after the play was finished. Like in Torres Naharro's *Ymenea*, in *El infamador* we see the occurrence of "imaginative authority." In this case, Leucino actions are the opposite of noble and decorous behavior since he represents the negative side of a noble class driven by money, imprudence, and greed. Although most certainly an unsavory fellow, Leucino is still interesting. His moral shortcomings make for a dramatic character that reaches out from the stage and draws the public into his world. His despicable behavior is not exemplary, of course, but it is theatrical and maintains the interest of the public. The play was written at a time of self-evaluation and *desengaño* in Spain, a reaction to the optimism of the Renaissance. This factor, combined with the influence of the unrefined characters seen in Lope de Rueda's *pasos*, for example, make way for the introduction of such characters to the stage. The tragicomic form, also lends to Leucino's characterization since he is a nobleman portrayed as

26. José María de Mena offers two other possibilities that could be tied into the theory that the character is based on a real person—or persons, in this case. In *Tradiciones y leyendas sevillanas* he mentions Pedro Ribero and Miguel de Mañara, noble gentleman of the seventeenth century. Although both lived much later than the 1581 premiere of *El infamador*, the idea that other similar figures known to Cueva is entirely possible.

low-class ruffian. Ultimately, his efforts are thwarted and he is punished. Other exaggerated behaviors are also tempered by Cueva's decorous playwriting in *El infamador*, but in a comical manner. Cueva ridicules his characters by means of their words and actions on the stage. Leucino's apparent womanizing is merely a false conception in his own mind and it is this pride that is at the base of his death at the end of the play.

Thematically speaking, a play needed to relate to the current-day circumstances of its audience, so the playwright is constantly challenged to present contemporary topics in an entertaining manner. In the case of *El infamador*, Cueva produced a simple and well-explained plot that questioned the honor code and demonstrated the ill fortune of those enveloped by pride. Such preoccupations anticipated the advice in *Ejemplar poético* that a play must have a purpose that conformed to contemporary times. The reinterrogation of the honor code in the play is another indicator of Cueva's cognizance of what was popular and how this affected playwriting. Most scholars agree that the dramatized honor code was not so much a faithful representation of societal regulations—though examples most certainly existed—but was more commonly presented on stage because of its popularity with the public; Lope notes the same in his *Arte nuevo*.

Like many of his contemporary playwrights, in *El infamador*, Cueva reworks the theme of honor. He demonstrates the shortcomings of the honor code in an exaggerated manner. Cueva's twist on a common theme, the defamation of a virgin, appeals to the public's sense of novelty but keeping the storyline recognizable and making the play both universal and "local" at the same time. By personifying the honor code in the figures of the fathers, Cueva interrogates the extreme nature of cultural norms and their excessive expectations since these men are more concerned with the family name than with the lives of their children. It takes a Roman goddess to fix the situation, perhaps an indication that the honor code is something too big for the common man. No matter the case, it also makes for good theater as the exaggerated honor code may shock the audience, but they are then appeased when poetic justice is doled out at the end of the play. The antagonism between established decorum and the characters' misbehavior builds tension throughout the play. The possibility of death lingers and maintains the interest of the audience, especially since it is the death of an innocent, undeserving woman.

Love also falls under the rules of decorum. Cueva states in the first epistle of the *Ejemplar poético*:

> Si de Amor celebrares l'aspereza,
> la impacience i furor de un ciego amante,
> de la mujer la ira i la crüeza,
> este decoro as de llevar delante
> sin mesclar en sus rabias congoxosas
> cosa que no sea desto semejante. (169-74)

Like in *Celestina*, *El infamador*'s didactic message criticizes the effect of *loco amor*. In addition to the actions of Leucino, the juxtaposition of the two goddesses is the most evident manifestation as is the death of Leucino. The only love found in the dramatic world is unbridled, passionate love, which is ultimately defeated and rejected by Eliodora with the help of Diana. This implies that it is better to not have love than to accept it in its irrational form. Although rational love is nonexistent in Cueva's play, when compared with Rojas's work, this dramatic world concludes with reason and justice prevailing in the form of Diana, who restores order in the dramatic world. This dramatic representation of the importance of reason in society transcends the stage and reaches out to the public.

Decorum is also used to interrogate society's contempt for women. After being falsely accused of having an illicit affair that ended in the death of one of her attackers, Eliodora accepts her punishment. She has no other alternative and it is her father who condemns her to death—in fact, he argues that execution is the only solution to resolve the situation. Tension mounts as she awaits her impending demise in a jail cell. Diana's wisdom and reason finally save her, dealing a blow to the commonly held notion of a woman's second-class position in society. In the play, Cueva builds tension by means of the characters' improprieties, which ensure an impending doom, but he does not cross the fine line that makes the play indecorous or unsavory. Poetic justice is the tool of decorum, assuring that everyone gets what they deserve.

The integration of fantasy adds an entertaining dimension to the story and makes the didactic lesson more palatable.

Imagination plays a big role in the composition of the play but, once again, it is developed in concert with decorum, and this imaginary aspect adds to the originality of the play. There is no loss of control in the play, though it may come close at times, the storyline remains constant and stable. Without the addition of the Roman gods, it would be just another story. Since the play is not historically based, there is much more room for imagination. Here, we see a split from Torres Naharro's use of imagination in his theater. Where Torres Naharro intended to recreate believable situations, Cueva's use of imagination was distinct because it added fantastic elements to the play. The introduction of supernatural beings and powers would not have been congruent in the works of Torres Naharro, but in Cueva's play these figures are fundamental to the story. Indeed, their inclusion is reminiscent of classical culture and mythology, reminding us of the Roman myths that were common to society. Gods served as stereotypes in an allegorical context that was easily understood. They also offered a local flavor. Cueva took advantage of this knowledge and offered an attractive element to the play. He understood the dramatic effect that they could provoke in an audience.

It is this imagination that separated a literary work from an historical one, a notion that Cueva clearly recognizes and mentions in his dramatic treatise. The play could well be based on a local situation but by adding the gods, he adds a universal dimension. The fantastic nature of the play also facilitates the didactic nature of the work. While the storyline and the human characters are most certainly believable and perhaps representative of some members of society, the gods add a dramatic effect. They remind us that this is a piece of literature and fantasy. Their presence breaks the dramatic illusion and provokes the public to contemplate the message. Also, this is done in an original manner, since they are not members of the Christian pantheon, so the message may be that much more effective since it is a new twist on a common theme often repeated in church services. Clearly, the use of the imagination adds to the dramatic spectacle of the play, of which the author and the public are fully aware. It serves as a constant reminder of the fictional nature of the work.

As can be expected, in the play, language also falls under the constraints of decorum. Cueva devotes much of the *Ejemplar poético* to the appropriate use of language. His opinions are based previous experience gained from writing his own plays, and they described precepts common to the contemporary stage and page. At the beginning of the dramatic treatise, he details the importance of simplicity and decorum in poetry in the following linked tercets:

> El verso advierta el escritor prudente
> que á de ser claro, fácil, numeroso,
> de sonido i espíritu ecelente.
> Á de ser figurado i copioso
> de sentencias i libre de diciones
> que lo hagan umilde u escabroso.
> La elevación de vozes i oraciones
> sublimes muchas vezes son viciosas
> i enflaquecen la fuerça a las razones.
> Vanse tras las palabras sonorosas
> la hinchazón del verso i la dulçura
> tras las sílabas llenes i pomposas.
> Entienden qu'está en esto la segura
> felicidad i luz de la poesía
> i que sin esto es lo demás horrura.
> Si el verso consta sólo de armonía
> sonora, de razones levantadas,
> ni fuerça a más, bien siguen essa vía,
> Mas si las cosas an de ser tratadas
> con puntual decoro del sugeto
> faltaran, d'esse modo gobernadas. (III, 49-69)

A return to the comparison between *El infamador* and *Celestina* reveals how this idea was reflected in Cueva's work long before it appeared in the *Ejemplar poético*. For all of the similarities between the two works that have been mentioned by numerous scholars since the end of the nineteenth century, it is clear that lexical choices and language usage are distinct. Of course, the fact that Rojas's work is written in prose and Cueva's in verse is certainly a factor, but it does not completely remove the possibility of including the colorful language seen in the earlier work. Cueva's dialogues are clear and simple; he does not use popular refrains and sayings as the base of the text. This is not to say that no word play or euphemism exist, but the instances of this are much more limited and less scandalous. The fact that the play was actually performed may have contributed to the conservative language since strict censorship would have been a common obstacle. But, on another level, acting would have supplemented the words being spoken; performance was placed on an equal plane with the play text since the two were mutually complementary.

As is the case with other aspects that characterize the play, Cueva's utilizes traditional and popular language, resulting in an austere and easy but refined style of writing. With regard to versification, Cueva esteems his classical predecessors throughout the text, but from the beginning he notes how Spanish poetry is the equal to its Greek and Roman ancestors. He states:

> [D]e nuestro español verso el elegante
> método, el armonía i la dulçulra,
> a la griega i latina semejante,
> ....
> Su noble antigüedad en las grecianas
> lyras se halla, en el trocayaco verso,
> qu'es el nuestro, i lo propio en la romanas.
> (II, 587-89, 593-95)

Although Edwin Morby suggests that some scholars exaggerate the combination of popular and traditional trends ("Notes" 214), this is something that cannot be denied or discounted. Cueva sought to produce poetry that conformed to the changing tastes in society while maintaining traditional conventions. José Cebrián gives a strophic breakdown of *El infamador* and we see that the majority of the verses are taken from Italian forms, though the Spanish *redondilla* is prevalent (Introducción 84) and is the only Spanish versification seen in the play.[27]

Consistent with the other strategies and conventions that dictate the playwriting process, Cueva combines new and old forms. At this time, in the early 1580s, the tragedy was a common albeit not very popular dramatic form. The more melodramatic School Dramas were more popular as were short dramatic forms

---

27. J. Caso González points out in his introduction to the play that of the 2,174 verses, 58 percent are hendecasyllabic or heptasyllabic forms, the rest are octosyllabic. Cebrián is more specific: 107 *octavas reales* = 856 verses, 12 *estancias* = 154 verses, 50 *tercetos encadenados* = 152 verses, 100 *endecasílabos en suelto* = 100 versos, 114 *redondillas dobles* = 912 verses. (84)

that were inspired by Rueda's *pasos*. This combination of poetic styles paralleled the need to mix traditional and innovative aspects to the play. This usage predates the *comedia nueva*, which also takes advantage of mixed verse form in the play text. It is, of course, impossible to know the influence of the play on future forms but no matter its influence, it cannot be denied that it was part of the evolution of theater in early modern Spain and anticipated future conventions. The balance of versification makes for a play text that is not monotonous, and the changes in verse vary and maintain the interest of the receivers.

As a response to earlier studies of Cueva, most notably Camillo Guirrieri Crocetti's *Juan de la Cueva e le origini del teatro nazionale spagnuolo*, Morby's "Notes on Juan de la Cueva: Versification and Dramatic Theory" rebuts previous suggestions that Cueva's theater is a mishmash of versifications. In *El infamador*, for example, the verse forms correspond with the interlocutors and the context of the situation. This strategy became commonplace in later years. It reinforced the characterization as the noble spoke in a more esteemed meter and the humble in a more popular meter. Interestingly enough, the vast majority of playwrights followed these guidelines, so when an exception was made, it would have been noticed by the contemporary public as well as by the modern reader or spectator. Most certainly the attribution of verisimilitude in its most basic sense is not applicable here since people did not speak in verse. Nonetheless, a looser interpretation of the concept can be applied to the correspondence between speaker and character in that the language becomes a metonymic characteristic that is associated with the character and their class. In *El infamador*, Cueva pairs meter with the characters' social position, which is not a surprise, since he was a stickler for following the rules of decorum.

Although Cueva enjoyed the luxury of having his plays performed in Seville, his prominence as a playwright throughout the rest of Spain and in the annals of Spanish literary history was not so great. This prideful man demonstrated a bitter side in *Coro febeo de romances historiales* (1587), the result of his peers not recognizing him as the grand innovator that he thought himself to be. An envious Cueva despised the recognition gained by the *comediantes*, and, as Cebrián notes in *Estudios sobre Juan de la*

Cueva, the last verses of the work contain implicit allusions to Lope (127).[28] Lope may have sparked this anger by omitting Cueva from the list of notable authors in Book 19 of *Jerusalén conquistada* in the second part of *La Filomena*, as well as by excluding him from the list of illustrious Sevillian writers in *El laurel de Apolo*. A reasonable explanation is that Lope did not know—or ignored—Cueva, though, in *Ingenios sevillanos del Siglo de Oro que vivieron en las Américas*, Santiago Montoto suggests that the two would have met in the literary circles of Seville (60). Lope's public omissions of Cueva in these lists could also suggest that the two were acquainted but simply did not get along;[29] in fact, Humberto López Morales opines that Lope used silence as a weapon, and by not mentioning his counterpart, destroyed his career (24). Correspondingly, Cueva attempted to use the same strategy but with different results, or more accurately, without any results, since Lope's career did not suffer from being omitted from Cueva's *Ejemplar poético*. Marcel Bataillon acknowledged the importance of the relationship between Lope and Cueva, maintaining that, since Lope was familiar with most dramatists at the time, he had simply ignored Cueva (207), contradicting his predecessor, Alfred Morel Fatio, who suggested

---

28. This citation is from an unedited manuscript of the *Coro febeo de romances historiales*:

> pues saqué el premio de aquellos
> que en su invención acabaron,
> cual fueron Perylo i Sçinis
> i de Antheo el crudo hermano
> Pigmalión, i Trassilo,
> i cual Diomedes el thraçio,
> que fueron sus propias obras
> causa de su mal i daño,
> cual a mí por mis comedias
> á salido el propio pago
> de aquellos que las imitan
> i siguen sus propios passos,
> i aprouechándose dellas,
> son a su invención ingratos. (qtd. in Cebrián 127)

29. In "El *Arte nuevo* de Lope de Vega o la loa dramática a su teatro," Porqueras Mayo notes that Lope was familiar with the literary theory in Spain at the time; so he should have been familiar with both Torres Naharro and Cueva, as both artists desired to explain their dramatic poetics (403).

that the omission by Lope actually illustrated the importance of Cueva, and the exclusion was a question of professional rivalry (34). Bataillon finally concluded that the importance of their mutual omission in the *Arte nuevo* and the *Ejemplar poético* is moot since both treatises trace classical history and not contemporary playwrights (208-09). He continues by positing that like Timoneda, Cueva was at the wrong place at the wrong time, writing plays during an epoch when new theatrical forms were not too successful (211).

Cueva, however, was not completely forgotten and his contemporaries praised his literary abilities as both a lyric poet and a playwright. In the prefatory remarks of the collection of amatory verse entitled *Obras de Juan de la Cueva dirigidas al ilustrísimo señor don Juan Téllez Girón* (1582), Téllez Girón applauded Cueva's poetic abilities. Francisco de Pacheco also honored Cueva in his sonnet "Francisco de Pacheco en loor de Juan de la Cueva." Furthermore, Montoto claims that Feliciana Enríquez de Guzmán alluded to the dramatic innovations of her fellow Sevillian in the 1627 play *Los jardines y campos sabeos* (67). Rodrigo Caro briefly mentioned Cueva in *Varones insignes en letras naturales de la ilustrísima ciudad de Sevilla*, and Nicolás Antonio, in his *Biblioteca hispana nova*, also recorded an incomplete list of his works (1672). Bataillon notes, referring to the play *Príncipe tirano*, that Agustín de Rojas mentioned Cueva in *El viaje entretenido* (1603) as being the first to introduce grave characters to Golden Age theater:

> Fue el autor primero desto
> el noble Juan de la Cueva;
> hizo del padre tirano,
> como sabeys, dos comedias. (209-10)

Cueva's innovative style received even greater critical praise in González de Salas's *Nueva idea de la tragedia antigua*, which applauded Cueva for writing classically inspired literature in a new vein, for combining classical and modern theory in the *Ejemplar poético* (qtd in Sánchez Escribano 177), and for marking a new direction in theatrical production.[30] All of this praise aside, Cueva would have certainly hungered for more recognition along the lines of González de Salas's acclaim and would have been disappointed by the censure, and even exclusion, of peers like Lope. Nonetheless, he clearly enjoyed some fame due to the performances of his plays and his attendance at the *tertulias* of Seville.

Cueva's role in the birth of a Spanish theatrical tradition has been recognized since the eighteenth century. Besides suggesting that Leucino is a prototype of Tirso's Don Juan, in *Orígenes del teatro español*, Fernández de Moratín, who, though critical of Cueva's plays, recognized his importance in the transformation of theatrical trends (270), a notion strongly contested by Francisco A. de Icaza and Gillet in the twentieth century. Menéndez y Pelayo noted that Cueva was a victim of the times: "La escasa cultura de Cueva, así como redujo sus comedias a embriones bárbaros y groseros, así le impidió fecundizar esta idea del progreso en el arte y reducirla a sus justas limitaciones" and most likely forgotten "atropellado... por los mismos a quienes había franqueado el camino" (772). Calling him a true pioneer of Spanish theater, Menéndez y Pelayo conceded that Cueva deserved more credit than he had received in the past.[31]

Debate over Cueva's importance became strong at the beginning of the twentieth century. In his edition of *Comedias y tragedias* (1917), Icaza extolled the virtues of Cueva while barely mentioning the merits of Lope.[32] Bataillon repudiated this idea,

---

30. One interesting but uncertain case is found when Cervantes mentioned Juan de la<u>s</u> Cueva<u>s</u> (stress mine) in *Canto de Calíope* in the *Galatea*, sparking debate as to the identity of the referent. Though probably a typographical error, careful scholars, among them Bataillon, are hesitant to accept the validity of this reference to the Sevillian playwright since the names Cueva and Cuevas were not rare in Spain (Canavaggio "Reflexiones" 208-09), but others, such as Glenn, accept the reference as real (32).

31. He recognizes Cueva's value in the following quotation: "No puede negarse a este ingenio incompleto el título de predecesor el más inmediato de Lope… Su mérito como iniciador es tan grande, que nos admira la poca justicia con que hasta ahora se le ha regateado, no viendo en sus laudables, aunque imperfectos ensayos, otra cosa que abortos informes" (*Estudios* III, 182).

32. A fervent supporter of Cueva, Icaza made the following exaggerated assertion: "[u]na de las mayores glorias de Juan de la Cueva es haber sido el

suggesting imprudence on Icaza's part in crediting Cueva, without concrete evidence, for innovations such as the introduction of ballads and mixed versification to the Spanish stage and hesitated to overemphasize the importance of the dramatist (212-13).[33] This stance elicited impassioned responses from other scholars, such as Morby, Bruce Wardropper, Rinoldo Froldi, and Jean Cannavagio.[34]

The study of Cueva's theater continues, and support for the playwright's importance has become more favorable, albeit

---

iniciador y en cierto modo el maestro de Lope. Y ambos fingieron ignorarse, en sus escritos no se nombraron jamás" (56).

33. He states: "Creo solamente que su importancia histórica no se la puede ya medir hoy, pues es uno de los rarísimos testigos de una enorme producción desaparecida y porque debe su supervivencia a una circunstancia material y no a la elección de sus coetáneos o de la posteridad."

34. In his 1936 doctoral dissertation, Edwin Morby noted the importance of Bataillon's article, but emphasized that much of the argumentation had been based on an insufficient study of Cueva's works. Morby suggested that Bataillon's theorizing about a little-known epoch was misdirected, remarking that it was more relevant to concentrate on Cueva's intrinsic value to Spanish literary history (Canavaggio, "Nuevas reflexiones" 103). Later in his career, Morby maintained in "Notes on Juan de la Cueva: Versification and Dramatic Theory" that Cueva's greatest contribution to Spanish literature was his spanning the gap between the classical and modern traditions, which facilitated a new dramatic tradition (218). Emphasizing the value of Cueva's appreciation of national history and his introduction of ballads to the stage, Bruce Wardropper then entered the fray as a proponent of the Sevillian playwright. In "Juan de Cueva y el drama histórico," Wardropper suggested that Cueva's dramaturgy outlined a conception of national historical theater that stemmed from the humanistic tendencies of sixteenth-century Seville (152). Cueva's fusion of the traditional and modern dramatic styles revealed how medieval traditions infiltrated Renaissance drama as popular poetry (i.e., ballads), coexisting with erudite art. Wardropper further opined that the natural progression of dramatic trends influenced Cueva's theater more than a desire to please the public, as would be the case with Lope (154), a view at odds with the numerous documents revealing Cueva's dismay with his lack of public recognition.

Support for Bataillon's assertions continued far into the twentieth century, especially in Europe. Froldi, for example, insisted in *Lope de Vega y la formación de la comedia* that Cueva cannot be considered a precursor to Lope because his popularity derived more from circumstance than merit. Most recently, Canavaggio reflected on the Cueva debate and offered support for Bataillon's arguments, suggesting that if Cueva had indeed been the "maestro" of Lope, he would have been mentioned by his "protégé" (37).

guarded, in nature; many recent critics have recognized Cueva as the most successful playwright of his time, but they do not necessarily applaud his abilities as a great dramatist. In the last twenty years, scholars continue to acknowledge the influence of Cueva on the *comedia*. In *The Legend of Bernardo del Carpio from Chronicle to Drama*, David G. Burton notes that Cueva envisioned the drama as a didactic tool, pioneering several new techniques that Lope may have adopted, refined, and improved, including topics inspired by Spanish history, a disregard for the unities of time and of place, and polymetric verse (55). Of course, we cannot legitimately assert or confirm the direct influence of Cueva on Lope because of a lack of evidence. In a later study, "The Historical Dramas of Juan de la Cueva," Burton takes a stronger stance regarding the influence of Cueva over Lope and even goes so far as to say that Lope mimicked Cueva, not only on the boards, but also when writing dramatic precepts (411-12).[35] More probable is that Cueva's work was forgotten by 1600, impelling him to write the *Ejemplar poético* as a reminder of his contributions, which just happened to coincide with Lope's *Arte nuevo*. It is, therefore, impractical to discount his influence as a transitional figure in the development of Spanish theater as he did, indeed, introduce innovation to the stage, and he utilized and refined other new trends. McKendrick sums up Cueva's importance in a neat and succinct manner: "Cueva was neither the initiator nor the precursor of the *comedia nueva*, but he was an important precursor" (53). Finally, in 2007, Jonathan Thacker noted that "[w]hether Lope would have approved or not, a search for the roots of the *comedia* must take Cueva into account (16).

The staging of his dramatic theories before discussing them in the *Ejemplar poético* was undoubtedly useful in ascertaining the factors that affected the playwriting process. By contemplating his own successes and failures, Cueva attempted to document the rise

35. Burton finds similarities in the texts of *Ejemplar poético* and the *Arte nuevo*. First, he suggests similarities in this line by Cueva: "Que ni a Ennio ni a Plauto conocemos / ni seguimos su modo ni artificio" with Lope's "Y, cuando he de escribir una comedia / encierro los preceptos con seis llaves: / saco a Terencio y a Plauto de mi estudio", and continues with references regarding the *vulgo* and the need to write to them. See "The Historical Dramas of Juan de la Cueva."

and success of the *comedia*, leaving by the wayside those techniques that were not as effective, including an introit linked to the play as well as the tragic dramatic form. We see a progression between the dramaturgy of Torres Naharro and that of Juan de la Cueva, a reorientation from the court to the commercial stage, whose demands were very different. Both playwrights are undeniable predecessors of the *comedia*, both in their dramatic output and their theoretical innovations.

The two playwrights and their works shared many common elements. As playwrights who wrote theory, they recorded their sensitivity to the importance of performance and reception, which they learned by seeing their plays performed. This invaluable experience buttressed the validity of their precepts as practical knowledge on which they based their ideas toward theater. For example, imagination was central to their innovation. In both cases, the men often strayed from typical sources of inspiration of the time and wrote fictional dramatic pieces that were creative and original works. Of course, they integrated imagination in distinct ways: Torres Naharro saw it as an instrument to develop lifelike storylines, where Cueva used it in a more fanciful manner. The use of imagination in the composition of theater opened infinite possibilities to the playwriting process. Both men also depended on the rules of decorum to direct the composition, production, and performance of their plays. They continually underscored its importance in their dramatic treatises and on the stage. The attention to orderliness suggests that the public, while hungry for change, was also fastidious, compelling the authors to be careful when introducing novelty into their art form.

Torres Naharro and Cueva are also linked by chronology, influences, and reception. In terms of chronology, both Torres Naharro and Cueva wrote at times of great transition in terms of Spanish theater. At the beginning of the Renaissance, theater was transitioning along with other forms of literature to become a reflection of the more modern culture. Torres Naharro and his contemporaries were directly responsible for the shift in styles and practices. Cueva, too, wrote during a transitional time, at the end of the sixteenth century, just as the dramatic tastes were changing directions from classically inspired work and directing themselves toward a tragicomic orientation. He dabbled in both styles, but abandoned the obsolete tragedy in favor of the more forward-thinking—and popular—comedy, which would evolve into the *comedia nueva*. Both poets shared common influences, too. Most obvious, is the desire to please the theatergoing public, which is seen in the innovative nature of their plays and reflected upon in the dramatic treatises. Also, Italy inspired Torres Naharro directly because of his residence there, and, in the case of Cueva, in a more indirect manner. Cueva was a well-educated humanist familiar with Italian literary theory, who even emulated classical theater and poetry styles. True, in the end he abandoned these practices, but he never lost esteem for them. Finally, and unfortunately, both men were received in much the same manner. As others have noted, these talented playwrights were writing at the wrong place at the wrong time, and have not received the recognition that they actually deserve. Most certainly, these men were not the only—or even the most influential or famous—playwrights at the time, but their great impact on Spanish stagecraft cannot be denied. Moreover, they were unique among the many because they formulated dramatic theory from their experiences and documented it for future guidance and reference.

The next chapter discusses two *comedias* written by two of the foremost playwrights of seventeenth-century Spain, Lope de Vega and Tirso de Molina. In both cases, these works serve as early dramatizations of both men's later dramatic treatises. By looking at the metatheatrical character of these works as well as the dramatization of audience reception, it is clear how the consideration of performance and reception was considered as important to the playwriting process as the play text itself.

CHAPTER 3: PERFORMING THE *COMEDIA*, ESTABLISHED NORMS AND CONTINUED INNOVATIONS

As a result of the commercialization of theater at the end of the sixteenth century, the production and the representation of plays began to diverge from the earlier secular contexts of courtly entertainment and street performances, as well as from the didactic scope of religious dramas. The *comedia*, a mixed-genre form, still entertained nobles and taught a moralizing lesson, but as the public and theatrical spaces changed, so did the dramatic landscape of early modern Spain, and a more democratic public went to see plays in the newly constructed and permanent *corrales de comedias*. The formation of this heterogeneous audience presented challenges for the dramatic poet, who was forced to face new and changing needs and expectations. The plays were escapist, and the public's thirst for novelty pushed the dramatic poet to develop original works within a familiar context. Most Spanish Golden Age playwrights met this challenge head on, changing with the times. Among the many great dramatists of the era, three stand out: Lope de Vega, Tirso de Molina, and Calderón de la Barca, and each one helped to establish the *comedia* as the national theatrical form of Spain. Where Lope took the existing—and evolving—dramatic tradition and molded it into what we know as the *comedia*, Tirso, an avid supporter of Lope, added his own touches to the innovative style, and finally Calderón, the youngest of the three, took the form, already deeply rooted in the culture, and enhanced it even further with philosophical and moral themes.

This chapter deals with the *comedia* and examines the dramatization of theater theory in two representative plays, *Lo fingido verdadero* by Lope and *El vergonzoso en palacio* by Tirso. In both cases, the works clearly manifest the concepts found in the dramatic treatises of the two playwrights. Lope's play stages most of the precepts set forth in his *Arte nuevo de hacer comedias*. Tirso's intercalates his *comedia* in the *Cigarrales de Toledo,* where it is sandwiched between critical commentary specifically about the play and, more generally, about the genre. The treatises themselves served to defend the *comedia* from the frequent attacks by the literati, and the dramatized versions served the same purpose, but they also conveyed the preoccupations and processes involved in composing the art form to the public in more accessible terms. These *comedias* demonstrate a prolific use of metatheatrical techniques that highlights the importance of performance and reception not only in the preliminary, or pre-performance, stages of the play: composition and rehearsal, but also when the dramatic spectacle is presented.

I. Lope de Vega's *Arte nuevo de hacer comedias*, examined from the perspective of performance and reception

Lope de Vega, one of the most prolific and influential figures in Spanish literature, was a successful poet, playwright, and novelist, composing literally thousands of works at a Herculean pace. In addition, he wrote the fundamental dramatic treatise of early modern Spain, the *Arte nuevo*, which established and defended the most popular dramatic form in Spanish history, the *comedia*. Lope's innovations, however, were not limited to theater, as he, along with Francisco de Quevedo and Luis de Góngora y Argote, was a major lyric poet of his day; he also wrote notable works in prose. Indeed, all of his literary creations inspired many admirers, who attempted to emulate and imitate his work, but it was his dramatic innovations that created the largest following of disciples, who, using Lope's plays as models, added their own original ideas to propagate the dynamic art form. In terms of early modern Spanish theater, Lope was the authority.

Though he was a hero to many, not all literary circles favored Lope's pioneering poetics, and there was an abundance of detractors who attacked his art and character from all directions. The Church disapproved of the representation of unseemly behavior on stage or, in some cases, the whole enterprise of theater in general. In the secular sector, the traditional neo-Aristotelians criticized his new approach to theater, the *culteranistas* led a furious debate over his poetic styles, and rival poets, envious of his popularity, slandered his character and attributed his name to second-rate works in order to sell them to unsuspecting theater owners. Indeed, Lope's fame and popularity sparked professional envy that led to vicious attacks by his enemies, illustrating the impact that his work had on the literary world of Golden Age Spain. Both his supporters and his enemies were impassioned in their opinions of the poet: while some, like Cervantes and Góngora, recognized the indisputable popularity of Lope de Vega, others, like Torres Rámila, challenged his popularity and consequently saw their own reputations ruined.[1] On a personal level, many noblemen, envious of Lope's artistic talent or his success with women, caused problems, too. These are just a few

---

1. Cervantes was, according to Joaquín de Entrambasaguas y Peña, Lope's worst and most brutal critic (22), whose attacks insisted that the *comedia* was an inferior art form when compared to the Greco-Latin theatrical tradition. Luis de Góngora was another bitter enemy of Lope de Vega but differed from Cervantes in that he brutally criticized Lope's lyric poetry, but admired his theatrical works. In fact, one of his *comedias*, *Las firmezas de Isabela* (1610), was edited and printed two times with two of Lope's *comedias* and another anonymous play in *Cuatro comedias famosas de D. Luis de Góngora y Lope de Vega Carpio* (1613, 1617). See Emilio Orozco-Díaz's "Sobre la actitud de Góngora ante el teatro de Lope" for more details.

Pedro Torres Rámila's *Spongia* was a brutal but ineffective attempt to discredit all of Lope's literary production. Lope did not take this attack lightly and that same year, responding swiftly and fiercely, he wrote two satirical poems that assailed the erudition of the author of and contributors to the *Spongia.* Thanks to the secret donations of many of the *literati* of Madrid, Toledo, and Alcalá, a formal response to Torres Rámila's *Spongia* was released and passed out free of charge in 1618 under the title *Expostulatio Spongiae a Petro Turriano Ramila Pro Lupo de Vega Carpio*, written by the invented author Julio Columbario. The *Expostulatio Spongiae* was a response to the libel of Torres Rámila, an attack on his theories, and a tribute to Lope, stating that his incomparable merits made him the renovator of poetry and the creator of drama. The attacks encountered in *Expostulatio Spongiae* matched and even surpassed the brutality of the *Spongia*. Lope's rebuttal did not end there, as he continued to insult Torres Rámila in the prologues and dedications of many of his plays between 1618 and 1620. Lope finally finished the job with the 1621 publication of *La Filomena*, where his detractors once again fell under the weight of his punishing pen, bringing an end to this literary battle leaving his critics' reputations pulverized by his harsh words, acoording to Entreambas (234). See Entramabasaguas's 1932 book, *Una guerra literaria del Siglo de Oro: Lope de Vega y los preceptistas aristotélicos*, in which he meticulously studies the polemic caused by the new dramatic form. His investigation of the precursors to the *Spongia*, its implications, and the resulting furor is fundamental to any study of dramatic precepts of seventeenth-century Spain.

examples of the groups who unsuccessfully tried to dethrone Lope as one of the reigning writers and drama theorists of his time.

The *Arte nuevo*, published in 1609, is a treatise defending Lope's *comedia nueva,* resulting from attacks by the Madrid Academy that challenged the dramatic form's innovative style. Many scholars claim that Lope hastily composed the work—Juan Manuel Rozas suggests he wrote it in a morning or an afternoon (*Significado* 51)—at the request of his patron, the Duke of Sessa, but he indubitably had recognized the importance of the *comedia* for some time and had been formulating a poetics that governed its production. The date of Lope's presentation of his treatise to the Madrid Academy is uncertain, but it is thought that it had circulated in literary circles much earlier than its publication in the 1609 edition of *Rimas*, stimulating and guiding dramatic invention.

It was well before the creation of the *Arte nuevo* that Lope had begun to chart the path that Spanish theater would follow. At the end of the sixteenth century, the introduction of permanent theaters and a proliferation of professional acting troupes added to the growing popularity of Spanish theater and provided a literal stage for Lope and his newly created texts. Lope emerged as a prominent playwright and, finding a virtual *tabula rasa* in theater, began to experiment with the form. During this first phase of Lope's playwriting, dating between the years 1579 and 1598 (qtd. in Morley et. al, 74),[2] he molded and informed the tastes of the public by reacting immediately to his successes and failures on the boards, illustrating how reception clearly shaped dramatic trends (Poteet-Bussard 345).

Though the treatise itself may have been written in a short time as the result of the stimulus provided by the Madrid Academy, its ideas were a long time in their formulation (Porqueras-Mayo, "El *Arte nuevo*" 402). Simultaneously a poetic soliloquy, a confession, and a self-defense, the extraordinary *Arte nuevo* outlined a new dramatic framework. In contrast to previous dramatic treatises that had taken a more developed, epistolary

---

2. Adolf Friedrich von Schack was the first to divide Lope's dramatic production into three stages, a notion commonly accepted among Golden Age scholars. This first stage ended with a fourteen-month closure of the theaters from November 1597 to April 1599.

form, the *Arte nuevo* was written in blank verse, which suggested haste, and its limited size set a new standard. These innovations, in addition to the use of rhyming couplets and aphorisms, underscore the theatricality of the work, since Lope assuredly read, that is, performed it for the Madrid Academy (*Significado* 56). The structure and themes of the *Arte nuevo* have been studied extensively through the years.[3] For example, Rozas suggested that Lope divided his testimony into a prologue, a doctrinal part, and an epilogue (*Significado* 179-80), and Porqueras-Mayo identified three basic concepts: the *vulgo*, *comedia,* and *arte* ("El *Arte nuevo*" 400). Both the structure and the themes of the treatise reveal Lope's interest in the relationship between audience reception and performance.

The preliminary section, or prologue, of the *Arte nuevo* is clearly delineated; it consists of a dedication and thanks to all of those who have supported Lope, with laurels being extended especially to the Madrid Academy, but one cannot help but notice the irony of the prologue. It is well known that Lope was a prideful and outspoken man. He assuredly would have been offended by any vilification of his work. In addition, being questioned by such an assemblage whose aesthetic orientation was bogged down by outdated precepts of art, would have been aggravating, especially because of the huge commercial success of his theater at the time. Unlike his critics, Lope grasped what the people wanted. His disdain is clear as he notes that the members' knowledge of literature is more theoretical than practical:

> Fácil parece este sujeto, y fácil
> fuera para cualquiera dc vosotros,
> que ha escrito mcnos dc cllas, y más sabe
> del arte de escribirlas, y de todo. (11-14)

This backhanded compliment is unmistakable. Lope suggests that while they may know about the established rules of literature, such

---

3. Many valuable studies of the *Arte nuevo* exist and are still being written. Excellent examples include those by Karl Vossler, Menéndez y Pelayo, José Manuel Rozas, Juana de José Prades, Donald Gilbert, John Weiger, Alberto Porqueras-Mayo, J. Pérez Magallón, Emilio Orozco, Rinaldo Froldi, Edward Friedman, and Miguel Romera-Navarro, to name a few.

precepts are not as valuable to successful playwriting as the actual experience gained from composing plays, from which one learns to fine-tune their creation according to what is effective. It is hard to accept that Lope's praise in the *captatio benevolentiae* of this first section is sincere, he had nothing to prove to this group, and his appearance was a favor to his current patron. Alberto Porqueras-Mayo suggests that the discourse in the treatise could be read on two levels: the first was serious, being destined for the literati, and the second, directed to his supporters, was sarcastic, couching much criticism for the Madrid Academy (412). Such ambiguity and disdain are corroborated by the comment at the end of the document when Lope suggests that the members of the literary circle actually attend a *comedia*, so that they may better understand his explanation and motivation to produce such a work: "Oye atento, y del arte no disputes, / que en la comedia se hallará modo / que, oyéndola, se pueda saber todo (387-89). Such clear irony closes a treatise tinged with sarcasm. Besides setting the tone for the treatise, this section establishes Lope's knowledge of past dramatic precepts and history, implying that his erudition should not be questioned by critics. Finally, the section concludes with a justification of his defense of the *comedia*.

Lope clearly positions the public at the forefront of the *Arte nuevo* while defending his style of playwriting. He always seems cognizant of his audience, whether they are in the *corral de comedias* or in the hallowed halls of the Madrid Academy, and he makes a distinction between the educated audience for whom he reads the defense and the ordinary person on the street. Lope's writing, he notes, is not guided by *arte*, that is to say, established precepts: "que lo que a mí me daña en esta parte / es haberlas escrito sin el arte" (15-16).[4] It was his experience writing for a contemporary public that guided the composition of his theater; it also taught him that tastes have changed from the original Greek notion of comedy. Playwrights who continue to write in the traditional manner are poor and starving: "y así, se introdujeron de tal modo / que, quien con arte agora las escribe, / muere sin fama y galardón…" (28-30); clearly, one must understand that popular

4. The verse numbers cited are from the version in the appendix of Rozas's study.

tastes prevail over classical tenets. Lope emphasizes the importance of presenting an appealing spectacle to contemporary playwriting in these often-cited lines:

> Y, cuando he de escribir una comedia,
> encierro los preceptos con seis llaves;
> saco a Terencio y Plauto de mi estudio,
> para que no me den voces (que suele
> dar gritos la verdad en libros mudos),
> y escribo por el arte que inventaron
> los que el vulgar aplauso pretendieron,
> porque, como las paga el vulgo, es justo
> hablarle en necio para darle gusto. (40-48)

Lope ends this section of the *Arte nuevo* by reiterating the theme that proves one of the most important to the document: knowledge of public tastes prevails over the understanding of literary precepts. He continues his lesson by demonstrating a profound knowledge of his predecessors and their dramatic theories. Lope leaves no room for doubt that his divergence from tradition is well informed and contemporary to the times. At the same time, he makes it clear that he has not forgotten about past dramatic traditions and considers many of them when writing his own plays.

After a brief analysis of past theoretical trends, Lope transitions into the doctrinal part of the document. This esteem of classical traditions serves as a counterexample for the novelty of the new dramatic variety. Throughout the *Arte nuevo*, Lope seems to denigrate the *comedia* by repeatedly highlighting its differences from classical theater. Although at first glance his arguments seem sincere, it is reasonable to interpret them in the opposite manner. He pokes fun at the members of the Madrid Academy, who are bored with his erudite references, even though such citations are precisely what they esteem most. He subtly demonstrates the outdated and tedious nature of past precepts by focusing on the boredom of the academy members as he reviews canonical literature and theory:

> Pero ya me parece estáis diciendo
> que es traducir los libros y cansaros
> pintaros esta máquina confusa.
> Creed que ha sido fuerza que os trujese

a la memoria algunas cosas de éstas,
porque veáis que me pedís que escriba
Arte de hacer comedias en España. (128-34)

Once again, we see to what extent Lope pays special attention to the audience, here, he recognizes the need to remind them of classical sources in order to further their understanding of his dramaturgy. This strategy strengthens the contrast between the two forms, forming a distance between the old and new styles. Although it may be perceived that Lope favors the classical works and theory, it seems that the opposite is the case. Lope does not overtly tout his dramaturgy; rather he lauds it in a subtler manner. He mentions how its creation is now beyond his control. It is a dynamic and gigantic force that does not rely on past tenets. When composing a *comedia*, he states that the playwright has no choice but to break from preconceived rules because it is the experience of what is successful on stage that matters most. That is, it comes down to a question of practice and not of theory:

[D]onde cuanto se escribe es contra el arte;
y que decir cómo serán agora
contra el antiguo, y qué en razón se funda,
es pedir parecer a mi experiencia,
no [al] arte, porque el arte verdad dice,
que el ignorante vulgo contradice. (135-40)

Lope ironically suggests that there is little *arte* in the new *comedia*, when the opposite is true. It is just a different *arte*, a new set of theoretical leanings that diverge from those of the past. His preoccupation with the changes brought about by public demand still arises and, in this case, a conflicted Lope surfaces when he reveals that he is at odds with his desire to produce works that please everyone:

Si pedís parecer de las que agora
están en posesión, y que forzoso
que el vulgo con sus leyes establezca
la vil quimera de este monstruo cómico,
diré el que tengo, y perdonad, pues debo
obedecer a quien mandarme puede,
que, dorando el error del vulgo, quiero

> deciros de qué modo las querría.
> ya que seguir el arte no hay remedio,
> en estos dos extremos dando el medio. (147-56)

Lope's repeated criticism of the *vulgo* reaches hyperbolic levels, which suggests another conclusion than a simple dislike for them or the idea of setting apart the literate from the illiterate. Clearly, the omnipresence of the *vulgo* in the treatise reflects their influence on the theater, both literally and figuratively. While some accept Lope's word literally, it is possible that this exaggeration is yet another manifestation of irony in the text. Indeed, Lope has no recourse but to criticize the lower, uneducated classes according to the circumstances of the *Arte nuevo*, but this could be done in a more succinct, less repetitious manner. Therefore, the act of concentrating so much on the common class may be understood as a positive acknowledgement of its contributions to the stage. Certainly, Lope forms a distance between the two groups, but perhaps he is not saving the literate from the illiterate, but rather the opposite.

In this middle part of the treatise, Lope concentrates on the process of playwriting. Clearly, the innovations introduced in the plays built upon one another in a constant, dynamic process, which resulted in an evolution of the dramatic form. The public, however, is never far from his thoughts since the *vulgo* now controls the "vile chimera of comedy" that results in the elimination of long-established notions of art since there is no middle ground between traditional and modern theater. Acknowledging the esteemed audience of the Academy, and in an attempt to placate them, Lope distances them from the *vulgo* by underscoring their importance in the literary world and praising their familiarity with theater. This situation presents an interesting, if not ironic, parallel as Lope is playing to the expectation of his audience. While such praise may not be entirely sincere, Lope hits the right buttons when presenting an explanation of his theatrical styles. Furthermore, in an attempt to appear refined and urbane in the eyes of the Madrid Academy, he downplays the quality of his own dramatic production, an unexpected strategy from someone not considered the most humble of artists.

By describing the *comedia* as a melding of various dramatic forms, Lope reveals a central point of his argumentation, presenting tragicomedy as the foundation of the innovative treatise. His metaphor of the Minotaur, half-bull and half-man, aptly describes the hybrid character of the tragicomedy:

> Lo trágico y lo cómico mezclado,
> y Terencio con Séneca, aunque sea
> como otro Minotauro de Pasife,
> harán grave una parte, otra ridícula,
> que aquesta variedad deleita mucho. (174-78)

Rozas pays special attention to these *conceptista* verses:

> Una atención especial merece la comparación de tragicomedia "como otro Minotauro de Pasife." Pasife engendró de un toro blanco el famoso Minotauro. El mito es bien expresivo—hasta genéticamente—del híbrido que era la tragicomedia para sus detractores. Era, como el Minotauro, un monstruo, fruto de un pecado de leso clasicismo por "lujuria" popular y barroca. (*Significado* 80)

In a clever use of language, Lope turns the specific symbols used to criticize his theater into a metaphor that applauds its mixed composition. This conceptualization of the Minotaur also effectively unites the savage aspect of the popular public with the dignified, rational characteristic of the learned class. By claiming that variety is pleasing, Lope gathers inspiration from nature: "buen ejemplo nos da naturaleza, / que por tal variedad tiene belleza" (179-80), giving it ultimate authority as the inspiration for all artists, both classical and contemporary. Furthermore, a hybrid form of theater adds even more variety since more possibilities can be staged, whether they be different themes, storylines, or combination of characters, to name a few. The form allows for new means of expression on the stage.

Next, Lope addresses to varying degrees the Aristotelian-inspired unities of action, time, and place according to his assessment of their importance. He readily accepts the unity of action—the one unity actually mentioned by Aristotle—suggesting that the storyline be clearly defined and connected, without great digression; the action should not be episodic because it becomes difficult to follow:

> Adviértase que sólo este sujeto
> tenga una acción, mirando que la fábula
> de ninguna manera sea episódica,
> quiero decir inserta de otras cosas
> que del primero intento se desvíen;
> ni que de ella se pueda quitar miembro
> que del contexto no derribe el todo. (181-87)

In contrast, recognizing that it is impossible to follow the dictum that all action occur in one day, Lope rejects the unity of time:

> [N]o hay que advertir que pase en el periodo
> de un sol, aunque es consejo de Aristóteles,
> porque ya le perdimos el respecto
> cuando mezclamos la sentencia trágica
> a la humildad de la bajeza cómica. (188-92)

In these previous lines, we see how Lope argues that breaking from Aristotle's suggestions is acceptable. Lope agreed with many Aristotelian concepts without believing them to be absolute. Remembering the comparison he makes between nature and theater, it is logical to accept that change is inevitable. He notes that a playwright must use the time necessary for the story to develop (193-200). For example, when Lope dramatizes historical events, he creates the illusion of the passing of time and forms a chronological distance between acts by means of the interludes and dances that take place during the intermissions. He does not, however, completely discard the unity of time because he follows the twenty-four hour time constraint within the acts, but rather his compromise lies in his allowing for the unlimited passing of time during the intermissions:

> [P]ase en el menos tiempo que ser pueda,
> si no es cuando el poeta escriba historia
> en que hayan de pasar algunos años,
> que éstos podrá poner en las distancias
> de los dos actos, o, si fuere fuerza,
> hacer algún camino una figura,
> cosa que tanto ofende a quien lo entiende,

> pero no vaya a verlas quien se ofende. (193-200)

Lope remains adamant about this decision based on his experience with the Spanish public, who, he states, has an insatiable hunger for as much information in as short amount of time as possible:

> ¡Oh, cuántos de este tiempo se hacen cruces
> de ver que han de pasar años en cosa
> que un día artificial tuvo de término,
> que aun no quisieron darle el matemático!
> porque considerando que la cólera
> de un español sentado no se templa
> si no le representan en dos horas
> hasta el Final Juicio desde el *Génesis*,
> yo hallo que, si allí se ha de dar gusto,
> con lo que se consigue es lo más justo. (201-10)

These concise yet profound observations grant us entry into the psyche of the Spanish populace of the time and reveals the importance of the theater to their everyday lives, as it supplied escape, national identity, eroticism, mysticism, news, and culture (Rozas, *Significado* 97), placing great responsibility on the playwright. He or she must fit in a lot of information and action into a limited amount of time. The duration of the play must also be limited since it helps to maintain order among the audience: Lope suggests an act be four *pliegos*, making the play last between two and two-and-one-half hours, since the public's span of attention lasts no longer: "Tenga cada acto cuatro pliegos solos, / que doce están medidos con el tiempo / y la paciencia del que está escuchando" (338-40). Such practical issues made necessary a change in theatrical practices in order to cater to the needs of the public, but it also set standards for the playwright, and, ultimately, for the public. The relationship between playwright and public was one of mutual benefit and influence.

Lope points out that the structural division of a play also affects audience reception, since it deals directly with how the public experiences the dramatic spectacle. He not only recognizes Virués as the pioneer of the three-act structure (215), but he also adopts this framework, establishing a standard for the *comedia*. Always keeping the public in mind, he offers further advice on composing a script, suggesting that the plot should be divided in two parts and warning against revealing the resolution too early, or making it too obvious, so as to keep the audience from leaving before the conclusion of the work:

> Dividido en dos partes el asunto,
> ponga la conexión desde el principio
> hasta que vaya declinando el paso,
> pero la solución no la permita
> hasta que llegue a la postrera escena,
> porque, en sabiendo el vulgo el fin que tiene,
> vuelve el rostro a la puerta y las espaldas
> al que esperó tres horas cara a cara,
> que no hay más que saber que en lo que para. (231-39)

Although not so flexible in its mechanical form, the tragicomic *comedia* offered infinite opportunities for original storylines. Furthermore, the plays often reflected contemporary news, situations, and events. This practice may have been inspired by established dramatic traditions in which the endings are predictable—most notably, the classical tragedy—and though the same could be said about the endings of the *comedia*, we must note that its finale was more varied. Two clear examples are seen in *Fuentovejuna,* which could have ended with the death of the villagers as opposed to their absolution for the murder of the *Comendador*, and in *El caballero de Olmedo*, which did not have to end with the death of Don Alonso. Such variety keeps the audience guessing; that is, they ultimately may intuit the resolution of the play, but not the specific circumstances.

Finally, Lope warns of the dangers of an empty stage or of one left with only non-speaking characters, indicating how both disturb the public, who then presumably become restless since there is no action to keep them entertained:

> Quede muy pocas veces el teatro
> sin persona que hable, porque el vulgo
> en aquellas distancias se inquieta
> y gran rato la fábula se alarga,
> que, fuera de ser esto un grande vicio,
> aumenta mayor gracia y artificio. (240-45)

Extended silences are never a good thing on stage because the public becomes uncomfortable. It is clear that the audience must remain involved in the theatrical exchange, or they become bored with the story.

Lope next examines the important role of language both in terms of the dramatic production and its effects on reception. Remembering Robertello and once again citing experience, he states that language must correspond appropriately to the situation and the interlocutors. Simple matters, for example, do not warrant eloquent words, which should be reserved for more serious or persuasive situations:

> Comience, pues, y con lenguaje casto
> no gaste pensamientos ni conceptos
> en las cosas domésticas, que sólo
> ha de imitar de dos o tres la plática;
> mas cuando la persona que introduce
> persuade, aconseje o disuade,
> allí ha de haber sentencias y conceptos,
> porque se imita la verdad sin duda,
> pues habla un hombre un diferente estilo
> del que tiene vulgar, cuando aconseja,
> persuade o parata alguna cosa. (246-56)

Verisimilitude ensures a believable, or recognizable, tenor of a conversation. Lope understands the need for prudent lexical usage as dictated by context. Word choice should also be accessible to the public, keeping them entertained and laughing:

> Dionos ejemplo Arístides retórico,
> porque quiere que el cómico lenguaje
> sea puro, claro, fácil, y aun añade
> que se tome del uso de la gente,
> haciendo diferencia al que es político,
> porque serán entonces las dicciones
> espléndidas, sonoras y adornadas. (257-63)

These lines remind us yet again of Lope's familiarity with classical sources and contemporary theory. His suggestions are reminiscent of Cueva's advice in the *Ejemplar poético*, in which he insists on the use of clear and unadorned language in contemporary theater.[5] Of course, the idea of adapting language to the public was not unique to these two playwrights, though it does point to a common preoccupation of pleasing the crowds. A similar notion of simplicity of language follows, where Lope notes that the unrealistic use of exquisite words has the tendency to offend the public: "no traya la escritura, ni el lenguaje / ofenda con vocablos exquisitos / porque, si ha de imitar a los que hablan" (264-66). Many members of the public were keen listeners and astute receivers of the spoken word. It was necessary, therefore, to follow decorum to keep them wrapped up in the dialogue without upsetting them. The public also loved word play and rhetoric, which entertained them and maintained their interest and attention throughout the play. Any break in dialogue, therefore, would have been seen as problematic, as Lope mentions a few lines earlier.

The *Arte nuevo* continues by outlining how characters need to speak in a manner befitting their role on stage. There were certain expectations that must be fulfilled while on stage. Lope mentions earlier in the treatise that King Phillip II did not appreciate seeing a king on the tragicomic stage (157-64), and this would have been even less likable to him if he was not acting in a proper manner. The audience paid attention to detail in the works and straying from rules of decorum or propriety was not looked upon in a favorable manner. Appropriate use of language is essential to the success of a play. Lope claims that language can direct the action of the play, suggesting that the playwright end scenes in a clear manner:

> Remátense las scenas con sentencia,
> con donaire, con versos elegantes,
> de suerte que, al entrarse el que recita,
> no deje con disgusto el auditorio. (294-97)

Another role of language is to inform the audience of actions that occur offstage or in the past: language acts as the vehicle of the dramatic text and also a conductor of the flow and comprehension

5. Rozas touches upon a few similarities between Cueva's and Lope's documents (*Significado* 55-56).

of the work. Lope's sets were not opulent, so he took advantage of other dramatic strategies to progress the action. It is because of its importance and primary role that Lope paid so much attention to language use.

Lope's experience guided him to use mixed meter and a varied rhyme scheme, which add a sense of verisimilitude, not because people commonly speak in verse, but rather because each type of verse represents a particular action or event:

> Acomode los versos con prudencia
> a los sujetos de que va tratando:
> las décimas son buenas para quejas;
> el soneto está bien en los que aguardan;
> las relaciones piden los romances,
> aunque en otavas lucen por extremo;
> son los tercetos para cosas graves,
> y para las de amor, las redondillas. (305-12)

The introduction of mixed meter to Spanish theater has been attributed to Cueva, both by himself in the *Ejemplar poético* and by recent scholars. If Lope was not familiar with Cueva and his treatise, which is unlikely, he most certainly intuited the benefits of mixing poetic forms in the composition and performance of a play. In *La preceptiva dramática de Lope de Vega y otros ensayos sobre el Fénix*, Romera Navarro explains that verse was preferred to prose because, sociologically speaking, it was easier for the actors to memorize the lines, and it allowed for an illiterate audience to follow the rhythm of the stanzas, and consequently, the style. Thematically and stylistically speaking, the use of verse in the *comedia* brought to mind the more conventional oral traditions, such as the ballad, epic, and song, which served as its foundation. Also, the use of verse allowed for the playwright to demonstrate his sharp wit and aptitude for manipulating the language. All three considerations tie in closely to performance and reception with relation to the delivery and interpretation of the text (98-109). The use of poetry offered countless possibilities for the good poets to show off their skills. The use of prose was limited to interludes and letters within the *comedia*, disrupting the poetic verse and consequently drawing the audience's attention to the function of language in the text. Poetry opened the doors for more creative use of the language, and he describes how verse should take full advantage of the literary devices and tropes to facilitate the expression of the artist and to entertain the public:

> [L]as figuras retóricas importan,
> como repetición o anadiplosis,
> y en el principio de los mismos versos
> aquellas relaciones de la anáfora,
> las ironías y adubitaciones,
> apóstrofes también y exclamaciones. (313-18)

These lines demonstrate the aesthetic and artistic character of the play and how it affects the reception of the work. The lines form the base of a performance, so they must be pleasing to the ear. By pointing out the rhetorical variation of the verse used in his *comedias*, Lope establishes that these were not poorly composed works but rather well thought out and constructed pieces of poetry. This adds to the defense of the validity of the *comedia*. Lope's reputation as a lyric poet was also great, so when he mentions the lyrical aspect of his theater, critics must take a step back and consider the plays within the context of Lope's great ability to write poetry; the *comedia* is, after all, dramatic poetry.

Lope states that thematically speaking, honor and virtue are at the core of the *comedia* (140), and in his own plays, he asserts, he exploits the power of honor since it evokes an emotional response in all audiences: "Los casos de la honra son mejores, / porque mueven con fuerza a toda gente" (327-28). He notes that the spectators passionately and emotionally respond to the events and characters onstage. In short, issues of honor simply made for good theater. Nevertheless, since the volatile public will react to the portrayal of dishonorable acts without appropriate reprisal, the playwright must exercise caution so as not to stage inappropriate actions, or the rejoinder of the public could ruin the performance. The fact that honor was a central theme of most plays corroborates its importance. This has led many to believe that honor was one of the central preoccupations in early modern Spain and, to a certain extent, it was. The honor code, however, was often dealt with an exaggerated manner, which sold tickets, and did not necessarily faithfully portray the current situation in Spain at the time.

In the *Arte nuevo*, Lope cautions about the explicit use of satire. Like the genre that it describes, the *Arte nuevo* is a reactionary and critical document. It subtly interrogates established norms while maintaining a decorous attitude. Lope states in the treatise that direct criticism and satire need to be kept in check, since overt displays infuriate the public. He reminds that this often occurred in classical theater, and strives to avoid explicit critique of contemporary issues:

> [E]n la parte satírica no sea
> claro ni descubierto, pues que sabe
> que por ley se vedaron las comedias
> por esta causa en Grecia y en Italia;
> pique sin odio, que si acaso infama,
> ni espera aplauso ni pretenda fama. (341-46)

This preoccupation is one of the reasons why many *comedias* were set in exotic locales, effectively deflecting any direct reference to leading figures in society. Of course, the subversive aspect of theater and its interrogation of societal norms was common and was what kept theater fresh, but it was not overly explicit, escaping the critical eye of censors. Again, we see how Lope takes into account all members of the public. It is not just the ticket-purchasing audience that is important, but also other critics who closely monitor the stage. Satire, too, could anger the public but it seems that Lope is pointing toward other receivers and interpreters of the text's message in this part of the treatise.

Lope did not highly value the use of extravagant sets, and in the *Arte nuevo*, he dedicated only six verses to scenery, noting that it varied greatly depending on the category of the troupe and the event being celebrated (350-55). Many playwrights concurred, believing that the stage setting tended to overshadow the play, and it was not until the beginning of the seventeenth century that stage properties became more extravagant and not until the 1630s that scenery was elaborated and used to its full potential. When the *comedia* became more prevalent in the royal court, staging became sumptuous, especially in the plays of Calderón and Bances, who viewed most of Lope's work as primitive because of its lack of sophisticated sets.

One of the underlying themes of the *Arte nuevo* is that experience and intuition have important roles in the production of a play. Lope highlights this from the very beginning, underscoring his extensive experience as a playwright while implicitly suggesting the lesser experience of the members of the Madrid Academy. Lope is proof positive of the success of the new literary form: he boasts of 483 *comedias* and claims that he would not have the same popularity had they been written in the conventional manner (369). He illustrates that, while being cognizant of traditional styles, he is able to deftly manipulate them to satisfy the contemporary concerns and desires of the paying public. Lope's defense exhibits a prescriptive character as he offers an explanation of a new, innovative style, inviting critics and supporters alike to go see a *comedia* while keeping his discourse in mind, and expressing the hope that they will then better understand his perspective: "Oye atento, y del arte no disputes, / que en la comedia se hallará modo / que, oyéndola, se pueda saber todo" (387-89). But Lope goes one step further since he was not concerned with explaining himself only to the *literati* of the times, but also to the theater-going public. *Lo fingido verdadero*, for example, dramatizes many of the concepts found in the *Arte nuevo*, offering a similar explanation of his work in terms accessible to a different audience.

II. Dramatic theory in practice: *Lo fingido verdadero*[6]

Lo fingido verdadero,[7] dated between 1607-08, offers an example of the degree to which Lope's innovative precepts may have inspired and directed his work. In fact, this play can be considered a dramatization of the theoretical model presented in the *Arte nuevo*. Lope's representation of public reception and performance within the play illustrates how the work portrays his preoccupations concerning the playwriting process. A comparison of the two texts is not a new idea: in 1976, Rozas, concentrating on

6. A version of this analysis, "The Dramatization of the *Arte nuevo*: Revisiting *Lo fingido verdadero*," was published in the *Bulletin of the Comediantes*.
7. In addition to the studies mentioned in the text, see Menéndez Pelayo, Warnke, Alan Trueblood, and Cecilia McGinnis.

the parallel usage of blank verse and rhyming couplets in both works, calls *Lo fingido verdadero* a sort of little *Arte nuevo*. That same year, in "Lope's *Lo fingido verdadero* and the Dramatization of the Theatrical Experience," Susan L. Fischer acknowledges that Lope was concerned with the art of playwriting in this dramatic text, but, she argues, "he surely did not intend, in *Lo fingido verdadero*, to dramatize an addendum to his tongue-in-cheek *Arte nuevo*" (157). Rather, Fischer emphasizes that the play is "self-consciously and self-referringly dramatic," an undeniable and accurate observation. In 1986, Michael McGaha published a translation of Lope's play, *Acting is Believing*, which includes an excellent preliminary study of the poet's life, the play, and their connection to early modern Spanish society. He describes *Lo fingido verdadero* in this way:

> It is at once a manifesto of Lope's dramatic theory, an invaluable documentary record of Spanish theatrical practice in his time, an embodiment of the playwright's most deeply held views on such important topics as religion and politics, and, above all, a superb example of his dramatic craftsmanship. (3)

A year later, María de Pilar Palomo describes how the extra-linguistic qualities of the text further communicate meaning to the *corral*-going public in "Proceso de comunicación en *Lo fingido verdadero*." In the late 1990s, Victor Dixon examines Lope's play in two valuable studies. The one, "<<Ya tienes la comedia prevenida...la imagen de la vida>>: *Lo fingido verdadero*," examines the play in a general manner. Dixon touches upon critical reception of the play, its Baroque nature, and its forward-thinking theatricality. Dixon also discusses the relationship between the actor and the poet—in this case, the protagonist, Ginés—and he talks about possible staging of the play, especially in terms of scenery. The other article, "*Lo fingido verdadero* y sus espectadores," convincingly argues how the work is "un ejemplo completamente excepcional de 'metateatro'" (98), by applying six of Richard Hornby's examples of categories of metatheater to the play. Indeed, previous scholarship proves invaluable to an understanding of *Lo fingido verdadero*, nevertheless, in light of several recent theoretical discussions, it is useful to revisit Lope's play to further explore the ways in which it embodies the ideas that drive his defense of the Spanish national theater.

Lope was certainly not the first to utilize metatheatrical techniques in a play; in fact, self-conscious strategies are frequent throughout the history of the theater and have sparked much discussion among theater critics, especially since the 1963 publication of Lionel Abel's *Metatheatre.* Catherine Larson observed in 1994 that metatheater is not a theoretical approach nor a critical methodology, but rather "a useful interpretive tool" that underlines the tension that exists between illusion and reality by the use of self-referential devices (206). Her outline of the controversy surrounding its application and validity summarizes a number of *comedia* scholars' views and clarifies how an appreciation of a text's metatheatrical strategies allows the critic to comprehend its meaning by exploring the interplay between the dramatic structure and theatrically self-reflexive themes.

The hagiographical *Lo fingido verdadero* has two main storylines: the conversion of the martyr Ginés, a Roman poet, actor, and director, and the rise to power of Diocletian, a humble Roman foot soldier who becomes emperor. The play begins with Diocletian complaining about the most recent military campaign and groaning about a lack of money but a surplus of hunger. After much scandal and intrigue, Diocletian rises to the throne and, in celebration, orders Ginés to prepare a play about love. During the play, the actor, heartbroken by the rejection of his costar, forgets that he is performing for the emperor and begins to lament and plead for her love. Diocletian and the public are confused by this break from character but all is resolved, and the emperor even orders that another play, about Christian conversion, be performed the next day. Ginés's actual conversion to Christianity during this performance is condemned by Diocletian, who punishes the actor for his newfound religious devotion.

Chronologically speaking, *Lo fingido verdadero* and the *Arte nuevo* are contemporaneous. Remembering how Lope's life often influenced his work, it is probable that a preoccupation with defending his dramatic theory manifested itself on the boards. Some scholars take a stronger stance, Dixon, for example, insists that Ginés is Lope ("Prevenida" 65-66), and he is not the only one to arrive at this conclusion. Without a doubt, the similarities between the two works are plentiful. Rozas specifically mentions a dialogue in the play that briefly defends the *comedia nueva* (57), a defense whose similarities to the *Arte nuevo* cannot be ignored. He also underlines the parallel lexical choices and rhyme schemes, pointing to the corresponding use of the couplet *arte* and *parte* (58): the treatise states "que lo que a mí me daña en esta parte / es haberlas escrito sin el arte" (15-16), compared to the play text's "Que los que miran en guardar el arte, / nunca del natural alcanzan parte" (57); both couplets address the necessity to de-emphasize "arte" since it detracts from the naturalness of the work. Rozas separates the *Arte nuevo* into three sections: a prologue, a central section that concentrates on precepts governing playwriting, and an epilogue (42-43). On a similar note, I would suggest that the play's *jornadas* echo this structure, with the second act highlighting the creative challenges of writing a play, adding to the long list of parallels between the two works.

Other scholars also explain the congruence between the two works by asserting that the play dramatizes of the treatise. Palomo, for example, presumes that the play is a dramatization of the *Arte nuevo* directed to the *corral*-going public, since they did not see Lope's presentation of his poetics as he presented it to the Madrid Academy (81). I most certainly agree with this conclusion. Besides the contemporaneousness of two works, other factors corroborate such an assumption. Lope's sensitivity to reaching all audience members, for example, is evident in his plays and recorded in the *Arte nuevo* itself. The most convincing evidence, however, is textual and found in the parallels between *Lo fingido verdadero* and the *Arte nuevo*. Although it is impossible to know if the similarities between the two works were purposeful or coincidental, it is clear that they exist. Throughout *Lo fingido verdadero*, Lope maintains the standards for writing a *comedia* that he had established years before on stage and recorded in the *Arte nuevo* in the early 1600s.

In both the *Arte nuevo* and *Lo fingido verdadero*, Lope discards the unities of time and place but retains that of action, the only one actually discussed by Aristotle. While some have suggested that the play is episodic—a peccadillo according to the *Arte nuevo*—Dixon repudiates this claim, neatly demonstrating how the three *jornadas* form a triptych of intertwined episodes, a purposeful strategy on Lope's part that appeased the Spanish audience's insatiable hunger for jam-packed storylines ("Prevenida" 59). True, one can separate the acts into episodes, but this is not sufficient to deem them unrelated. Dixon's astute conclusion further demonstrates Ginés's importance to the text. Besides being the title character, his artistic creation is the common link found in the three acts.

Dixon also discusses some possibilities of staging the play and how they relate to Lope's treatise. He points to how Ginés condemns ornate stage settings because they distract the public and overshadow the play text, reflecting Lope's similar reflections in the *Arte nuevo* ("Prevenida" 68).[8] Similarly, he discusses costuming in the two works ("Prevenida" 70). Correspondence between the play and the treatise does not stop with these thoughtful observations. One aspect in the play not mentioned by Dixon is the duration of a dramatic work. Two times the ideal length of a play is described in *Lo fingido verdadero*, as one and one half hours, (48). Although this deviates from Lope's suggestion of two and one half to three hours (338-40), it does identify the necessity for standards to ensure optimum enjoyment of the public and good performances by the actors.

Further specifics highlighted in the *Arte nuevo* are also present in *Lo fingido verdadero*. For example, at the end of the play, each actor goes before Diocletian to swear that they are not a Christian and to describe the roles that they play on stage (77-78), the latter information expands on Lope's description in the *Arte nuevo,* which briefly discusses the comportment of the characters of king, old man, and woman and their relation to language (269-79). In *Lo fingido verdadero*, we see that the number of actors was limited but their repertory was extensive, giving them flexibility to stage a variety of works while maintaining consistency by ensuring that each actor played a specific role. The specific roles of each player were established by age, gender, and talent; they were type cast. This specific designation is seen earlier in the play when

8. The overall spirit of the *Arte nuevo* is that no rules are forever binding and we see that even Lope broke his own rules. For example, his 1629 production of *La selva sin amor* was complemented by ornate staging designed by the reknowned Italian set designer Cosme Lotti.

Fabio shows concern that when he is asked to play the part of an angel, one that he has not played in over a year as well as a role currently reserved for Marcela (72). Much like today, the public had certain expectations about certain actors playing specific roles.

Similar to how it is described in the *Arte nuevo*, the agile use of mixed meter in *Lo fingido verdadero* corresponds to particular situations. The play benefits from a variety of verse forms, whose variation breaks the monotony that any one meter may offer. Octosyllabic verses were most common, but McGaha points out that Lope used ten different meters throughout *Lo fingido verdadero* (Introduction 35). In the play, Ginés mentions the difficulties involved in finding the right meter to describe the noble deeds of Diocletian:

> Si tus glorias,
> si tus grandes hazañas, si tu raro
> divino entendimiento, César ínclito,
> fuera capaz de versos y de historias,
> ginés representara tu alabanza,
> y todos los ingenios que celebra,
> no sólo Roma, pero España y Grecia,
> se ocuparan, señor, en escribillas. (57)

Here, Ginés suggests that it is not easy to compose poems that suitably relate the glories of Diocletian, since a poet's duty includes portraying events in an appropriate, and often hyperbolic, manner. As one of the best poets of early modern Spain, Lope had no problem creating the appropriate meter for each situation that arose in the play. This is reflected by Ginés, who composes and recites two sonnets in the third *jornada* that express his feelings of love, the first directed toward Fenisa and the second to God. Since the sonnet is the ubiquitous form of love poetry at the time, it is no surprise that it is used by Lope in the play. In his notes on translating the play, McGaha mentions that the sonnet was the only poetic form that he maintained because of its poetic impact and ability to express deep emotions—the rest of the work was translated into prose (35). Because of the long tradition of the sonnet as the ultimate poetic expression of love at the time, its usage was most certainly not lost on the public, whether in the past or the present.

As mentioned earlier, the episodic yet related *jornadas* frame a compelling story and develop numerous themes in the play. The notion of *theatrum mundi*, for example, is clearly developed in the three acts. This theme has been adequately explored by scholars, most notably by Warnke in *Versions of the Baroque: European Literature in the Seventeenth Century*. The themes of honor and virtue also are fundamental to the play's meaning—as Lope suggests in the *Arte nuevo*. In fact, breaking the honor code proves central in the deaths of Carino and Apro. They were not honorable men, falling victims to lust, greed, and ambition. Their deaths are welcomed by the public. This same notion is seen in the *Arte nuevo* where Lope says that "pues [que] vemos, si acaso un recitante / hace un traidor, es tan odioso a todos / que lo que va a comprar no se lo venden" (331-33). Conversely, Diocletian is the opposite of his predecessor: he is prudent, just, and generous. The varying degrees of each figure's virtuous behavior develop compelling characters with which the audience may sympathize or ostracize since "[l]os casos de la honra son mejores, / porque mueven con fuerza a toda gente" (327-28). It is Ginés, however, who personifies virtue both as an actor and a Christian. In the *Arte nuevo*, Lope notes that "con ellos las acciones virtuosas, / que la virtud es dondequiera amada," (329-30), and this is the case with Ginés. Within the former, professional context, he is a consummate actor, dramatist, and poet—the best in the Rome—and his works move the public because of their sublime nature. Within the religious context, his role as a martyr demonstrates his exemplary faith. His talents cannot be wasted on pagan society, with its terrestrial sins and vices; he must use his talents in the name of God. So, while not the most obvious themes developed in *Lo fingido verdadero*, honor and virtue remain important as a foundation as they help develop the characters and organize the storyline.

Such thematic and textual allusions are unmistakable, but an additional examination that concentrates on audience reception and performance grants us, the modern-day critics, further understanding to the complexities of the playwriting process in early modern Spain. During the first act, the emperor Carino demands that Ginés perform a comedy on the spot, which, the actor/director tells him, is impossible, so the emperor then orders one for the next day with an indecorous and outrageous storyline (49). Carino's misunderstanding of the art of playwriting reflects simultaneously the ignorance and the supremacy of the public: he simply does not understand the mechanics of writing a play and producing it for the stage, while at the same time he dictates its content and style in accordance with his own taste. In that sense, Carino represents the theatergoer who enjoys the final product without understanding the preparations necessary for its production. We see how the playwriting process presupposes experience and intuition, two qualities embodied in the figure of Ginés, as integral to commercial success. Ginés stresses the important role of the playwright, arguing that a play cannot be hurried, but Carino suggests that another, more prolific, playwright be employed, in perhaps an ironic commentary on Lope's own prolific production. Ginés responds that a new writer will also observe the same rules, but Carino quickly rejects his argument: "Representa como sueles; / Que yo no gusto de andar / Con el arte y los preceptos" (50). The emperor shrugs off Ginés's concern about the scorn of the intellectuals. He demands that the play simply pleases the ears and not confound the mind with absurdities:

> Pues déjalos cansar.
> Deleita el oído, y basta,
> como no haya error que sea
> disparate que se vea. (50)

Clearly, the modern audience member is concerned more with being entertained than interested in what is entertaining them. Furthermore, in the play, Carino is otherwise occupied with the potential pleasure promised by his nocturnal forays with his servant and lover, so he has no time—or desire—to delve into the depths of theater composition or theory. His words suggest a desire for immediate gratification that should come from the theatrical work. The theatrical experience is lowered to a base level; its intellectual potential is not realized—in either sense of the word—by Carino since the Roman emperor is driven more by his appetites for physical satisfaction than for mental exercise. His predilection undoubtedly relates to the similar sensibilities of society. These words offer a sense of disillusionment or resignation. Lope, like Ginés, sees himself forced to succumb to the less refined tastes of the contemporary public. These words relay the message of ambiguity that courses through the *Arte nuevo*, where Lope seems to be simultaneously proud of his innovations but nostalgic for the practices that they have replaced.

In the second act, a similar exchange occurs between Ginés and the new emperor, Diocletian, who rejects several plays as being too old-fashioned or tragic, finally describing what he wants:

> Dame una nueva fábula que tenga
> más invención, aunque carezca de arte;
> que tengo gusto de español en esto,
> y como me le dé lo verosímil,
> nunca reparo tanto en los preceptos. (57)

The notion that the modern playwright writes to please a public unconcerned with restrictive guidelines is also prevalent throughout the *Arte nuevo*, especially in the following description of the new and predominant style of theater:

> Mas porque, en fin, hallé que las comedias
> estaban en España, en aquel tiempo,
> no como sus primores inventores
> pensaron que en el mundo se escribieran,
> mas como las trataron muchos bárbaros
> que enseñaron el vulgo sus rudezas. (22-27)

Such parallels are hard to ignore; indeed, it would seem reasonable to assume that remnants of Lope's insistence that the election of subject matter and style are dictated by the uneducated surfaces in this play. Both Lope and Ginés are, as Burningham puts it, condemned to write for barbarous crowds ("Barbarians" 291); Lope's audience is the seventeenth-century Spanish theater-going public, and Ginés's audience is ruled by men who arguably are not intellectual and whose sensibilities are grounded in the interests of the lower classes. Also, it should be noted that the emperors are asking for the new style of drama, which Ginés was initially trying to avoid staging by recommending classical plays. This metaphorical use of the absolute leader of the Roman Empire to represent the desires of the common public demonstrates the unstoppable force of the public's desires and its influence on theater. Like in the *Arte nuevo*, the playwright is defending the classical playwrights, but this is a losing battle. Ginés proves to be just as capable to write contemporary plays as the classical, replicating the reality of the dramatic environment of Lope's Spain. Carino generously rewards the playwright for his willingness to cater to the emperor's needs and present a new dramatic piece, exactly how Lope explains in the *Arte nuevo*.

It is not only Diocletian who rejects past theatrical practices, making way for new trends, but also Camila, whose tastes influence the emperor's entertainment choices. At the beginning of his reign, he wants to celebrate his rise to power with a banquet that includes the performance of a play. He asks Ginés for a tragedy, since presumably these plays were esteemed as noble dramatic works, but, at the urging of Camila, he rejects the performance of a tragedy:

> DIOCL. ¿Tienes tragedia alguna?
> ....
> CAMILA. No le pidas tragedia; así los cielos
> tu imperio ensalcen de este polo al otro:
> que si tragedias son ruinas del imperios,
> no es buen agüero de tu lauro el día.
> DIOCL. Pues hazme una comedia que te agrade,
> y quede á tu elección. (58)

Camila's words describe the tragic nature of previous emperors. She advises Diocletian to diverge from previous trends. She not only recognizes the need for a reformed government but also for a different dramatic style. Innovation and reform are necessary in both the political and theatrical contexts. Similarly, Camila later refuses to attend the gladiatorial battles with exotic animals, compelling Diocletian to cancel this obsolete form of entertainment, too, and insist on the immediate staging of Gines's comedy:

> CAMILA. Porque son hombres
> no los quiero ver matar;
> porque eres hombre, y por ti
> todos los hombres respeto.
> ....

DIOCL. No se trate más
esta fiesta de las fieras,
que no es fiesta la crueldad
véalas por novedad
Roma. (69)

The connection between literal deaths of the Roman Emperor and the figurative death of the tragedy and gladiatorial games—that is, the classical forms of entertainment—once again brings us to the conclusion that a new form of theater is imminent. Tragedy and gladiatorial games were outdated forms of entertainment that did not appeal to the modern audience. Both spectacles are characterized by blood and death, which were unsavory to the Emperor's soon-to-be love interest, Camila; her attitude and rejection of the past reflects the modern taste in theater that was also seen in Spain as the *comedia* continued to gain ground and the tragedy lost what little footing it had on the stage. The desire for change came from all members of the audience, as represented by Camila and Diocletian. Moreover, as time progresses, so does the theater, as common concerns and interests change. Lope understood this, noting in the *Arte nuevo* that the needs of the Spanish public differ greatly from those of earlier audiences (24-32) as he argued for a new dramatic form.

Lope obliges the public to reexamine the role of reception in the production of a dramatic work. The contemplation and representation of two plays within the work create an on-stage audience that addresses the importance of recognizing the distinction between illusion and reality by breaking the theatrical illusion, forcing the audience members to see themselves reflected on the stage and to contemplate their position in the interaction between the dramatic work and the public. Lope's use of *mise en abîme* challenges the public perception of the play and the distinction between reality and fiction.[9] As the audience members

9. The perception of the external—or "real"—audience has been a point of conflict for some scholars. On one hand, María del Pilar Palomo states that the theatrical illusion remains clear and unequivocal to the external audience (92). On the other hand, Victor Dixon asserts that the use of *mise en abîme* confounds the spectators, and erases the fine line that exists between reality and fiction ("Prevenida" 64, "Espectadores" 112). A look at earlier studies shows that like

see the reaction of the "interior"—or onstage—audience, the "real life" theatergoers are led to think about the theatrical event that they are experiencing at the time. Making the public aware of its position in the theatrical process therefore helps to communicate the audience's vital role in the production and performance of a dramatic work. At first, Diocletian and his entourage react favorably to the touching performance of the actors, but as the distinction between illusion and reality begins to blur, Diocletian is confused and angered, not knowing if the drama is real or fantasy or if he is an audience member or an actor within the play (67). He finally decides that he has been a participant in the drama since he has actually addressed the actors during the spectacle. The dramatization of this issue further underscores the relationship between the audience and the playwriting process. The interior audience is disoriented, demonstrating how the play's production needs to remain within the grasp of understanding of the audience. The real audience, of course, is not as confused as their onstage counterparts, but rather, the scene demonstrates the fragile balance that is maintained during the dramatic spectacle between losing oneself in the dramatic illusion and remembering—and contemplating—the issue of theater as a reflection of life. The spectator must remember the artificial nature of theatrical performance or risk being swept up in the spectacle. The *comedia* in general bore a message for the public to interpret but it was not the idea to leave the audience feeling unsettled and confused about their position in the dramatic exchange; *Lo fingido verdadero* warns us as to what can happen when loss of control occurs. Luckily, Diocletian also represents a forgiving audience because he gives Ginés a second chance to stage another play, which reflects the hunger for the art form since the public tolerates bad theater as long as the opportunity for more productions exists.

Lope analyzes audience reception a second time in *Lo fingido verdadero*. During the second performance, Diocletian is not so receptive to the disruptions and digressions of Ginés, who, once again, is overwhelmed with passion, but this time as the result of his conversion to Christianity. Diocletian once again addresses

---

Palomo, Warnke sees a clear distinction between fantasy and reality in the play (84-86); Fischer says it is not so clear ("Theatrical Experience" 156).

the players, criticizing their abilities and finally condemning the star to death—the ultimate bad review. In addition to its religious implications, such an extreme reaction to the drama offers a subtle commentary on the unruly theater-going public of the Golden Age, who always threatened to ruin a performance and whose judgment was final. Lope's use of an invented audience and plays within the text focuses the spectators' and readers' attention on the public's role in the dramatic exchange as well as the integral function that performance plays. This allows Lope to invent common situations and typical reactions to the *comedias* that convince the public of the veracity of his arguments presented on the stage and on the pages of the *Arte nuevo.*

An examination of performance in *Lo fingido verdadero* emphasizes Lope's concern with the playwriting process. Due to the metadramatic nature of the play, we actually see performance on three levels: the audience watching the play, the actors on stage, and the actors off stage. Each level encodes different cultural meanings and illustrates the processes and the relationships that constitute audience reception.

The performative aspects of the audience watching Ginés and his Roman acting troupe embody the cultural values of Golden Age Spain. In the *Arte nuevo*, Lope mentions that a rowdy audience was commonplace in the *corrales de comedia*:

> Quede muy pocas veces el teatro
> sin persona que hable, porque el vulgo
> en aquellas distancias se inquïeta
> y gran rato la fábula se alarga. (240-44)

Diocletian and his entourage act and react in a manner consistent with the norms of Spanish culture. Like the theater-going public of early modern Spain that they represent, this onstage audience is amazed and intrigued by the performances of the actors, reacting to and participating in the stage production in an enthusiastic manner. Indeed, Lope and many other playwrights feared the "furia del mosquetero" (217), as Suárez de Figueroa called it in the 1617 publication *El pasajero*. The Roman public created by Lope in *Lo fingido verdadero* further demonstrates the important role of the audience in the entire process of playwriting: the public determines the subject matter of the play, and, depending on how it is received, influences the popularity and future of the playwright, the acting troupe, and, ultimately, the play itself.

In addition to emphasizing the influence of the public on the dramatic spectacle, *Lo fingido verdadero* also underlines the inherent power of the onstage performance. At the beginning of the first play, Ginés's superb skills as both a prologuist and an actor astound the crowd:

MAXIM. Éste, señor, es Ginés.
DIOCL. Notable representante;
no he visto acción semejante.
LENTULO. Único entre muchos es.
DIOCL. ¿Dijo aquesto de improviso!
CAMILA. Sí, señor, que es gran poeta.
DIOCL. ¡Gran comparación!
....
Da aqueste anillo á Ginés
por la loa, que después
tendrá todo el premio junto. (61)

Ginés is a gifted orator who deserves material recompense, and this scene recalls Lope's observation in the *Arte nuevo* that the good poets live well, and the old-fashioned poets are dying of hunger (29-32). Later in the production, however, things take a turn for the worse when Ginés breaks decorum, strays from the script, and begins to improvise even more, leaving the actors and—more importantly—the audience bewildered:

¿Es esto representar
y á invención convenible,
o quieres mostrar, Ginés,
que con burlas semejantes
nos haces representantes? (67)

Such a reaction to Ginés's performance reveals the interconnectivity of performance and reception. The audience is indeed an active player in the dramatic exchange even though they are not necessarily on the stage. Diocletian's uncertainty as to his role on the stage is a microcosmic reflection of the *theatrum mundi* topos that runs throughout the play. Although he has always been a participant in the theatrical spectacle, the emperor has unwittingly taken an active role in the production.

This confusion on the part of the audience is not, however, confined to the first intercalated play but is also experienced in Ginés's second performance. The beginning of this interior play, too, delights the crowd but such pleasure quickly diminishes because of Ginés's unexpected actions on stage, which include his conversion to Christianity, leaving the other actors perplexed:

CAPITÁN. Aquello no está
en la comedia.
SOLDADO. Bravo humor gasta
el día que representa
al César.
....
CAPITÁN. El fin deste paso dudo;
que no se ensayaba así.
SOLDADO. cace y dice de improviso
Cosas de que no da aviso.
CAPITÁN. ¿Á dónde va por allí?
SOLDADO. No sé; mas ya se cubrió
de una cortina. (74)

Clearly, these examples of Ginés's performance acknowledge the power that the actors held on the dramatic spectacle, not only in relation to the public but also to the other actors. The actual performance on stage synthesizes the creative and receptive aspects of the artist and the public. Sometimes failure can be attributed to numerous factors, including bad playwriting or inadequate acting. In the case of both intercalated plays, it was the acting that ruined the show. Not only Ginés, but also his costars went off script, causing an onstage fiasco.

Ginés's preparation for the plays is another element related to the issue of performance. His desire to please the public, in this case the emperor, is made clear by his inquiry as to what themes he should address in the play. Ginés must contemplate, he asserts, the drama and his role in creating and acting in it, as both the poet and the actor must be consumed by the work for a successful performance to take place (58). By using his own play, Ginés willingly puts his reputation on the line: "Haré la mía / Porque si acaso no te diere gusto / no pierda la opinión ningún poeta" (58).

This overtly articulated emphasis on public approval transcends the stage to Lope's admission and acceptance of the burden to please the audience in the *Arte nuevo.* This could also reflect Lope's egotistical side, since he was the top playwright, no other dramatic piece could satisfy as his did.

Ginés's rehearsals of the upcoming plays become central to a discussion of reception and performance in the play because this self-conscious attitude leads us closer to a better understanding of the concepts that drove Lope's poetics. By addressing performance issues, Lope demonstrated his understanding of the playwriting process: actors rehearse because of the desire to please the audience (58). Francisco Portes describes an actor's preparation: "El actor reflexiona sobre su arte, afina su intelecto, cultiva su sensibilidad, prepara su cuerpo, medita sobre lo que puede aportar como artista y como ciudadano…" (31). The intercalation of such rehearsal emphasizes the crucial role of performance in the dramatic spectacle since the spectacle is deemed successful or not based on the abilities of the performers to act.

It is probable that Lope de Vega also felt a tension between his roles as a creative writer and as a composer of a poetics of theater. Clearly, writing theater to please the *vulgo* did not appeal to many poets of the age; in fact, scorn for the uncultured audience was readily evident in the comments of many writers. Lope, too, cherished the notion of preserving *arte* in his works, but he understood the practical and economical aspects of writing for the popular public: "Las Musas dan honor, más no dan renta" (qtd. in Amezúa 143). In a 1612 letter to the Duke of Sessa, Lope, possibly utilizing a *conceptista* allusion to the expression "costar un ojo de la cara," critiqued the quality of his own work, but underlined that he must write to live: "Duque mi señor, de escriuir disparates para uiuir he tenido un ojo para perder…" (qtd. in Amezúa 104). Lope's preoccupation with money was not new; years earlier he had explained in the *Arte nuevo* that he wrote for the common people since they buy the tickets to see the plays (46-48). Nevertheless, Lope did finally receive the critical and financial compensation that he coveted with the great commercial success of his dramatic works.

So far, it has been my intention to illustrate how a focus on audience reception and performance can influence our approach to the *comedia* or at least one typical early modern Spanish play. As critics before me have noted, Lope contemplated his theater over a long period of time, and it is certain that the *Arte nuevo* circulated among the *literati* before its publication in 1609. The *Arte nuevo*'s chronological correspondence to *Lo fingido verdadero* suggests that Lope's obsession with defending the new dramatic principles of the *comedia* might also have inspired him to develop them in dramatic form, thereby reaching yet another audience besides that of literary *tertulias* and the Madrid Academy. Due to the *comedia's* smashing success, there was really no need to defend these innovations to the *corral*-going public, but since Lope wrote theater for the *vulgo*, perhaps he felt that they, too, deserved an explanation of his work in an accessible form. Lope was driven by two main influences in his playwriting: his experience and the audience, a notion clearly demonstrated in the *Arte nuevo* and dramatized in *Lo fingido verdadero*.

The next section of the chapter is dedicated to Tirso's defense of the *comedia* as described in the literary discussions of *Cigarrales de Toledo* and dramatized in one of the intercalated *comedias*, *El vergonzoso en palacio*. Tirso was a strong defender of the dramatic form, which did not go unnoticed by Lope, who dedicated the 1621 publication of *Lo fingido verdadero* to the priest in gratitude for his adamant stance on the virtues of the *comedia* that was recently released in the *Cigarrales*. In the *dedicatoria* of the play, Lope applauds the priest for his craft. Lope notes that vulgar people are not those that enjoy *comedias*, but rather those that criticize the *comedia* without actually writing them. He continues that those who have *arte* can write successfully in any genre they choose. Clearly, Lope still found himself entrenched in a literary battle while defending the *comedia* thirteen years after the publication of the *Arte nuevo*, but he was in good company with Tirso, among others.

III. Tirso de Molina's *Cigarrales de Toledo*: a noble defense of the *comedia*

Tirso de Molina helped to further entrench the *comedia* as the dominant dramatic form of early modern Spain by means of his ingenious wit and writing skills, establishing himself as one of the greatest playwrights of the time. A self-proclaimed disciple of Lope (*Cigarrales* 230),[10] Tirso did not rely on simple imitation to attain popularity, but rather worked within the frame Lope had constructed, offering in different works a polemical, moralistic, and often racy breed of the *comedia* that simultaneously pleased the public and shocked the clergy.[11] Writing an impressive 400 plays, of which approximately eighty-five still exist (Hesse, introduction to *Vergonzoso* 14), Tirso's best-known contribution to world literature is the Don Juan figure in *El burlador de Sevilla y convidado de piedra,* published in *Doze comedias* in 1630.[12]

Unlike Lope but similar to Calderón, Tirso never wrote a formal defense of his poetics, but several passages found in his works reveal his tendencies and beliefs regarding theatrical practice and production. The most important and studied examples are found in the novelistic frame and intercalated plays of his first miscellany, the *Cigarrales de Toledo* (1621); other examples are seen in the dedication and the story *El bandolero* in *Deleytar aprovechando*, his second work of prose, also a miscellany; and also in *La fingida Arcadia* (1621). Like Lope, Tirso does not hesitate to openly express his opinions about theater, and, as Henry Sullivan points out in *Tirso de Molina & The Drama of the Counter Reformation*, he follows his eclectic ideas faithfully (71). This chapter discusses Tirso's defense of the *comedia* as found in the various debates in the *Cigarrales de Toledo* and, while paying special attention to public reception and performance, examines the way in which the play *El vergonzoso de palacio* dramatizes these ideals.

---

10. See Ruth Lee Kennedy's "A Reappraisal of Tirso's Relations to Lope and his Theater," and Alexandre Ciornescu's "Tirso de Molina y Lope de Vega," for more detailed information about the relationship shared between the two men.

11. Gerald Wade discusses the conflicts that arise between the two vocations in "Tirso de Molina: Priest-Playwright."

12. Though now it is commonly accepted that Tirso wrote the play, in the past there was some discussion as to the authorship of *El burlador de Sevilla* with some scholars suggesting that the play was actually written by Andrés de Claramonte. See the introduction to Alfredo Rodríguez López-Vázquez's edition of *El burlador* in which he discusses past questions regarding the attribution of the play.

Tirso's three works in prose, *Cigarrales de Toledo, Deleytar aprovechando,*[13] and *Historia de la Orden de Merced de nuestra Señora de las Mercedes,*[14] demonstrate his transformation from the contentious and profane playwright Tirso de Molina into the subdued and pious monk Gabriel Téllez. The texts, representations of two distinct eras in his life, include lucid defenses of the dramatic tendencies that inspired Tirso during each

---

13. *Deleytar aprovechando* follows the same mixed-genre structure as the earlier *Cigarrales* but diverges from its predecessor in both content and purpose, and, as a possible result, did not enjoy high esteem in the past, only being reprinted twice: in 1677 and in 1765. More recently, the work has suffered from the same lack of enthusiasm on the part of literary critics: Margaret Wilson, for example, highlights the difference between the brilliance of Tirso and the pseudo-scholarly piety of Téllez when comparing the two works ("Aspects"19). It would seem that the reprimand and threat of excommunication of the Junta's 1625 edict definitely took its toll on both the abundance and subject matter of his creative works. After 1626, Tirso wrote only eleven dramas, a drastic change from his earlier and more prolific production. One constant, however, is Tirso's concern with entertaining, as he attempted to present the moralizing texts in an engaging manner. The action in *Deleytar aprovechando* takes place during a three-day religious festival that occurs during *Carnaval*, a setting approximating that of the *Cigarrales*, and similarly displays works inserted into the novelistic framework. This second *miscellanea*, however, stands apart from the *Cigarrales* in terms of the literary genres and themes treated in the text: *autos* replaced *comedias* and hagiographic biographies replaced the secular *novellas,* demonstrating Tirso's more pious attitude and offering an instructional, and still entertaining, work, as the title implies. The substitution of religious works for secular ones, in addition to the outright condemnation of the *entremés,* signaled a complete reversal of Tirso's opinions regarding theater. Moreover, in his criticism of the *culteranista* playwrights, rampant plagiarism, cruel audiences, and greedy playwrights, Tirso expressed within the text even more resentment of the secular theater (II 77-81). These attacks took on a personal tone in *Deleytar*, revealing antipathy and disdain for the art form he had defended so fervently in the past.

14. Tirso's third work in prose, a history of the Mercedarian Order from its foundation in the Middle Ages to the 1630s, offers a comprehensive account of the religious group. Regarding Tirso's poetics, the work is of no consequence, though Gerald Wade mentions that in the past some scholars suggested that its *acto de contrición* expressed the poet's repentance for past oversights and improprieties regarding his production of *comedias.* This notion is quickly discounted and not verifiable since the confession does not even mention his past theatrical output, in fact, Wade doubts Tirso even wrote the *acto* ("Priest" 122).

epoch of his professional life.[15] Tirso's first two books are generic miscellany (*miscelanea*) made up of prose, poetry, and drama. According to Gerald Wade, this literary form, reminiscent of Boccaccio's *Decameron*, appealed to Tirso's predilection for liberty of expression and creative freedom (119-20). E. B. Place disagrees, noting that Tirso's works are distinct precisely because of their eclectic nature, which differs greatly from Boccaccio's novelesque works (qtd. in M. Wilson, "Aspects" 19). André Nogué offers yet a third point of view, suggesting that Tirso follows Lope's advice in the *Arte nuevo* to write in prose, which can later be put into verse: "el sugeto elegido escriba en prosa" (84). He also suggests that the works can be seen as prosified *comedias* due to the intrigue, love interests, conflicts, and other common devices and themes found in both genres (85).

In *Cigarrales de Toledo*, the summer *tertulias* of the Toledan noble class not only frame the intercalated literary texts within the work but also present an independent story that offers a forum to develop and demonstrate Tirso's literary theories. The work contains five episodes, called *cigarrales*,[16] that are connected to form a cohesive unity but each one also exists as a separate, independent work. In the introduction to his edition of the *Cigarrales*, Luis Vázquez asserts that the work is in a state of permanent contrast (62), while Nogué characterizes the *Cigarrales*

---

15. Nogué agrees with the assertion that Tirso denounced the secular dramatic tradition in *Deleytar aprovechando*, but also adds that he did not completely eliminate remnants of the *comedia* in its most famous intercalated work, *El bandolero,* the history of the Catalan Saint Pierre Armengol (292). Paying special attention to the behavior of the principal characters, the complexity of intrigue, and the interrogation of such themes as honor, social class, and vengeance, Nogué suggests that the story retains many theatrical attributes common to the *comedia,* but expressed in prose form (292). Other similarities include Tirso's use of characters corresponding to those found in the *comedia.* Finally, *Deleytar's* abundant use of disguises, horoscopes, the thematic conflict between fate and destiny, as well as night scenes causes Nogué to point to how characteristics common to the *comedia* also inspired the progression of the action and the structure of the work (293). So, it would seem, that although Tirso may have wanted to distance himself from his past productions, he did not completely succeed in doing so, whether on purpose or subconsciously.

16. A *cigarral* is the name for a country estate, but Tirso also uses the title to separate each episode.

as having artistic density because of the combination of so many styles, representing, in an original manner, a perfect manifestation of Baroque art (400). The literary climate invented by Tirso creates, explores, critiques, and defends the representation of various poetic forms in an imaginative fashion while reproducing the arguments that must have permeated the literary circles, giving a unique perspective on the literary criticism and social climate of early modern Spain.

The multifaceted character of *Cigarrales* provides a different approach to the defense of Spanish national theater by creating an atmosphere in which Tirso presents his poetics in an intelligible and playful manner. Don Alejo, the host and owner of one of the summer villas where the gatherings take place, is the voice of reason, and through him Tirso explores and criticizes the attacks on the *comedia*. Though not a purely theoretical treatise, the *Cigarrales* offers a convincing and definitive justification of the *comedia*, placing an explanation of Tirso's poetics within the frame of literary discussion. Furthermore, Tirso's strategy of introducing dramatic texts into the miscellany allows for the play to be fresh in the readers' minds as they reflect on the reviews and comments of the spectators within the text, which follow each work. Such a metatheatrical device compels the reader of the *Cigarrales* to recognize and reconsider the relationship shared by the playwright and public, bringing to light the roles of each participant in the reception of the work, and making us, the real readers, reflect on the role of the interior audience. The dramatic characteristics of the work, however, do not stop here. Nogué proposes that the story in the *Cigarrales* itself is set up like a Golden Age play, because of the introduction of stock characters, typical storylines, and complicated intrigue (85, 87).[17]

Most contemporary editions of the *Cigarrales* omit the intercalated works due to publication demands and a lack of space, and although reading the omitted plays can help us to fully grasp the meaning of the collection as a whole, the contiguous material can stand alone as both critical and literary pieces. In the *Cigarrales*, Tirso resolutely defends the *comedia* three times,

17. Nogué draws the same conclusion with the structure of *Deleytar aprovechando* (85, 87).

addressing different aspects of dramatic theory: *Cigarral* one discusses the omission of certain unities and the preservation of verisimilitude in the plays, *Cigarral* four addresses performance and the importance of the actors to the success of a production, and *Cigarral* five reinforces the necessity for decorum in the *comedia*. What this concise defense of the *comedia* lacks in extension, it makes up for in veracity and viability. In fact, many scholars consider Tirso's *Cigarrales* as one of the most important examples of drama theory of the times.

The relevance of the first *Cigarral* lies in its fervent defense of the *comedia*; it takes the form of a heated debate that concentrates on the theater's duty of fulfilling the expectations of the audience. After seeing the performance of *El vergonzoso en palacio*, the characters praise the play and acknowledge its well-deserved popularity in Spain, Italy, and the Americas, as well as among the spectators within the *Cigarrales*, who actually complain of it being too short (218). The only dissenter, "un presumido, natural de Toledo," offers a distinctly different view of the play, complaining that the play is too long, diverges from historical fact, abuses the unities of time and place, and desegregates the social classes. Tirso obviously intends for this figure to represent those who have not accepted the *comedia* as the new national theatrical form, preferring to support past traditions, and the character's complaints about the genre set the stage for Tirso's defense of contemporary dramatic trends (224). By portraying the man as uncultured and ignorant, Tirso continues a trend that his predecessors and contemporaries have adopted when describing their critics as uninformed. This is not a surprising reaction, as many expressed similar opinions, including Lope in the *Arte nuevo*.

Don Alejo immediately takes the floor and responds to the previous comments in a direct manner. First, he remarks that it is bad conduct to criticize the play, since it insulted the host (225); this marks a clear reflection of Tirso's opinion of the poorly behaved common public. He then states that it is illogical to follow the unity of time since a gentleman cannot meet, fall in love with, court, and marry a damsel in such a limited time frame. Such a whirlwind romance, he asserts, compromises the verisimilitude of the play because the audience simply will not buy into such a relationship, especially since factors that are fundamental to the intrigue—jealousy, desperation, faithfulness, and love—have no time to develop (225). He states:

> [L]a comedia, que es una imagen y representación de su argumento, es fuerza que, cuando le toma de los sucesos de dos amantes, retrate al vivo lo que le pudo acaecer, y, no siendo esto verisímil en un día, tiene obligación de fingir pasan los necesarios, para que la tal acción sean perfecta; que no en vano se llamó la poesía *pintura viva*.... (226)

The playwright, therefore, must consider the audience's reception of the story when producing his plays, subordinating mechanical rules to psychological veracity. Don Alejo further argues in favor of omitting the unity of time, drawing parallels to the ways in which history texts and novels both detail the span of many years on a few pages, which Sullivan deems a "capital point in Tirso's defense" of the *comedia* (*Tirso* 75). Evidently, Tirso agreed with Lope's assessment in the *Arte nuevo* that because the Spanish audience hungers for as much information as possible, it is the playwright's responsibility to give it to them.

Much like the case with the unity of time, Tirso also discounts the relevance of the unity of place in the *comedia,* arguing that it hinders the formulation of an entertaining story that entails movement between distant locales (226). According to Menéndez y Pelayo, these remarks are analogous to Alessandro Manzoni's letter to a critic of his 1820 play, *Carmagnola* (789), an interesting suggestion, since the two were born 100 years apart but they still shared many opinions regarding the process of playwriting.[18]

Tirso's exclusion of the unities of time and place is logical and does not actually betray classical thinking, especially since Aristotle did not explicitly mention them in his *Poetics*; they were

---

18. Manzoni states that verisimilitude in a play and interest in the dramatic characters—like in all parts of poetry—derives from the truth. He maintains that it is logical to reject the unities on the historically based argument that great things take more than twenty-four hours to complete (qtd. in Menéndez y Pelayo 789).

suggested in the Renaissance by Italian playwrights.[19] Of course, Tirso recognized some characteristics as immutable such as the unity of action—the only unity actually alluded to by Aristotle—verisimilitude, and decorum, three aspects whose dismissal could provoke the displeasure of the public. In the *Cigarrales*, Don Alejo notes that although the classical pioneers of drama still deserve much credit, modern playwrights should strive to augment and perfect the foundations set down before them; he concludes that it is not ambitious, nor is it natural, to maintain standards, but rather, to change them (227). He illustrates the point by describing the evolution of music and how it has changed from banging on drums with hammers to a more complex and delicate art form (228). Also, by using the analogy of God as the first tailor who originally gave man animal skins as vestments, Don Alejo notes how fashion has evolved into utilizing fine materials and creating intricate articles of clothing, drawing a parallel as to how the modern *comedia* likewise has been handcrafted and improved over time (228). The ideas presented in the *Arte nuevo* regarding the dynamic and evolutionary characteristics of nature, most notably, its ever-changing and heterogeneous makeup, further inform Tirso's explanation of the tragicomedy, which he considers a graft of the best qualities of both tragedy and comedy to yield a new form. Finally, putting it in botanical terms, he remarks how fruits and vegetables are crossbred to produce variations that are equally as tasty as their constituent parts (227-28).

Tirso concludes this section with earnest praise for Lope, placing him on a pedestal alongside the classical poets of the past because of his unparalleled literary production, but perhaps the greatest praise is Tirso's proclamation that he considers himself a disciple and defender of Lope, the man who perfected the *comedia*.[20] Interestingly enough, however, Tirso does not accept

---

19. Giraldi Cintio introduced the unity of time in 1543, Maggi introduced the unity of place in 1550, and it was Lodovico Castelvetro who was the first to mention the three unities together as inseparable (Parker, "Defensor" 43).

20. The two would have at least known of each other as early as 1615, as Lope mentions Tirso in a letter to the Duke of Sessa, and Tirso would have been familiar with Lope's enormous success on the boards. But Lope later left Tirso off his list of great contemporary poets in *El jardín,* published with *La filomena* in 1621, an interesting note, since the two had a strained, but respectful,

the notion that the common public influences Lope's writing, even though Lope himself states this in the *Arte Nuevo*. Rather, he believes that the statement was made due to modesty (230). Tirso's assertion is debatable, however, since we know that Lope never had the reputation of being a humble artist.

Tirso's fourth *Cigarral* concentrates on how performance affects the reception of the play. The beginning of this chapter describes a courtly crowd and the numerous forms of entertainment that they enjoy. It relates one afternoon's festive atmosphere, full of musical performances, a lunch that includes a spectacle of *máscaras* and *mimos*, and an afternoon nap, which precedes the performance of *Como han de ser amigos* in the gardens of one of the Toledan estates. As was the case with the previous day's *comedia*, the public enjoyed the production so much that the only general complaint was about the duration of the play, which was too short, in their opinion. Of course, the play was no longer or shorter than others, it was simply so enjoyable that the time passed by quickly. The participants agree that the ideal length of a play should be roughly two hours: "Entretenidas dos horas (dijo don Melchor) tiene el entendimiento en una comedia cuando es buena" (449). Much longer plays are not looked upon favorably, especially when they are of poor quality: "Martirio de tres o treinta padece el alma (replicó don García) cuando es mala" (449). Such parameters outline a limit enjoyable for the public and performable for the actors. To mention such concerns speaks for itself regarding Tirso's cognizance of the needs of all participants in the theatrical event, and it coincides with Lope's assertion regarding the desired duration of a play in the *Arte nuevo*. A play script should not be He written on more than twelve sheets ("cuatro pliegos"), which would last between two and three hours, according to Rozas, (*Significado* 151). Time is truly of the essence when composing and performing a play to ensure that the public remains entertained during the peroformance in the house of a possibly uncomfortable theater space.

Another topic eliciting lively dialogue during the *tertulia* arises over the importance of the playwright knowing his audience

---

relationship during those times. See Kennedy's "A Reappraisal of Tirso's Relations to Lope and His Theater."

and playing to their needs. Ideally, the dramatic poet will be able to cater to all members of his audience—or at least a vast majority—when composing his plays. If not, he runs the risk of alienating a great part of the public, as Don Melchor states, referring to Don García's observations about good and bad plays:

> Decís la verdad (respondió don Melchor), la diferencia que yo hallo en esos dos encontrados poemas es que hace el sabio entre la conversación del necio y el discreto, que si la una satisface y entretiene, la otra atormenta y martiriza. (498)

In short, the fact that different audience members have distinct needs is seen here. While within the fictional context of the *miscelanea*, the public was homogeneous: the upper echelon of society, but in reality, the theater-going public was more diverse. The thought processes involved in writing a play for an exclusively courtly audience, therefore, would have been different than that for a mixed crowd. This is an issue that Lope struggled with, also, as we see in the *Arte nuevo* and in *Lo fingido verdadero*, where he claims to have no choice but to write for one public, the less-refined members, at the expense of artistic expression and the enjoyment of the better-educated upper classes. Don Melchor recognizes this conflict of interest, which confronts not only dramatic poets but also other authors whose works enjoy a mixed audience. Clearly, the playwright faces many challenges. The reception of the play, it is noted, is very much dependent on the script but there are also other factors that elicit a positive or negative reaction to the performance. Some of these factors are outside the control of the playwright, and Don Alejo points to one example: bad acting.

Bad acting can ruin the best of scripts. Don Alejo acknowledges the power that performance holds over the reception of dramatic spectacle. Unskilled actors often ruined great plays: "ya por errarlas, ya por no vestirlas, y ya por despropositados los papeles para las personas que los estudian" (448). In fact, Tirso was affected by bad reviews first-hand and he mentions an actual performance of *El vergonzoso en palacio*, panned by the critics, as an example of how bad acting can spoil a great work. These bad reviews had obviously affected Tirso, who felt inclined to mention the later success of the play and blame the incident on poor acting, costuming, and misinterpretation of the text by the actors (450). It is mentioned, however, that just as a work can be adversely affected by bad acting, its good name can be restored by a qualified acting troupe (448). Here, Tirso's frustration surfaces since the success or failure of his plays is often the result of other people's abilities or shortcomings, and not his own. This is not a unique grievance because other contemporary playwrights also complained of issues that were outside of their control: poor copyists, inaccurate *memoriones*, forgeries, misrepresentation of authorship, to name a few; these factors are set apart from bad staging and acting, or an inhospitable public. As much as this section is a defense of the *comedia* in general, it is also Tirso's outlet to explain why a couple of his previous works were criticized harshly.

Another nobleman, Don Melchor, substantiates Don Alejo's comments and mentions further causes of a bad performance and the ensuing poor reception by the audience. His explanation highlights and corroborates how the constituents of the dramatic spectacle bear some responsibility for the success of a work. Indeed, the positive reception of a play is not guaranteed by any one person or group, Rozik suggests that the constituent participants of the spectacle can be considered the combined author of the text (*Acting* 151). In the *Cigarrales*, Tirso warns that improprieties committed by the author may shock and displease the public (451), an obvious observation that stems back to Horace's *Ars poetica*, in which he insists on following the rules of decorum when writing not only theater, but all imaginative literature. The director, he adds, must also take special care not to mismatch the actors and their roles since the public enters with predetermined conceptions of the characters that are expected to be maintained (451-52). Finally, an actor can completely spoil a play by delivering his lines poorly, which not only insults the poet but also the text; Don Melchor concludes that offenders of such a crime should be punished by the audience (453).[21] The simple

21. In his *loa* to *La burladora burlada*, Ricardo de Turia suggests that the audience react in a similar, although less extreme, manner: if the play is good, applaud, if it is not, remain quiet (418-19).

notion of chastisement underlines the fundamental role of the actors and the great responsibility that they shoulder with relation to the theatrical experience.

Don Melchor does not specifically mention the public in this discussion of the interrelationship and responsibilities of the participants in the dramatic spectacle, but the audience is subtly represented in the discussion by him and his colleagues. By carrying on the conversation, the role of the public as receivers of the performance, interpreters of the message, and critics of the spectacle is established. The public's opinion of a work obviously affects its popularity and the composition of later plays but also the success of those who were responsible for the various stages of its production, demonstrating the relation between the participants of the production.

In this *cigarral*, the public is portrayed in a positive light, but in other works Tirso does not hesitate to express his disdain for the theater-going crowds, who are often characterized as fickle, rude, and ignorant. His critique came to a head in *Deleytar aprovechando*, where Tirso expresses his disenchantment with the theater-going crowds in Madrid. Sullivan notes that Tirso points out five main complaints: first, the public is unenthusiastic about sacred objects. Second, the public is filled with envy and ignorance. Third, the piety of the works tended to be overshadowed by elaborate scenery. Fourth, the plays represented grand events and far-fetched miracles despite warnings from the Council of Trent. Fifth, the longest-run of a play in Madrid was two weeks, and in the provinces two or three days; he fears a play will be forgotten in three years (87). So the public clearly affects the playwright's perspective as to composing plays, or at the very least, Tirso's.

The final *Cigarral* wraps up the defense of the *comedia* by reinforcing and restating its decorous nature. After another successful performance, this time of *El celoso prudente*, the spectators comment on that day's play. It is without fault, and one of the attendees, Don Juan de Salcedo, challenges anyone to find a shortcoming in the play, satirically naming such a person Zoilos, referring to the Classical Greek literary critic's penchant for harsh literary reviews (497).[22] The work exemplifies proper behavior and prudence from which the spectator should benefit. The *comedia* has reached a high level: "y todos presentes a estimar el entretenimiento de la *comedia,* que en estos tiempos, expurgada de las perfecciones que en los años pasados se consentían a los teatros de España, y limpia de toda acción torpe, deleita enseñando y enseña dando gusto" (498). Here, Tirso sums up his idea of the quintessential role of a dramatic production: to teach while entertaining. This may also be a response to the censure that Tirso faced in the past, especially from his religious order, the Mercedarians, from whom he faced strong criticism. This censure led to the 1625 prohibition of writing more secular plays, backed by the threat of his excommunication.

Don García continues the praise and offers his own perspective to the didactic and entertaining character of the *comedia*, which is subtle and delightful at the same time. He mentions how the play's artifice and story tend to disguise a somber lesson, making it more attractive. He makes an analogy between food and the challenging, and even cathartic, lessons often contained in a play: both are easy to swallow as long as they are well-prepared (498). Though probably not directly related, Torres Naharro also compared his theater to food—or feed—suggesting that it served to satiate the appetite of the masses. In both cases, the idea of making an enjoyable experience out of theater comes through, highlighting the important need to entertain and teach simultaneously, which Bances Candamo will take to the extreme at the end of the century, and which will be discussed in the next chapter.

The commentary in the fifth *Cigarral* neatly sums up Tirso's positive and optimistic attitude toward the *comedia.* He fervently defends the art form from its detractors, and his own work from his critics. He shows great pride in his own works and and admires how far the dramatic form has advanced. While the fictitious nature of the supporters and critics in the *miscelanea* is irrefutable, a quick glance at Cotarelo's *Bibliografía* demonstrates that these arguments were based on actual criticism of the time. These discussions found in the *Cigarrales* defended the

22. Cervantes also pokes fun of Zoilos in the prologue of *Don Quijote.*

exemplarity and usefulness of his dramatic works; in Tirso's opinion, his own works served as models for other playwrights due to their decorous and entertaining natures. As a priest-playwright, Tirso faced additional obstacles that he had to overcome since his work would have been judged by Church critics and censors in a different light since he also was a religious figure; he was held to a different set of expectations.

In the *Cigarrales* Tirso presented his dramatic precepts in an effective and innovative manner. Of course, by its very nature, this defense of the *comedia* is very subjective. Within the fictional framework, Tirso placed specific topics of discussion that had been of concern in his times, and then responded to them in a direct yet playful manner. The work concentrated on what he perceived as the aspects that needed to be discussed. He controlled the conversation of the fictional *tertulias*, teaching and entertaining at the same time, which is also his stated goal of the *comedias*. Tirso used his creativity to diverge from the restrictive and perhaps daunting model of the dramatic treatise, which can be dull and difficult to understand, opting for a more "hands-on" approach. The presentation of the plays and their immediate critique was a manner to make an often weighty topic lighter but no less important.

In very little space, Tirso is able to lay out a comprehensive approach to writing and watching a *comedia*. Innovation and change are expected. Since theater is an imitation of life, variety is normal as theatrical trends transform with the tastes and needs of a dynamic society. He demonstrates his predilections for theater throughout the work. His preference for a noble crowd is also clear. The *tertulias* are populated by the upper classes, the lower class is *invisible* in the *Cigarrales* but there are the *graciosos* or the servants in the plays. Tirso was not hesitant to express his disdain for the unruly, lower classes that filled theaters and often affected the performances of his plays. Like others before him, he accepts the need to regulate action in the drama but sees no need to restrict time and place. Verisimilitude is stressed, so the validity of the latter two unities is nullified since following them would affect even further the artificiality of the play. Decorum is also a priority for all members of the dramatic exchange. Breaks in decorum cause immediate reaction with the public.

Tirso also points to numerous factors that affect the reception of a performance. Acting is of the utmost importance, since it is the vehicle by which the dramatic text reaches the public. The actors have a great responsibility to ensure that a play is acted well and within the expectations of the public. So the actors, like the playwrights and directors, must be cognizant of who they are playing to, which will help them to better understand the tastes of the audience, because the reverse is also true: the public always has specific expectations about a performance. This same notion pertains to the playwrights and directors. Unlike other playwrights at the time, however, Tirso did not see himself as dependent on the public. He most certainly was conscious of them, but he insinuates that they did not influence him as much as others. This is possible, of course, because Tirso was not forced to live on his earnings, since his vocation supported him. In the eyes of the playwright, the *comedia* had reached a climax—apparently with his works—and a state of perfection. A prideful Tirso saw his works as the ideal and decorous means to simultaneously teach and entertain the early modern Spanish public.

The commentaries found in *Cigarrales de Toledo* clearly show that performance and audience reception concerned Tirso. Though he may not have benefited from a familiarity with the stage to the degree of Lope, he clearly understood the basic ingredients that comprised a successful performance. Tirso knew, or at the very least intuited, the concept of didactic entertainment and the need to stay within the boundaries of accepted societal and dramatic norms, but at the same time, the risks he took on stage resulted in his triumph as a successful playwright. Such popularity was not necessarily beneficial to his religious career, and Tirso felt the need to produce and to defend the virtues of *comedia*. Within the framework of a mixed-genre novel, his arguments were not as formal as those in other defenses, but they were nonetheless strong, poignant, and well defended. Much like Lope, Tirso also used some of his own dramatic texts to manifest the defense of his dramatic tendencies, and a clear example of this is *El vergonzoso en palacio*, where Tirso's art is not only displayed by the structure of the play, but also within its metatheatrical aspects. These elements express the importance of performance and audience reception, and make the audience contemplate their own position in the dramatic exchange.

IV. Performance and reception in the intercalated play, *El vergonzoso en palacio*

Written and performed in 1611 but not published until 1621 in *Cigarrales de Toledo*, *El vergonzoso en palacio* premiered in Madrid and received disastrous reviews, the result of poor acting. The play later enjoyed critical success once performed by a top-notch acting troupe led by one of the finest actors of the times, Fernán Sánchez de Varga (Ayala 42).[23] Despite its rave reviews, Tirso was still affected by the initial performance's failure, however, and he attempts to explain the reasons in the *Cigarrales* in a discussion about acting. Complex intrigue characterizes this particular play, as Tirso utilizes common dramatic techniques: mistaken identity, confusion, disguise, and nocturnal encounters, to obfuscate the story.

El vergonzoso centers on the amorous escapades of the Duke of Avero's daughters, Madalena and Serafina, and their respective suitors. Sensing that he was nobler than his shepherd's life might suggest, the title character, Mireno, leaves home in search of a better life but his journey is cut short when he finds himself apprehended by the Duke's posse, the result of mistaken identity. Upon seeing Mireno (who has changed his name to Dionís), an enamored Madalena arranges his release from prison and hires him as her tutor. Unable to express their mutual love because of apparent class differences, they do finally reveal their feelings as Madalena feigns sleep. The couple marries at the end of the play after his noble roots are revealed. When a visiting Antonio sees Serafina, he decides to seduce her. After learning that she will be in the garden rehearsing her part for an upcoming performance, he hides in the bushes to see her stunning performance and hires a painter to paint her portrait, in which she is dressed as a man. After an argument, Antonio throws down the portrait in anger and Serafina instantly falls in love with the "man" in the picture.

23. In his introduction to *Vergonzoso,* Francisco de Ayala states that Blanca de los Ríos proved this without a doubt (8).

Antonio makes up a lie that the portrait is actually a nobleman named Dionís. A skeptical Serafina orders Antonio to bring Dionís to the garden that night, when, by playing the role of both men, he gains entrance to Serafina's room under false identity and they marry the next day.

This comedy of intrigue expounds on erotic love as its central theme, a common topic in early modern Spanish drama, through the characterization of Antonio. Madalena and Serafina, too, fulfill expectations of how young women are commonly portrayed in the Golden Age theater: they refuse to be controlled by contemporary societal convention. Madalena is indeed receptive to love, but with whom she chooses, and, by the end of the play, she sheds the prejudice of predetermined class structure, which commonly determined relationships, by articulating her love for Dionís; on the other hand, Serafina is simply not interested in men, until she falls in love with the portrait of herself dressed as one, ironically undermining the accepted tradition of marriage as a stabilizing force of society. Tirso interrogates women's role in early modern Spain by representing them in his plays as plucky and independent characters who challenge established norms; such dynamic and dramatically charged individuals were vital elements because they made for such good material for his dramatic works.

El vergonzoso examines various aspects of the theatrical spectacle through its interwoven levels of audience, familiar themes of the times, and exploration of dramatic practices. The play actually stages the dramatic precepts that Tirso followed when composing plays, the same ones that he later elaborated on in the *Cigarrales*. For example, in *El vergonzoso*, Tirso presents a brief literary discussion, later copied in the *Cigarrales*. After Serafina appears dressed in male attire to rehearse her part in an upcoming play, the two engage in the following exchange:

JUANA. ¿Qué aquesto de veras haces?
¿Qué en verte así no te ofendas?
SERAFINA. Fiestas de Carnestendolas
todas paran en disfraces.
Deséome entretener
Deste modo; no te asombre
que apetezca el traje de hombre,
ya que no lo puedo ser.

JUANA.	Paréceslo de manera, que me enamoro de ti. En fin, ¿esta noche es?
SERAFINA.	Sí
JUANA.	A mí más gusto me diera que te holgaras de otros modos, y no con representar.
SERAFINA.	No me podrás tú juntar, para los sentidos todos los deleites que ha diversos en la comedia.
JUANA.	Calla. (2.734-48)

Here, Tirso presents a debate about the propriety of the *comedia*, with each woman representing either the detractors (Juana) or the supporters (Serafina) of the form and of theater in general. This same model is seen later in the fifth *Cigarral*, when the playwright expresses his absolute support of the dramatic form. In *El vergonzoso*, Juana is not convinced by Serafina's arguments and proves hesitant to accept her friend's vocation as an actor (2.789). In fact, in an earlier discussion with her cousin Antonio, Juana described Serafina as having lost her mind over theater (2.481-82). Nonetheless, Juana unwittingly plays two roles ubiquitous to theatrical productions that facilitate Serafina's successful performance. First, she is a promoter; by telling Antonio about the time and location of the rehearsal, Juana essentially arranges for the public to attend (2.479-80). Second, she is the director, and her role is even more important to a successful staging. Juana tells Antonio and the painter where to sit, so that they are not seen but still have a clear view:

> Desde este verde arrayán
> donde el sitio el amor hurta[s],
> estos jazmines y murtas
> ser tus celosías podrán;
> pero que calles te aviso
> y tendrá tu amor buen fin. (2.647-52)

Her insistence that the two men remain quiet is a clear jab at the rowdy audiences of the times. As mentioned earlier in this study and in many studies dealing with early modern Spanish theater, the crowds were often loud and disruptive.[24] Juana's lines instruct the public that if they behave, good things will come to them from the stage. Immediately after, she promises that she will direct the rehearsal, setting up the blocking for the actor, ensuring that Serafina will be in plain sight:

> Yo haré que ensaye el papel
> aquí para que esté enfrente
> del pintor, y retratalla
> con más facilidad pueda. (2.657-60)

While her actual intention was to facilitate the courtship of her cousin Antonio and Serafina, her other roles in the spectacle are not to be ignored. They show Tirso's recognition of yet another aspect of theater that ensures positive reception of the work by the public. The importance of all participants in the preparation and performance of a play is also highlighted in the fourth *Cigarral.*

Other, frequent references to theater expose the self-conscious nature of the play and Serafina's description of the *comedia* echoes Tirso's own delight in the art form, as described in the *Cigarrales*, where he praises the entertaining and even consoling nature of the genre. Reminiscent of Mateo Luján's comments in *Segunda parte de la vida del pícaro Guzmán de Alfarache*: "la comedia es imitación hecha para limpiar el ánimo de las pasiones por medio del deleite de la risa," (258), Serafina asks:

> En la comedia, los ojos
> ¿no se deleitan y ven
> mil cosas que hacen que estén
> olvidados tus enojos? (2.751-54)

She continues explaining how the *comedia* entertains the public because of the play's ability to please the various senses with its variety of stimuli: "La música, ¿no recrea / el oído, y el discreto / no gusta allí del concerto / y la traza que desea? (2.755-58). Similar comments resonate in the observations made in the literary discussions of the *Cigarrales.* With regard to how the

24. Jane Albrecht's study, *The Playgoing Public of Madrid in the Time of Tirso de Molina*, is an excellent example of the scholarship dedicated to the topic of early modern Spanish audiences.

entertainment value of the *comedia* relates to the senses, we are reminded of the comparisons made at the end of the first *Cigarral*.

Explaining that variation is expected in theater, Don Alejo compares the often hybrid nature of many fruits and vegetables with the *comedia* (227-28). The analogy is effective because it, too, invokes more than one sense—in this case sight and taste—making it much more striking and comprehensible. While taste is not the sense that one would relate specifically with the *comedia* (though there was certainly some eating taking place in the *corrales* during the afternoon's activities), the notion highlights the importance of stimulating the spectator in a number of ways to make the production more enjoyable. Most certainly, an afternoon in the *corral de comedias* had to be a stimulating sensorial experience, with the sights and sounds of the production mixed with offstage activities.

Serafina continues her convincing statements, noting how the *comedia* has something for everyone. It appeals to all publics through a combination of interesting content and original subject matter:

> Para el alegre, ¿no hay risa?
> Para el triste, ¿no hay tristeza?
> Para el agudo, ¿agudeza?
> Allí el necio, ¿no se avisa?
> El ignorante, ¿no sabe?
> ¿No hay guerra para el valiente,
> consejos para el prudente,
> y autoridad para el grave?
> Moros hay, si quieres moros;
> si apetecen tus deseos
> torneos, te hacen torneos;
> si toros, correrán toros. (2.758-70)

These comments expound on the heterogeneous theater audience of early modern Spain that paid admission to see plays. Serafina describes the tragicomic form, explaining how the hybrid theatrical styling took advantage of the best aspect of both forms and presented current subject matter in an appealing manner. Serafina insists that the *comedia* has become a theater of the masses that pleases most audience members:

> ¿Quieres ver los epítetos
> que de la comedia he hallado?
> De la vida es un traslado,
> sustento de los discretos,
> dama del entendimiento,
> de los sentidos banquete,
> de los gustos ramillete,
> esfera del pensamiento,
> olvido de los agravios,
> manjar de diversos precios,
> que mata de hambre a los necios
> y satisface a los sabios.
> Mira lo que quieres ser
> de aquestos dos bandos. (2.771-84)

At the end of the discussion in the fifth *Cigarral*, a similar notion is introduced, when the Toledan nobles talk about how the *comedia* succeeds in presenting a serious message in an enjoyable manner. Also, the need to please the entire audience is mentioned in the fourth *Cigarral* when the participants discuss the need to make a work accessible and enjoyable to both the *sabio* and the *necio*.

This preoccupation of appealing to the entire public became more complicated as commercial theaters, where a heterogeneous audience gathered to see plays, became more ubiquitous. In a similar circumstance discussed in Chapter two, Lihani mentions that playing to all members of the audience was also a concern of Torres Naharro when he was writing in Italy at the beginning of the sixteenth century. Lihani states that Torres Naharro's plays were targeted at both the noble spectators and the servants in attendance but in distinct ways and with unique messages. While certainly a possibility, especially since Torres Naharro alludes to his solidarity with the working class in the *Prohemio* to the *Propalladia*, the true challenge of writing for a mixed audience arose much later when tickets were actually purchased by all and there was the explicit need to please the audience, not just the patron of the playwright. In fact, in Torres Naharro's time, I doubt that the playwrights' priority was pleasing the service staff that saw the plays while they worked, though it may have been a minor concern. Lope, on the other hand, chose to please the lower classes with his *comedias*. Of course, the goal of staging a play is for the enjoyment of the general public, so pleasing the majority must be a priority for most playwrights. Turning a deaf ear to one constituency, no matter who it is, seems counterproductive. This particular aspect of composition would have been challenging to the playwrights as their plays had to appeal to all audience members.

Serafina's rehearsal in the garden is central to a discussion of reception and performance in the play; the metatheatrical aspects found in this scene lead us closer to a better understanding of the concepts that drove Tirso's poetics and his playwriting. The garden scene can be considered an early dramatization of Tirso's defense of the *comedia* later presented in the *Cigarrales*. In "*El vergonzoso en palacio:* duplicaciones y multiplicaciones," Margit Frenk draws parallels between the play and the *Cigarrales*, noting that Serafina's rehearsal in the garden is not coincidental. In fact, Frenk likens the scene to a performance of a *comedia*: Serafina's description of the *comedia* acts as a *loa*, her three different performances compare to the three-act structure, and the presence of a public and the elaborate costuming was emblematic to the spectacle (78). I would add that just as we have a "mini" *comedia*, we also see a miniaturization of a diverse public representing three distinct demographics: Juana is a mid-level noble woman as the maid-in-waiting, Antonio is a duke, and the painter is a commoner. Also, the introduction of Serafina's rehearsal within the play—Frenk's *loa*—reproduces a similar dynamic that is seen between the play and the *Cigarrales*, in which *El vergonzoso* is intercalated within the text of the miscellany. Such resemblances further support the notion of the dramatization of Tirso's poetics and point to a definite recognition of the actual playwriting process, in the mind of both Tirso and the public.

Further analogous structures in the *Cigarrales* and *El vergonzoso* offer new levels of audience within both texts that force the public to further contemplate their important role in the process of reception. In the *Cigarrales*, the intercalation of the play forms an interior audience consisting of the characters within the miscellany that go to see the play. This structure allows Tirso to address typical criticisms by means of the invented reactions of the characters in the *Cigarrales*, ingeniously developing the debate and convincing the reader of the veracity of his arguments. The multiple levels of audience focus readers' attention on the public's role in the dramatic exchange as they see how Don Alejo and the others react to a particular work.

In *El vergonzoso*, Tirso reproduces a similar audience perspective when Serafina rehearses her part for Juana while Antonio and the painter are spying on the two women. The addition of one more level of intratextual audience reemphasizes the importance of the public to us, the readers, by clearly demonstrating the reactions of characters within the *Cigarrales* and consequently demonstrating the role of the public in the reception of the play. By calling attention to the multiple layers of audience in his play, Tirso draws attention to the importance of the spectator to the dramatic spectacle, reminding the theatergoers of their vital role as receivers of the text: a play is not a play without an audience.

This scene also demonstrates the different ways in which a *comedia* affects an audience according to their expectations and desires: the painter is impressed, Juana is amazed and even tricked by Serafina's gripping performance and the enamored Antonio falls deeper in love with the actress. Indeed, Juana's reaction to the realistic acting skills of Serafina further uncovers the audience's role in the reception of a play as she becomes frightened by Serafina's characters, believes they are real, and, involuntarily, begins to act within the play, blurring the lines between reality and fiction. These various reactions to the performance of Serafina once again reveal the interconnectivity of performance and reception. Tirso does not explicitly address reception in the play but his views are clearly presented. In fact, the garden scene is a clear exposition on the reception and the factors that affect it. Like Lope's *Lo fingido verdadero*, Tirso's play clearly demonstrates the importance of performance and reception to the dramatic spectacle.

The performative aspects of the play further demonstrate Tirso's understanding of the playwriting process. Serafina rehearses, she claims, because of a desire to please her audience and improve her already notable acting abilities: "Deséome entretener / deste modo (2.736-37). In "Sentido y forma en *El vergonzoso en palacio,*" Joaquín Casalduero asserts that Renaissance and Baroque aesthetic are manifested in Serafina's performance, since to be a good actor, it is not important to feel the role, but to know how to fake the role (208). Even more convincing is Dawn Smith's assertion in "*El vergonzoso en palacio*: A Play for Actors" that Tirso is obviously poking fun at the over-dramatic actor (93). She comments on the comic aspect of this scene, noting that Serafina and her "virtuoso" performance are so exaggerated that "we may imagine that the actress playing the part of Serafina gave free rein to every melodramatic trick of which she was capable" (93). The over-the-top performance could also be a commentary on how many actors overact their parts, making this another example of justifying the poor performance of the play that bothers Tirso so deeply. A contrasting view is presented in Portes's "Reflexiones sobre el actor." Portes, who was one of the most respected actors of classical Spanish theater during the second half of the twentieth century, describes how the actor becomes the character:

> El actor no es simple transmisor. Cuando en ello se le convierte aparece la mentira, la impostura. El actor en su más alto concepto es una extraordinaria máquina de transformación y depuración de materiales intelectuales, emotivos y fisonómicos. Si se le vacía sólo quedará el continente. Que no es poco. El cuerpo es un imán. Pero en el contenido está la razón última y moral de su existencia sobre el tablado. (30)

This perspective differs from Casalduero's since Portes does not describe acting as faking a role but becoming a role, making the performance that much more convincing and imitative. In *El vergonzoso*, Serafina takes her rehearsal in the garden very seriously, and the effects on her public are notable. According to many actors and scholars, acting is not faking but assimilating a character. Maria Aitken states that "[a]ctor, character, and language combine to make their own reality. That's what any actor wants..." (13-14). So, within Serafina's performance is found the desire to become a character and an acknowledgement of the power that the actors hold on the dramatic spectacle.

Instances of role-playing and disguise abound in *El vergonzoso,* constantly reminding the public of the artificial nature of theater. As already mentioned, Serafina rehearses her part dressed as man, reflecting a popular theatrical tend of the time. Glenn comments on the use of camouflage in "Disguises and

Masquerades in *El vergonzoso en palacio,*" noting that poetic justice is doled out according to the nature of the disguise, that is, the purpose for adopting another identity (17). For example Mireno's case was justified, while Antonio's was not. In *Irony and Theatricality in Tirso de Molina,* Jane Albrecht states that the play is a series of falsehoods because the characters constantly refer to fiction, drama, and painting, constant reminders of the fabricated nature of the dramatic event (59). These examples clearly demonstrate the Baroque preoccupation of the deceptiveness of appearances, underlining the desire for *desengaño.*

Other significant examples of role play within the work occur in Act 3, when Madalena feigns sleep and proclaims her love for Mireno. Though not a professional actress like her sister, Madalena's performances are just as convincing, stirring emotions—namely fear—in Mireno. Madalena sees no other recourse than to feign sleep in order to transmit a message, illustrating how acting is simultaneously an effective vehicle for information and a fictional construct. It is in this scene that I suggest that we see a manifestation of the Golden Age aesthetic proposed by Casalduero. Madelena's performance embodies many concepts treated in the Renaissance and Baroque theater of Spain. Her feigning deep slumber and talking in her sleep as if she was dreaming is reminiscent of the uncertainty of man's existence, which Mireno personifies in the scene. We also see how the scene manifests a suspicious feeling toward what is real or illusion. A simple reading of the text cannot reveal to the critic how the scene was performed. It seems just as reasonable that Serafina took her acting of her roles to heart, and tried to assimilate herself to the character. This is an attitude that Ginés discusses in Lope's *Lo fingido verdadero.*

This scene also demonstrates the split persona of the actor. Trancón describes how, before entering on stage, the actor is actually two people, the actor and the character. This transformation is clear in this case. Before Mireno enters the room, Madalena is awake and scheming as to how to elicit a statement of love from her tutor. By feigning sleep, Madalena becomes a fictional character and is acting as she recites her amorous lines to the young man. He is confused, but finally he believes she is sleeping. This ruse underlines further the power of acting and its potential to manipulate the public. It is through this scene that emotions become clearer and a potential romance becomes more tangible. When Madalena "awakens," she returns to her normal self, she is no longer acting, but the effect of the performance remains, especially for Mireno. In this case, the actor does not break from her role, as Ginés did in *Lo fingido verdadero*, and the performance was much more successful. To ensure a good performance, the actors themselves must separate from their actual persona and adopt that of the characters they are portraying.

Another example of metatheater materializes in the portrait of Serafina and hints at Tirso's innovative tendencies. The portrait in *El vergonzoso* differs from other examples of ekphrasis in the *comedia* because it adds the extra layer of confusion.[25] It still fulfills the typical expectations of increasing suspense, but, in this case, the painting actually subverts the notion of a portrait representing the beauty of a woman because she is painted in men's clothing. Albrecht states that Tirso's skewed conception "ironizes" a theatrical device (65). In addition, further tension between the plastic arts and theater becomes evident as the convention of the transvestitism of women (*una mujer vestida de hombre*) within the dynamic dramatic text is juxtaposed with the fossilization of the subject in the painting, who is captured at one moment in time. This contrast between the ability and inability to change could suggest the heightened importance of the dramatic arts. Such an experimental use of convention again demonstrates Tirso's interrogation of established norms.

Although he agrees with Lope's opinions regarding the vast diversity of art, Tirso had a different explanation as to what spurs artistic creation, noting that internal inspiration drives art more than external stimuli. In the dedication to the *Tercera parte* of his *comedias*, he comments, comparing the artist to a silkworm, that since art is the expression of the poet's inner substance, a premium is put on originality. Tirso further develops this notion in the play,

---

25. See Frederick A. de Armas's volume *Ekphrasis in the Age of Cervantes* for numerous studies dealing with use of the rhetorical device in early modern Spanish literature.

within the context of the painting.[26] Returning to the rehearsal scene in the garden, Antonio speaks to the artist in Aristotelian terms, explaining that he, too, is a painter of spiritual works in his mind, using his understanding of beauty (2.718-19, 669). Antonio describes painting as colors and forms that fill in a preconceived outline, but understanding of the form comes from within and defines the figure:

> Las colores y matices
> son especies del objeto,
> que los ojos que le miran
> al sentido común dan;
> que es obrador donde están
> cosas que el ingenio admiran,
> tan solamente en bosquejo,
> hasta que con luz distinta
> las ilumina y las pinta
> entendimiento, espejo
> que a todos da claridad. (2.673-83)

Tirso's suggests that the meaning of the works stems from inside the poet, thereby liberating the public from the responsibility of driving the creative process. Because of this opinion, his dramatic poetry seems more subjective and less dependent on audience expectations, a notion we also see in the *Cigarrales* in his refusal to admit that Lope had been encouraged by the public. Also, as mentioned earlier, Lope's different motivations, specifically, making a living, may have affected his perspective with regard to pleasing the audience. Of course, there remains the possibility that Lope's *Arte nuevo* was simply a compilation of excuses to justify his writing style to the Madrid Academy, but this is doubtful since he wrote so many *comedias* and very few classically inspired works—at the beginning of his career—to sate his hunger to write with *arte*.

By dealing with its own theatricality, the play interrogates the issues of metatheater, performance, and audience reception with the intention of discovering their influence on the playwriting process. Like Lope's *Lo fingido verdadero*, Tirso's *El vergonzoso*

---

26. In addition to Smith's study, Sullivan discusses this concept in Chapter four of *Tirso de Molina and the Drama of the Counter Reformation.*

en palacio accentuates the playwright's poetics and dramatic tendencies. As a writer of the popular *comedia*, Tirso had to acknowledge the public's fundamental role in the playwriting process, and though he apparently was more hesitant than Lope to accept the notion, his plays reflected an understanding of its importance to the success of a dramatic work. In fact, it is possible that the *Cigarrales'* invented audience was intended to serve as a model for the theater-going public to follow. He clearly wrote his text with public opinion in mind, as evidenced by his reaction to bad reviews and his attempt in the *Cigarrales* to justify the poor performance of *El vergonzoso*.

The early date of the play clearly indicates that Tirso had been contemplating the mechanisms and theories that drive the production of theater for a long time. By placing an explanation of his dramatic poetics within the framework of the *Cigarrales*, Tirso illustrates his awareness of the interrelationship of reception and performance; he literally creates the literary forums in which his works are discussed. This strategy allows for the original presentation of both sides of the literary debate, and its actual representation of the discussions within the texts obliges the reader of the *Cigarrales* to further contemplate his or her role as a receiver of the text. This work does not have as its central focus the actual playwriting process, as in Lope's play, but it does highlight the importance of reception and performance, underlining their importance by means of several metatheatrical techniques.

A careful look at the two dramatic treatises reveals that they share much in common. In both cases, the poets offer an original and entertaining manner to present their dramatic precepts. Lope's use of blank verse suggests a playful attitude, and one that facilitates the presentation of the text to his audience, the Madrid Academy. Similarly, Tirso's *Cigarrales* also defends the dramatic form in an innovative manner. These two theoretical manifestations echo the dynamic nature of theater and literature in general. They both build on old styles and ideas, presenting an enjoyable manner to explain what could be perceived by some as an uninteresting topic.

Both the *Arte nuevo* and *Cigarrales* emphasize the need to appeal to the tastes and expectations of the theater-going audience, the receivers of the dramatic text. This acuity results from a playwright's experience staging plays; in short, theatrical styles evolve in conjunction with the changing preferences of the audience, leading to shifts in dramatic theory. Lope and Tirso discuss factors that directly affect the reception of the plays: a dynamic and hybrid character, the unity of action, the predilection for change, and sustained decorum, to name a few. The dramatic poets recognize the interrelation between composition, performance, and reception, and that these factors should be considered during all stages of the dramatic spectacle: pre-performance, performance, and post-performance.

Differences between the two treatises exist, too, but they are less striking than the similarities. They do not stem from a divergence in common beliefs but are the result of the evolving nature of theatrical practices. For example, there is much more detail in Lope's piece than in Tirso's. This is to be expected, however, because Lope had already laid out the foundation of the *comedia* in the *Arte nuevo*, so Tirso, a supporter of Lope, built upon those established ideas. Tirso deals with other facets of the dramatic spectacle, continuing the dialogue defending the tragicomic form. Tirso concentrates on the roles of the actors, directors, and public and how they all affect the success of a play. Where Lope's *Arte nuevo* may seem at times apologetic, Tirso's *Cigarrales* is much more assertive, possibly the result of being composed during the heyday of the *comedia* in Spain.

Perhaps the biggest thematic difference is the esteem given to the general public. In the *Arte nuevo*, Lope repeatedly mentions the influence that the *vulgo* has had over the composition of his plays. The common public is always on his mind, compelling him to change his writing style by not following classical dramatic precepts. Of course, there is a degree of irony in his words, especially since he was addressing the literati of Madrid, who saw themselves as authorities of literature. Lope seems to intuit their criticism of his less traditional theater by responding that he recognizes that it is a lesser form—more irony—but he must write for those that buy tickets to the plays; so the influence of the *vulgo* is strong according to Lope. In his dramatic treatise, Tirso does not give as much weight to the general public with regard to their influence on dramatic trends. The audience in the *Cigarrales* belongs to the noble classes and the members of the common classes do not enter into the picture. Tirso does not sympathize with the lower classes and does not admit to being affected to such a great degree by their demands. He recognizes, however, that they do have an affect on the creative process of writing theater. It seems that Tirso refuses to acknowledge the public as contributors to his particular art. Of course, he did not face the same conditions as Lope, since his audience was more established and cognizant of the dramatic practices typical to the *comedia*, allowing for a more ambivalent attitude.

An inclusive examination of the two plays demonstrates a similar dynamic. The dramatic process is a common theme in both works, but it is dealt with in more detail in Lope's *comedia.* This is not surprising since, as a dramatic representation of the *Arte nuevo*, *Lo fingido verdadero* frankly had more ground to cover. Its earlier date corresponds to a time when the *comedia* was still being established as the primary dramatic form, so Lope presented a more comprehensive view and explanation of the dramatic context of the time. Tirso, was able to be more selective, and while his message is no less convincing, he was certainly not compelled to repeat established norms.

The use of metatheater is common in the *comedia*, and these two plays clearly demonstrate how its application helps us to further understand the dramatic landscape of the time. As Larson points out, metatheater is a valuable tool in the study of theater, and through its use, Lope and Tirso dramatize the precepts that affected the composition, preparation, performance, and reception of their work. *Lo fingido verdadero* directly addresses the process of writing a play in the exchanges between Ginés and the various emperors. It is not as simple as some imagine, nor is it a fast process. A lot of consideration and careful planning go into the composition of a good play. Tirso, too, addresses the complexity of the *comedia* in *El vergonzoso* through Serafina, who describes how the *comedia* appeals to the interests of all members of the audience. Neither playwright forgets—or lets his audience forget—that the public is important to the success of a play since it is for them that a play is performed.

The importance and power of the actor is also highlighted in the two plays, which dramatize the stages of a performance from rehearsal to representation to reception. We see how rehearsal is fundamental to successfully playing a role. Since a good actor becomes the character that he or she plays, it necessary for a certain amount of preparation and familiarity with the role. The *comedias* also show that when acting it is imperative not to break from role, which causes negative reactions in the public, and to maintain composure and decorum within the role, which results in a powerful performance that moves the public. By seeing an intercalated performance, its importance becomes clear since it is at center stage, both in literal and figurative terms. These plays demonstrate the intrinsic role of performance to theater in a way that becomes clear to the audience as they see it onstage. The direct influence of performance on the public is clear and compelling by the reactions of the public.

The use of internal audiences, or ones that actually appear onstage, is another metatheatrical technique used in both plays. This strategy continues to highlight the connection between performance and reception because the real audience sees the reactions of the staged public, a mirror image of themselves. Both *comedias* discussed in this chapter share a similar dynamic of an "interior" audience, which gives the "exterior" public a clearly delineated view of the relationship between performance and reception. In both cases, the audiences are rapt by the performances. The members are lost in the dramatic illusion produced by the actors, to such an extent that they unwittingly become players in the productions. Diocletian cannot distinguish Ginés's break from character during the first performance and usurps a role. Similarly, Juana is spellbound by Serafina's rehearsal and her reactions reveal that she believes the roles played by her friend and demonstrates actual emotions as a result of the performance. The affective power of acting is presented right before the eyes of the public and this metatheatrical moment serves to remind the public of the fictional nature of theater. The public should not get lost in the dramatic illusion of the play. Tirso mentions that his theater teaches as it entertains, a common goal among most playwrights, and if the public becomes too enveloped in the storyline, they lose perspective of the message of the play.

These *comedias* differ from the plays of Torres Naharro and Cueva because they focus more on the practical aspects related to the commercialization of seventeenth-century theater. It is during the time of Lope and Tirso that the *comedia* emerged as the national form of theater in Spain. Performances were frequent, making them lucrative investments for many of the parties involved. The *comedias* were so popular that theater managers were often likely to accept most scripts, which led to a number of problems: forgery, false attribution, and poor quality, to name a few. Also, with such a great demand for theater at the time, acting troupes popped up everywhere, many of which were made up of unskilled actors, which also affected performance. The public became more demanding at every performance. They transformed into an educated—in theatrical terms—crowd, so their increasingly high standards coupled with a hunger for originality posed a challenge for most playwrights.

The *comedia* continued as the most popular form of theater in Spain until the 1640s, when commercial theaters were closed a number of times to observe extended periods of mourning, which, in conjunction with other factors, greatly affected their future and popularity. But tastes change and at this time the popularity of court theater and plays celebrating religious holidays grew, upstaging the *comedia*, so popular at the beginning of the seventeenth century. The next chapter mirrors this trend, dealing with the ways that dramatic theory was represented in an *auto sacramental* by Pedro Calderón de la Barca and a court play by Francisco Bances Candamo.

CHAPTER 4: OUT OF THE *CORRALES*: RECEPTION AND PERFORMANCE IN THE *AUTO SACRAMENTAL* AND COURT DRAMA

In *Theatre in Spain: 1499-1700*, McKendrick notes that the religious and the profane were never far apart in Spain (209); an examination of reception and performance in the *auto sacramental* and court drama is the subject of this chapter. Besides some similarities in staging, they also share numerous characteristics regarding reception and performance, affecting their creation and evolution. The placement of a discussion of these two forms at the end of the study is not coincidental because, in addition to illustrating the chronologies of the playwrights themselves, these subgenres reflect the progression of the state of theater in Spain in the last half of the seventeenth century: as the *comedia* enters a state of decline, the *auto* and court drama enjoy a resurgence in popularity, anticipating the theatrical trends of early eighteenth-century Spain.

This chapter discusses the work of two prominent playwrights at the end of the seventeenth century: Pedro Calderón de la Barca and Francisco Antonio de Bances Candamo. The first part examines Calderón's *La segunda esposa y muriendo triunfando* and how this *auto* staged the dramatic theory both unique to the form and ubiquitous to theater in general, poetics that he later described in the prologue to his collection of liturgical dramas. This study then exits the religious milieu and addresses how the court dramas of Bances influenced dramatic theory at the close of the Spanish Golden Age by looking at *Duelos de Ingenio y Fortuna* and the parallels it shares with his *Theatro de los Theatros*, the last notable dramatic treatise of the epoch. Not only do the religious *auto* and the secular court drama highlight the culmination of the importance of reception and performance on theater in early modern Spain, but also they conclude a long and vibrant dramatic tradition that prospered during the sixteenth and seventeenth century.

I. Calderón de la Barca's religious poetics and the *auto sacramental*

One of the greatest playwrights in Spanish literary history, Calderón was a fervently religious man, and although the *auto* best illustrated the influence of Catholic doctrine on his life, his orthodoxy drove his entire theatrical output. In his edition of Calderón's *autos,* Ángel Valbuena Prat praises the playwright for creating a synthesis of history and human theology, asserting that the art form peaked under his pen (10-11); A. A. Parker concurs, noting that Calderón's *autos* were scrupulously and perfectly structured (*Allegorical* 14-15).

The search for the perfect definition of an *auto* has been undertaken by numerous scholars throughout the twentieth century, but the most satisfactory is that of Valbuena Prat, who presents a clear, concise description of the genre: the *auto sacramental* is a religious, one-act dramatic piece, most commonly represented during the celebration of Corpus Christi, which refers to the mystery of the Eucharist, using allegory as a basic element of its structure and of the development of its message (*Obras* 9). Parker expands on the description by dividing the types of *autos* into a manageable list of five categories: dogmatic, scriptural (historical-theological), apologetical, ethical, and devotional/hagiographical (*Allegorical* 62).

Since the nineteenth century, critical reactions to the *auto* have proven polemical. Menéndez y Pelayo was undecided if the dramatic style was an artistic aberration or aesthetic exception to theater (*Calderón y su teatro* 103). Later, Parker praised the form in his comprehensive study, *The Allegorical Drama of Calderón*; Valbuena Prat successfully restored Calderón's religious plays to their rightful place in Spanish literary history, and, more recently, the works of Ángel Cilveti and Donald Dietz have offered intriguing insight into the study of the subgenre. Valuable scholarship dealing with the *auto* continues, some of the major contributors include Shergold, Varey, Arellano, José María Díez Borque, Viviana Díaz Balsera, Barbara E. Kurtz, and Dale Pratt, to name a few. These scholars explore such topics as the form's cultural implications, staging, performance, and use of allegory. The number of excellent studies continues to grow but, as Díez

Borque has recognized, research on the reception of the *auto* still needs to catch up with similar studies of the other prominent dramatic forms of early modern Spain (*Fiesta* 25).

Calderón did not write a lengthy, formal dramatic treatise explaining his approach to theater; nevertheless, descriptions found in the prologue to *Autos sacramentales alegóricos y historiales*, published in 1677, and the *loa* to one *auto* in particular, *La segunda esposa y triunfar muriendo*, illustrate that he, too, was concerned with reception and performance and their connections to the creative process.[1] The prologue provides a point of departure for a discussion of the factors that may have influenced Calderón while writing these religious plays. In it, he describes the regretful state of publishing—especially in terms of the *comedia*—at the time, the result of the theft and plagiarism of other playwrights and the alteration of many texts at the hands of censors, printers, and copyists.[2] Calderón assures us, however, that this particular collection of *autos* has been spared such desecration for two reasons: first, because of the sacred nature of the plays, and second, because they were destined to be performed for the royal court on holy days; their only defects are his own: "que para defectos bastan los míos" (41). Clearly, more care was taken to retain the original message and form of the *autos* because of their religious nature. The message of the plays should not be changed in any way in order to maintain the integrity of the religious message and the structure was well established. Apparently, the threat of textual corruption was so great that Calderón often found himself obliged to edit his own works to safeguard their authenticity. Sadly, no work was completely safe from censorship,

1. This is not the only instance where Calderón defines the *auto sacramental*. Descriptions of the form and its public are seen in several of the *loas* or in the plays themselves, on example is seen in the *loa* to *El verdadero Dios Pan*.

2. Calderón complained of the sorry state of publishing in the prologue to his *Cuarta parte,* a collection of his dramatic works, noting textual errors and erroneous attribution of his works, including forty-one plays falsely attached to his name. This has been a topic of interest for many scholars. For example, see Everett W. Hesse's "The First and Second Editions of Calderón's *Cuarta parte*" and "The Publication of Calderón's Plays in the Seventeenth Century." For a more general overview, see Catherine Larson's *Language and the Comedia* for a discussion of the various filters that mired the transmission of many Golden Age texts.

which changed far too many plays in the name of the Counterreformation. This did not prove too problematic for the *autos* due to their inherent religious nature and unvarying form and subject matter.[3] Indeed, it seems counterintuitive to censor the same literature that exalted Catholic dogma and openly confronted the spreading threat of Protestantism throughout Europe. Furthermore, once a playwright established his reputation in a certain city or town, that government often contracted him year after year to write the play for the celebration of Corpus, making it easier to receive the approval of ecclesiastical censors. Nevertheless, Calderón's concern with preserving his works points to a preoccupation with their desired reception. Of course, changes inevitably and uncontrollably occur after the text leaves the possession of the poet.

Strict thematic and structural guidelines dictate the production of the *auto* and although the contrary may seem more logical, the creative limitations imposed by these dramatic precepts actually guided the creative process and fostered innovative playwriting. Parker identifies two aspects basic to all *autos*: the *asunto*, or Eucharistic theme, and the *argumento*, the plot, of the *auto* (*Allegorical* 59). The *asunto* does not change but the *argument* does vary, leaving innumerable options for the playwright to express the religious doctrine. Addressing possible criticism that the *autos* always deal with the same subject matter, Calderón astutely points out that this repetition actually contributes to the originality of the plays since the dramatic poet must create original works around the same theme, a clear acknowledgement of the influence of reception on the creative process. Similar to Lope and Tirso, Calderón draws a parallel between creation and the delicate originality found in nature. In his explanation of the

3. In early modern Spain, institutionalized censorship imposed blatant control over literary texts, especially in the case of the *comedia*. See Edward Wilson's "Calderón and the Stage-Censor in the Seventeenth Century: A Provisional Study." Anthony Close suggests in "Lo cómico y la censura en el Siglo de Oro," that censorship actually contributed to the originality of the plays. Although Calderón's *comedias* often fell victim to the censors, the only case of prohibition of one of his *auto* was that of *Las órdenes militares* in 1662. See Juan Eugenio Hartzenbusch, Emanuel Walberg, and Barbara E. Kurtz.

use of the same allegorical figures in many of the *autos*, Calderón states:

> [Q]ue le mayor primor de la naturaleza es que con unas mismas facciones haga tantos rostros diferentes, con cuyo ejemplar, ya que no sea primor, sea disculpa el haber hecho tantos diferentes Autos con unos mismos personajes.
> Hallaranse parecidos algunos pasos; también en la naturaleza se hallan algunos rostros parecidos.... (42)

Like his predecessors, Calderón reverts to the ultimate source of inspiration and creation, Nature, in search of a pattern to follow when composing his *autos*; he produces different faces from the same features, justifying the use of the same allegorical figures. This repetition is not negative, since the standard theme presented in an original manner proved compelling to the audience.

In terms of the reception of the *autos*, the limitations on theme and form aided the comprehension of the message. This formulaic approach does not seem coincidental, and it was most certainly effective since the *auto* remained virtually unchanged for hundreds of years; the only major differences would have been the plots and the growing extravagance of the sets. Since the plays were staged only once a year, the Eucharistic theme and fixed form actually facilitated the public's understanding, which can be attributed to the theatergoers' cultural background. Since the audience entered the dramatic exchange knowing what to expect, the novelty of the performance came to center stage as it related the Eucharistic message in an innovative manner. The playwrights often reflected and responded to the cultural, political, or social climate prevalent at the time, which is the case with *Segunda esposa*, for example.

Since this particular collection was compiled to be read, its prologue instructs the reader how to effectively approach the texts when they are not performed. Calderón, however, continually emphasizes the impact of the *auto's* spectacle. As with all forms of theater, the *autos* are meant to be performed, not read from a book. Díez Borque notes that the spectacle of the *auto* is even more complex than that of many secular theater forms since it combines ceremony and dramatized action (*Fiesta* 34), effectively embodying the dogma of the Spanish Counterreformation and many of the values that characterize the times. Victor Turner's suggestion that theater is a cultural and aesthetic mirror couldn't hold truer here, he states: "[c]ultures are most fully expressed in and made conscious of themselves in their ritual and theatrical performances" (qtd. in Schechner *Performance Studies* 15), and in the case of the *auto*, we have both ritual and theater. Acknowledging the multiplicity of the spectacle is fundamental to examine the work; a study of the *auto* from a purely textual approach is insufficient. Of course, Calderón, too, recognized the performative potential of the *auto*, noting how the brilliance of the works comes from their actual representation and that a simple reading "no puede dar de sí ni lo sonoro de la música, ni lo aparatoso de las tramoyas" (42).[4] The festive nature of the *auto* and its performance appeals to numerous senses and can only be fully appreciated when staged.

As an encounter between liturgy and theater, the *auto* incorporates two different forms of representation, the ceremony of the Eucharist and scenic action, and this combination draws the spectator into the message produced by the play. Since the idea of the work is to amaze the faithful and reaffirm the greatness of the Church and its sacraments, the playwright uses whatever means necessary to achieve this effect. By appealing to not only the visual but also the other senses, the *auto* often provides a barrage of sensorial stimuli. Díez Borque suggests that the dramatic event not only consisted of a spectacular visual and musical production but probably integrated the other senses too, where the presence of incense, flowers, food, and drink added to the festive atmosphere (76). Along similar lines, Pratt suggests that the materiality of the plays causes sensual deceit among the public (41). The emblematic nature of the whole experience awes most spectators and reinforces religious beliefs. Of course, a spectacle that appeals to several senses is not unique to the *auto*, but to all theatrical productions, as Serafina points out in the garden scene of *El vergonzoso* when she defends the propriety of the *comedia*. By stimulating the senses, Calderón attempts to stir the imagination of the receiver, who should enjoy the texts, but never forget the sacred and

---

4. See Alice M. Pollin and Jack Sage for useful studies of Calderón's treatment of music in his *autos*.

performative natures of the plays: "y si ya no es que el que lea haga en su imaginación composición de lugares, considerando lo que sería sin entero juicio de lo que es, que muchas veces descaece el que escribe de sí mismo por conveniencias del pueblo y del tablado" (42). The outright mention of the stage clearly emphasizes the performative nature of these works.

In conjunction with the sensual appeal of the works, the use of allegory is fundamental to promoting the appropriate reception of the play. Parker notes that what is performed on the stage cannot be approximated off stage. As such, the public recognizes the important themes because the staged actions coincide with the conceptions in the mind; the conceptual and the experiential intersect (*Allegorical* 83). In "Defining Allegory, or Troping Through Calderón's *Autos,*" Kurtz notes that Calderón succeeded at defining allegory, which became a repeated metaliterary tool because of its frequent use in the dramatic form (228).[5] The visualization of a complex idea is imperative in order to understand it. When the audience member see a connection between what is seen on stage and real life, complex ideas become more relatable.

Like other Golden Age playwrights, Calderón shows some degree of frustration with the public, which appears in the closing paragraph of the prologue when he addresses the reader as "¡Oh lector amigo o enemigo!" (42). His expression of disdain for anyone who ravages his work continues:

---

5. Calderón mentions the use of allegory in numerous *loas* to his *autos* or in the *autos* themselves. Two clear examples—besides that in *Segunda esposa*—are in the *loa* to *El Sacro Parnaso*, when the character *Alegoría* explains herself as "dando cuerpo al concepto / aun lo no visible animo (3 b), and in the *auto El verdadero Dios Pan*:

> La alegoría no es más
> que un espejo que traslada
> lo que es con lo que no es;
> y está toda su elegancia
> en que salga parecida
> tanta la copia en la tabla,
> que el que está mirando a una
> piense que está viendo a entrambas.
> Corre ahora la paridad
> entre lo vivo y la estampa. (1242 b)

> [S]i en lo dicho o por decir hubiere una sola voz de disuene a la pureza de la fe o al decoro de las buenas costumbres, desde luego, la delato, la detesto y la retracto, y de ella pido a Dios el perdón y a ti la enmienda. (42)

This commentary reveals Calderón's conception of the *auto* as an instrument fundamental to Catholic worship and whose production is driven by unfaltering faith. The prologue also points out the participatory role that the receiver plays with the text. Of course, the public did not act on the stage, rather, by reflecting on the message and the way that it was relayed, they worshipped through contemplation. Pratt suggests that the people came to the play to commit—in this case, to see and experience—sin, and then to be saved. The visualization of the plays wakes up the desire for emulation of the sacred (41-42). Therefore, an accurate interpretation of the *auto* was imperative since these works served as another means of worship in addition to the sermon and other religious rites.

Besides what is found in the prologue to his first collection of *autos*, Calderón uses the *loas* to the plays to address the issues that influence the composition of the works. In general, these introits reveal numerous aspects that drove the playwright's dramaturgy. The clearest example is found in *Segunda esposa*.[6] The *loa* presents a discussion between a shepherd and a peasant woman about the festivities surrounding the celebration of Corpus. The prologue begins as the Shepherd excitedly makes his way to Madrid to celebrate the religious holiday:

> [P]ues hoy el Pan de los Cielos
> se da balde a los Hombres
> que yo me parto a Madrid
> a ver danzas, procesiones,
> pues ya retumba en los valles
> el eco de sus tambores. (425 a)

The description of the festive atmosphere sets the tone of the spectacle, and reflects the jubilant nature of the holiday, which is

---

6. The *loa* to the *auto* is mentioned by numerous scholars specifically because of its description of the dramatic form that it introduces. The *auto* itself, however, has received less critical attention, see Víctor García Ruiz and Hans Flasche.

dedicated to commemorating the Last Supper and the Eucharist. Although religious in nature, the day's festivities take on an almost secular character in the variety of forms of entertainment enjoyed by the attendees.

Like the *auto* that it precedes, the *loa* instructs and prepares the public for the upcoming moralizing of the principal work. The *loa* to *Segunda esposa* serves as a primer, reminding the audience of numerous basic issues of their faith. The first one deals with the greatness of God.[7] When they first meet, the Shepherd inquires about the Peasant Woman's familiarity with the mystery of God, and she replies that this is something greater than herself "porque Misterio tan alto / tiene muy grande primores" (425 b). She proceeds to give her astute perspective of God, which she has learned from sermons and general discussion in her small town. An earthy logic guides the woman's religious beliefs and she describes the omnipresent and omnipotent grace of God in clear metaphors relatable to her social position, and, presumably, to that of much of the public. She uses two simple images, one of sunlight shining through a sieve and the other of sunlight reflecting off the pieces of a broken mirror, to describe God's glory, which is spread out and shines brightly all over (426 a). Here, Calderón takes advantage of understandable symbolism to demonstrate his point. This simple imagery perfectly expresses the concept and anticipates the more complex use of allegory in the *auto*. Since the *loa* serves as an introduction to the principal work, it is possible to see that this facile explanation of God's grace also serves to prepare the public for more grandiose concepts.

The *loa* teaches that religion is for everyone and that the faithful are expected to put forth an effort to understand its teachings. The Peasant Woman informs the Shepherd that women need to know as much as men: "[p]ara que no nos apoquen / los Hombres, cualquiera estudia" (426 a). At the end of the *loa*, Calderón revisits and reiterates how the *auto* attempts to reach out

---

7. In general, the early modern Spanish public had a well-developed background in religion. Kurt Spang goes so far as to say that it was more profound than current day knowledge, while Ludwig Pfandl suggests that religious understanding may not have been profound, but at least it was systematic and comprehensive.

to everyone by describing its wide audience. The Eucharistic message targets all members of society.[8] There is a sort of "trickle-down effect" that starts with the King, who is expected to recognize the play's message and then lead by its example:

> Y pues en piadosos pechos
> es a la razón conforme
> y el animar los humildes
> se ejercita en pechos nobles,
> recibid nuestros deseos. (427 b)

As it turns out, we are all accomplices and participants in the exchange of religious ideas; the public learns from the work itself and from the other members in order to accept the dogma of the Counterreformation at the time. The parallels between theater and religion are clear: both are performative and didactic actions that reach out to a wide audience.

Next, the Shepherd's description of the mysteries of the Eucharist acknowledges the difficulty that a common man encounters when trying to comprehend them. This suggests that abstract concepts need to be presented by other means, ones that can be understood by a simple man and another indication of the public's role in the composition of dramatic literature. Addressing the various mysteries of God, the Shepherd notes that they are difficult to imagine because of humanity's limited mental capacity:

> … No sé cómo contemplaros
> ni cómo sabré quereros
> quien hoy para conoceros
> no ha de poder alcanzaros;
> y así, en Misterios tan raros,
> difíciles de entender,
> conténtese con saber
> la inteligencia atrevida,
> que morir para dar vida,
> sólo Dios lo pudo hacer. (426 b)

---

8. Manfred Tietz discusses the heterogeneous public that enjoyed the representations of the *autos*.

This citation expresses several ideas related to the *auto*. It points to the complexity of religion for the common man, as well as the imperative need to understand and believe its teachings; it also highlights how the performative aspects of the *auto* facilitate the audience's visualization of abstract notions as presented in a play that reinforce or establish a belief system. Calderón's understanding of the advantages of presenting religious doctrine in an alternate form other than simple preaching compelled him to teach in an effective, entertaining manner. This strategy was not unique to the *auto*, of course, as it was common in all dramatic forms. Tirso, for example, discusses in *Cigarrales* how an unsavory topic becomes more palatable when offered in an attractive manner.

Besides examining the benefits of staging abstract topics in a tangible and accessible manner, the *loa* also addresses details about the performance space of the *auto*. Intrigued by the extravagance of the festivities, the Peasant Woman inquires as to its purpose, while simultaneously describing the staging of the plays on the *carros*:[9]

> [D]ecidme, aquellas torres,
> o triunfales carros, que
> el aire ocupan disformes,
> ¿para qué fin aquí están? (426 b)

Clearly, the spectacle succeeds in impressing the audience by means of technologically advanced stage machinery and extravagant sets. The Shepherd then explains to her that the spectacle augments the greatness of the religious message. The next passage informs the audience as to what to expect during the play and emphasizes the embedded religious message:

> PASTOR. A fin de hacer las mejores
> fiestas que pudo la idea
> inventar.
> LABRADORA. ¿Qué son?

9. See Shergold's and Varey's *Los autos sacramentales en Madrid en la época de Calderón*, and José M. Ruano de la Haza's "Los carros de los autos sacramentales de Calderón (1659-1681), for more information about the staging of the plays, including the scholars' conceptions of the *carros*.

PASTOR. Sermones
puesto en verso, en idea
representable, cuestiones
de la Sacra Teología
que no alcanzan mis razones
a explicar ni comprender,
y el regocijo dispone
en aplauso deste día. (426 b-27 a)

Here, Calderón not only underlines the opulent staging techniques on the moveable carts, but he also discusses the representation of theological doctrine, stressing the importance of performance and its role in facilitating comprehension of the play's themes. The reference to sermons presented in verse further emphasizes the performative characteristics of the inherent message of the *auto*, which would be more difficult to comprehend otherwise. Finally, by highlighting the desire to provide delight to the spectators, Calderón reveals that he has the public in mind when writing his plays.

These admittedly brief references to his religious theater highlight Calderón's stance regarding the actual playwriting process and demonstrate that reception and performance of the play guided his creation of liturgical drama. As a complement to the official religious service, the *auto* plays an integral part in the holy celebration of Corpus Christi. The dramatic form wields great didactic power as a result of its extravagant symbols, staging, and themes, making the dogmatic message more comprehensible than a simple sermon. By offering a storyline that is conceptual, not realistic, the *auto* differs from other contemporary theatrical forms because it does not rely on verisimilitude. The comprehension of such unique subject matter depends on presenting an abstract lesson in a tangible form, which coincides with the conceptions of the audience; it becomes necessary, therefore, to dramatize ideas and not human actions (Parker, *Allegorical* 65, 83). This conceptual and experiential phenomenon suggests that the public recognized its role as the interpreters of the event, a fact that certainly did not escape Calderón. Furthermore, due to its embellished, religious nature, the spectacle of the *auto* imposes itself on the public, forcing the participation of the audience in the contemplation of the work.

The description found in the *loa* comes after Calderón had written numerous *autos* and the prologue of the collection was presumably written even later. We see that throughout his career, Calderón provided constant reminders of the *auto's* purpose and the manner to reach it. These two introductory pieces highlight the necessity to represent complicated and often abstract religious doctrine in a more understandable manner, which is done through staged allegory in a spectacular and awe inspiring manner. More than in other forms, reception is a complicated phenomenon that affects composition of the play because the didactic aspect can overshadow the entertainment value but, at the same time, cannot be completely eliminated, since the goal of the work is to teach in an amenable and entertaining manner to a wide audience. *La segunda esposa y triunfar muriendo* exemplifies the proportional presentation of didactic content with entertainment value. This particular *auto* represents a comprehensive vision of Catholic beliefs and sacraments while, simultaneously, endorsing the second marriage of Phillip IV.

II. Dramatic poetics represented on the liturgical stage: *La segunda esposa y triunfar muriendo*

The historical-theological *La segunda esposa y triunfar muriendo* not only celebrates the Eucharist but also the second marriage of King Phillip IV to Mariana of Austria, daughter of Ferdinand III, the Emperor of the Holy Roman Empire.[10] Though the wedding ceremony took place November 8, 1648, scholars date the performance of the *auto* either in 1649 or 1652 (Valbuena Prat, "Notes" 423).[11] The play begins with Matrimony urging the King to remarry after the unfortunate death of his first wife. He agrees and chooses Ana as his bride-to-be. The story then moves to a

---

10. In *The Play of Allegory,* Kurtz complains that "in the midst of these theological details the *auto*'s circumstantial pretext–the royal wedding of 1648–tends to disappear" (134).

11. Logically, Valbuena Prat deduced that the play would have been performed after the wedding in 1649 or perhaps in 1652. It seems that there is no clear record of the *autos* performed in those years, but it is evident that *Segunda esposa* was not performed in 1650 or in 1651, because there is record of the other plays represented during those years.

conversation between Death and Sin, who, tracing their origins, cite events from both testaments of the Bible. Pleasure, the *gracioso* of the play,[12] tells them the good news of the wedding, causing the pair to begin complaining that the union of Jesus (King) and the Church (Wife) will affect them greatly. Meanwhile, Man appears with a symbolic axe decorated with six candles; he is accosted by Death and Sin, who extinguish all but one of the flames, informing him that his destiny is to be pursued eternally by Sin and to follow Death. The Holy Sacraments appear and save Man by showing him the spiritual path to heaven. After a brief holy war between the Sacraments and Sin and Death, the King sacrifices himself for mankind and is reborn, promising salvation and eternal life for his followers through the Eucharist, which serves as a symbol of the covenant between God and Man. As with all *autos*, the use of symbol and allegory is explicit, making the endorsement of the King's second marriage as clear as the emphasis in the importance of the Eucharistic tradition.

To prepare the public for the upcoming play, Calderón takes advantage of direct address at the beginning of the work. The religious message is clearly stated, and though other distractions caused by the spectacle may be present, the true purpose of the work is never lost. The metatheatrical strategy forces the audience to consider its position within the spectacle and in the world as both spectators and congregants. Here, the allegorical character, Música, promises eternal life:

> Venid, mortales, venid,
> si queréis no serlo,
> y eternos vivir,
> que aquí está la Vida,
> puesto que está aquí,
> quien muriendo, a la Muerte
> ha de destruir. (428 a)

This song is an attention getter, which settles the public, both spiritually, reinforcing their religious faith, and theatrically,

12. See Kurtz's "Guilty Pleasure: The Comic, the Sacred, and *Placer(es)* in the *Autos Sacramentales* of Calderón de la Barca" for an examination of the character Placer in *La segunda esposa y triunfar muriendo.*

preparing them for the upcoming spectacle. Música repeats the refrain throughout the *auto*, especially after highly emotional scenes, where the lines serve as relief and reassurance for the public. Díez Borque comments how the music in Calderón's *autos* acquired meaning within a framework of the functionality of religious music in the Baroque (*Fiesta* 43). Songs in general, and in particular in *Segunda esposa*, offer an exposition of direct religious doctrine. He also notes how songs inscribe a second text on top of the first, made up of the dramatic action, introducing a form of communication not only to contemplate but also to take part in (*Fiesta* 45). The participatory aspect becomes clear with the inclusion of the refrains throughout the plays, which would give the public an opportunity to sing.[13] Participation in the event is an effective way to further draw the spectator in to the production. As they become a part of the spectacle, the message becomes personal. Song forms a perfect balance between content and form, underlining the celebratory nature of the Corpus celebration, which Placer underlines:

> Mil extremos he de hacer
> de contento y alegría:
> albricias, que hoy es mi día,
> pues es día de Placer.
> Cantar, bailar y tañer, sean todos mis intentos,
> digan voces e instrumentos,
> que hoy en metáfora un Rey
> hace de Gracia una Ley
> con todos sus Sacramentos
> repitiendo alegres en cláusulas mil. (428 a)

Like the *loa* to the play, this introductory description of the purpose, tone, and form of the festivities further prepares the public for things to come.

Allegory is basic to all *autos*. In *Segunda esposa*, its use conveys both a religious and political message. The dissemination of propagandist messages was nothing new or uncommon during

---

13. Of course, celebratory singing is not a new convention in theater or in liturgical services.

the epoch.[14] In this play, allegory is explicitly mentioned two times, pointing to its importance to the *auto*. Reminding the public of a major theme of the play, the *auto* allegorizes the wedding, calling it "una nueva Alegoría" (428 b) and, having been endorsed by Matrimony itself, highlights the divine nature of the nuptials. Sebastián Neumeister notes that the newlyweds are alluded to in holy terms throughout the play (38-39), and though the merging of the royal houses remains important, it is the other union, that of Jesus Christ and the Church, represented here in the form of King and Wife, that takes precedence.[15] Calderón underlines the unification by presenting the idea of the wedding and by tracing the foundation of humanity's relationship with the Church: the Sacraments repeatedly save Man from Sin and Death until he (Man) finally agrees to share his life with the King, establishing another holy union symbolized by the passing of a torch (441 a). The portrayal of these ceremonies would have inspired the public to observe and contemplate the actions portrayed on the stage, and to hopefully adopt the embedded positive message. The *auto,* therefore, represents a metatextual bridge between the sacramental act and its significance. Allegory is mentioned a second time later in the play when a repentant Placer describes the wedding in the following terms: "me atreviera a decir, dando / Alegórico Sentido / a estas Bodas y Guerras" (442 a), and continues by repeating the nature of the union: "Bodas de Segunda Esposa / que son la Iglesia con Cristo" (442 a). The metatheatrical implications of the entire text are clear in its constant reference to sacraments and ceremonies. More specifically, the play's self-awareness of its use of allegory reminds us of the rhetorical device's effectiveness in relaying the message of the play. By explicitly mentioning allegory—as well as any other metatheatrical or literary strategy—the dramatic illusion is broken, reminding the public that they are seeing a staged performance, which also includes a didactic message.

---

14. See Neumeister's "Las bodas de España: alegoría y política en los autos sacramentales" for a discussion of weddings in various *autos*.

15. Calderón refers to Isabel, Phillip IV's first wife, as "la hermosa Sinagoga" (429), and Mariana symbolically represents the Catholic Church because her father was the Holy Roman Emperor.

In *Segunda esposa*, the importance of allegory and its effectiveness in transmitting a complex concept in relatable terms are further developed and represented on stage. At the beginning of the play, Calderón explains the different stages of a Christian's religious life, referring to the sacraments that govern the faith. While informative and most certainly familiar to the public, a simple oral presentation may not be the best means to transmit the message because it is simply a description of abstract beliefs. The concept and importance of the sacraments become clear toward the end of the *auto* when each sacrament, represented by an actor, appears on stage again, but this time each character confronts Death and Sin in a manner corresponding to that particular stage in life. A clear example occurs when Sin insists on following Man, even shackling his hands; Man's subsequent liberation is brought about by his acceptance of the sacrament of Baptism (437 a). The representation of this scene demonstrates the power of performance, as a splash of holy water destroys the confining steel manacles as well as the character's symbolic imprisonment. Other examples abound in the play, illustrating actual visual manifestations of religious actions. The action impacts the public as a mimetic representation of the sacraments and Catholic doctrine.

A second instance of the explanation of an abstract idea that is then represented on stage is seen in the description of Death and Sin. A long and fairly complex discussion of the concepts of death and sin introduces the public to the extent of their power over mankind. But one can become easily lost in the sea of wordy rhetoric and obscure references. Nonetheless, the concepts become obvious as we follow Death and Sin throughout the play, seeing their contact with the holy sacraments and eventual imprisonment. So, this staging represents in a clear manner the more complex issues that may arise when contemplating religious dogma. This pattern emphasizes how performance brings the play text to life. Calderón was aware of his varied public, of course, and the presentation of the same idea in different manners proves this. It also corroborates Tietz's suggestion that the public was heterogeneous, one which is widely accepted now. What the members of the audience lost in the exposition of Catholic doctrine was reintroduced and presumably better understood in its performance.

As Calderón states in the prologue to the *autos*, faith and proper decorum serve as part of the foundation of the play. This is seen in the performance of *Segunda esposa*, which presents cultural ideals in *Segunda esposa* by effectively reinforcing virtuous actions while discouraging corrupt ones. The *auto* demonstrates both good and bad acts, with the hope that the public will emulate the virtue seen in the play. In *Calderón y las quimeras de la culpa,* Díaz Balsera warns of the possibility of misguided reception that would have been triggered by the performance of evil acts or ideas against which the *auto* warns (6).[16] This would be more of a concern in secular theater, where the religious context does not exist. Of course, there is some danger of such misinterpretation, but the overt message and obvious symbolism grounds the play within the context of a righteous system of behavior and belief; therefore, the temptation should not be problematic in this or other works. Since good characters maintain righteous moral behavior and evil ones commit sins and are punished, there is no guesswork in the *auto* because the doctrine of right and wrong is Manichaean. Indeed, temptation is something that everyone must confront and overcome on a daily basis. In the case of *Segunda esposa*, its presence adds to the religious experience and the veracity of the message since it is presented on stage but then literally imprisoned. *Segunda esposa* offers examples of sinful behavior as the character continually attempts to corrupt Man by means of earthly temptations. Generally speaking, the playwright has to tread a very thin line so that the public is not beguiled by the attractive nature of the sins presented onstage, though they need to be titillating and interesting. As a result, notoriously immoral characters commit dishonest actions and suggest corrupt ideas, symbolizing the evil nature of the choice. Of course, at the end of the play, the prudent alternative overshadows the bad one, convincing the audience to follow the exemplary path.

---

16. Such misinterpretation has always been a hurdle in religious theater, and King Alfonso X warned in his *Siete partidas* against priests acting in plays in which their characters or actions were seen as sinful. See footnote 6.

Clearly, performance and reception play a significant role in composition, presentation, and interpretation of the *auto*. Because of the *auto's* standard Eucharistic theme, the playwright searches for original means to represent a familiar idea in an entertaining manner, commonly resorting to elaborate scenery fused with music and verse, with the intention of creating a grand spectacle that served to awe, entertain, and teach the spectators. But it was not only the genius of the playwrights that drove the evolution and innovation of the art form, but also the desires and tastes of the public, Cilveti states:

> El concepto de continuidad cultural garantiza y verifica el valor ideológico y artístico del auto calderoniano. Por continuidad cultural entiendo la permanencia y también la innovación de motivos, formas de pensamiento, de expresión y de conducta análogos y constantes a lo largo del tiempo. (46)

In addition to providing relatable and familiar subject matter, the use of contemporary or familiar events as inspiration succeeds in grounding the audience members in their contemplation of the message and prevents their being overwhelmed by the fantasy of the whole production. The *auto* is first and foremost a religious play that utilizes performance to produce a sacred message that is comprehensible to the congregants, and both the Church and the playwright must have understood the importance of entertainment in this theatrical drama. The Spanish public, too, would have recognized the entertainment value of the *autos*, delighting in their splendor while simultaneously absorbing their holy message.

The impact of performance was an important factor connected to the composition of the *auto*, a celebratory and religious work with an explicit theme. In the *loa* to *Segunda esposa*, Calderón described the language of the play as "sermon written in verse" (427 a). He recognized the power of the form to change and reinforce the religious beliefs of the public, who utilized the *auto* as an alternative form of worship. Always aware of the needs and desires of his public, he, as well as many other dramatic poets, created original works that were based on the same theme, the Eucharist, and using the same strategies, especially allegory, to develop and explain religious abstractions to a heterogeneous public. By placing familiar stories, legends, and myths, as well as current events in a religious context, the *auto* celebrated the liturgical holidays, the contemporary culture, and the theater-going public, who benefited from the religious teachings that were presented in original manners. Exuberant scenery added to the spectacle of the dramatic event, reinforcing the power of the Church and of theater to move its audience. It was a challenge to introduce new and entertaining ways to present a familiar topic within the same dramatic structure. Since the plays were written for one-time performance during a specific epoch of the year, the playwright must have found himself compelled to demonstrate his poetic prowess by introducing a familiar form and message in a new way. In terms of the numerous factors that affect the evolution of poetry, Bataillon states that:

> Toda poesía es un producto de los poetas. Un género *no se crea* por sí sólo: *es creado* por una serie de innovaciones y adaptaciones, que no se deben forzosamente a la iniciativa de poetas de genio, pero que responden a lo que el público o sus elementos directores esperan. ("Ensayo de explicación" 455)

These words are applicable to all forms of poetry, but they are especially relevant within the discussion of the *auto* because the form continued to respond to all members in the dramatic exchange with the intention of entertaining and teaching its public.

Another theatrical form, the court drama, also utilized elaborate staging and often contained a didactic message in order to simultaneously teach and entertain the royal court. Like the *autos*, these celebratory plays represent another form of theater that takes us away from the *corrales*, but unlike their religious counterparts, they catered to a much more elite and educated audience. Although Calderón was a brilliant writer of court drama, so was his disciple, Francisco Antonio de Bances Candamo, who composed an important treatise on dramatic theory as well as a notable collection of plays.

III. *Theatro de los theatros*: Bances Candamo's dramatic poetics in the court theater of Charles II

Bances closed the curtain on the theater of the Spanish Golden Age as the last of the important playwright-theorists of the seventeenth century. His ideas exemplified the culmination of the evolution of dramatic trends and practices throughout early modern Spain. As the court dramatist of Charles II, Bances faced a distinct set of challenges and created his plays under circumstances different from those of his predecessors.[17] First, he wrote at the end of the seventeenth century, after the *comedia* had already been established as the dramatic form of choice. Nevertheless, the *comedia* still sparked controversy, and fierce attacks—especially by the Jesuit priests—challenged the morality of the theater, compelling Bances to write his dramatic treatise, *Theatro de los theatros* (1689-94) in an attempt to legitimize and defend the theater of his day. Second, Bances wrote for a more homogeneous audience, whose ideologies and aesthetics were better defined; his plays, therefore, closely followed the rules of decorum, portrayed the high nobility as infallible, and used *culteranista* language in an attempt to produce a fusion of the arts, that is, a total spectacle. According to Bances, the nobles needed to see these historically based dramas to learn from the great feats of their ancestors (*Theatro* 57).

The impact of Bances's work on the trajectory of Spanish theater has been a point of contention throughout the twentieth century. In his 1916 study *Don Francisco Antonio de Bances y López-Candamo: Estudio bio-bibliográfico y crítico*, Francisco Cuervo Arango recognized the importance of the playwright, as did W. Shaffer Jack in 1929, who commented on the significance of his dramatic treatise in "Bances and the Calderonian Decadents," while in 1937 Valbuena Prat called him the last great figure of Spanish national theater (*Historia* 1.464). Enthusiasm for Bances later faded as many scholars, including Ludwig Pfändl and Juan Luis Alborg, considered him merely a member of the

17. See Carmen Sanz Ayán's *Pedagogía de reyes: el teatro palaciego en el reinado de Carlos II* for an in-depth study of the challenges and means undertaken in an attempt to educate Charles II.

Calderonian decadents who unsuccessfully attempted to mimic their predecessor. It was not until Rozas published "La licitud del teatro y otras cuestiones literarias en Bances Candamo, escritor límite" in 1965, and Moir released his comprehensive edition of *Theatro* in 1970, that an interest in Bances as both a gifted playwright and an astute critic was resuscitated. In recent years, such scholars as María Cristina Quintero, Santiago García-Castañon, Ana Suárez, Arellano, and Carmen Díaz Castañon have analyzed his works. Varey and Margaret Rich Greer have also contributed much to the study of court drama in Madrid, offering great insight into the theatrical world at the end of the seventeenth century.

The fruit of an incestuous relationship between Philip IV and his niece Mariana of Austria—the same matrimony that inspired Calderón's *Segunda esposa*—in a desperate attempt to secure a successor to the throne, Charles II personified the decline of the Hapsburg dynasty and Spanish culture in general at the end of the seventeenth century. Though such intermarriage was not uncommon within the Hapsburgs, Charles II was the best known, and arguably the most negative, case in the family's history. Described as slow, indifferent, torpid, and without his own will (qtd. in Kamen 21), this sole male survivor of the six children that Mariana bore to Philip IV was physically weak and mildly retarded. Such physical and mental deficiencies gave rise to an impotent king: Charles never won the respect of his court nor did he produce a male heir to the throne, and both shortcomings became the topic of both hushed and outspoken criticism. Numerous people, including his mother and a series of ministers, alternatively ruled the country as regents since Charles II could not capably make political decisions.

Outside of Spain, the continual decline of the Spanish Empire did not go unnoticed. Foreign visitors, including Marquis Pierre de Villars, the French ambassador to Spain from 1668-69, 1671-73, and 1679-81, noted that Spain's status as a world power had faltered earlier in the century (qtd. in Díez Borque, *La vida española* 33). Upon seeing Charles II at nineteen years of age, the Marquis described him as follows:

> Como no se han aplicado desde su juventud más que a hacerlo vivir, sin pensar en su educación, no sabe ejercicio ninguno, ni tiene el menor conocimiento de ciencia ni de letra, apenas si sabe leer y escribir. Tiene la cara de una longitud extraordinaria, estrecha y enjuta, cuyas facciones desmesuradas les forman una fisonomía extraña. (García Mercadal 881)

Such candid descriptions of the King serve as a metaphor for the sorry state of Spain at end of the seventeenth century, and function as a point of departure for an examination of possible motivations behind the theatrical works of Bances in relation to his patron.

In the prologue of his edition of *Theatro,* Moir asserts that Bances is both a court dramatist and a political dramatist (15), which is an affirmation that the playwright himself made in the treatise:

> Yo, pues, que he cursado diez años esta profesión y que me hallo ellegido de su Magestad por su Real decreto para escrivir unicamente sus festejos, y con renta asignada por ello, he juzgado tocarme por muchos títulos estudiar *ex profeso* quanto pudiese conducir a hacer arte áulica y política la de festejar a tan gran Rei, cuios oídos se me entregan aquellas tres horas, siendo ésta una de las mairoes confianzas que se pueden hacer de una doctrina. (56)

Moir also mentions the uniqueness of the document's declaration of drama's political intentions, and he insists on the notion of a purely politically-motivated theater since Bances describes the playwright as a dignified teacher of the people, who uses his art to reform and improve society (prólogo 95). Such a lofty mission for a playwright is not a new idea; Juan de Zabaleta's *El Emperador Cómmodo, historia discursiva, según el texto de Herodiano* (1666) demonstrates how decorum should be used to educate Charles II, an admittedly difficult pupil, and how the theater could serve as a means to guide the king to a life ruled by truth and virtue (qtd. in Moir, appendix III 160-63). García-Castañón posits in "La presencia del ideario de Saavedra Fajardo en Bances Candamo" that Bances's familiarity with Niccolo Machiavelli's *Il principe* and Diego de Saavedra Fajardo's *Idea de un príncipe político cristiano en cien empresas*, had also helped to formulate the political and didactic nature of his dramatic works (409).

Motivated by the rules of decorum, the concept of *decir sin decir* clearly lies at the center of the argument supporting the political impetus of Bances's works. In "Political Intentionality and Dramatic Convention in the *Teatro Palaciego* of Francisco Bances Candamo," Quintero states that Bances subverted the panegyric vein of theater in order to influence and change existing political circumstances (41); in another article, entitled "Monarchy and the Limits of Exemplarity in the *Teatro Palaciego* of Francisco Bances Candamo," she reaffirms Moir's assertion that Bances saw his job as court dramatist instilled with the obligation to educate the king (310). This assumption originates from an examination of the last three plays written by Bances, especially *El esclavo en grillos* (1692), which portray the role of the monarch as both ruler of and slave to his people.[18] Quintero's articles point out how the plays clearly contain unspoken messages directed at Charles II, but at the same time, they offer a somewhat limited viewpoint since she makes sweeping generalizations about Bances's intentions based on a limited number of his plays.

Though the political aspect of Bances's theater is irrefutable, Arellano suggests that it has been over-emphasized, and his research diverges, without completely straying, from the commonly accepted ideas of Moir. Arellano, too, notes that the strict rules of decorum steer Bances's dramatic works and highlights the honesty, merit, and dignity of the *comedia*, but he suggests another impulse besides politics that plays an equally important role in the production of the plays: the necessity to exalt and praise the royal family ("Poeta áulico" 44-46). The objective to teach while entertaining implies that certain common themes and motives found in the court are represented in standard scenes, including duels, the hunt, and clever gallantry, which conform to an ideal vision of the king. Although Bances qualifies his own work as political, Arellano contends that Moir's perspective is too limiting, observing that we must consider Bances more as a court

---

18. For other valuable studies that deal with the play and Bances's political intentions as a playwright, see Juan A. Sánchez Belén, García-Castañón, and Díaz Castañón.

playwright than a political dramatist, though the political aspect definitely exists ("Poeta áulico" 49). He backs his assertions with examples of Bances's fusion of extravagant scenery and flamboyant language, making for a spectacle as complex and noble as its audience. Furthermore, noting Bances's belief in the necessity to always respect the king and follow rules of decorum while in his presence, Arellano rejects García-Castañón's suggestion that Bances's theater was subversive. He also questions previous assumptions about the motivations behind Bances's theater since they were based only on the trilogy of politically allegorical plays ("Teoría dramática" 183). He concurs, however, that the theater was aligned with politics but rejects the notion that political intentions drove his theater; in fact, these motivations stand out much more in his commentaries than in his works as a whole ("Teoría dramática" 184). Certainly, the courtly nature of the dramas stems from the magnificence of the overall spectacle ("Teoría dramática" 190), though, I might add, the political aspect also proves valid when reception is foregrounded and we take into account the elite audience that saw the plays and the last three plays that Bances saw performed in Madrid.

Further highlighting the courtly nature of Bances's theater, Arellano points out in *Convención y recepción: estudios sobre el teatro del Siglo de Oro*, that the playwright characterized his own work as both "áulica y política" and defended the decency and dignity of the *comedia* (180). He believes that this statement, taken so seriously by previous scholars, does not represent a declaration of political intentions, but rather offers a guideline mandating how a playwright should present his lesson (180). Arellano's astute analysis is valid, especially when all of Bances's works are considered. The representation of his plays drove the defense of his theater, since most were staged before writing the last version of *Theatro*. By looking at the collection, the political characteristic is present and undeniable, but it is not the only aspect that his plays demonstrate. Simply by definition, the court drama is characterized by its entertainment value and, as court playwright, Bances's works included dazzling spectacle in an effort to please Charles II and his court. I tend to agree with Arellano that the idea of "áulica y política" may have been taken too literally, especially when we take a comprehensive look at all styles of his works, *amatorias, historiales, fábulas*, and how they form the basis and stage the precepts later described in *Theatro*.

In *Estudios escénicos: Cuadernos del Instituto del Teatro,* E. Wilson recognized that, along with Friar Manuel de Guerra y Ribera's *Aprobación, Theatro* offered one of the most profound examples of drama theory in early modern Spain (50). Bances wrote three versions of the treatise, all of them incomplete, and only the third bears the title we know today. The first version defended the late seventeenth-century *comedia* from a brutal 1689 attack by Camargo,[19] whose pessimistic vision of the condition of theater fueled a wide-ranging assault on the dramatic arts; the priest believed that drama corrupted the weak human spirit and caused decadence in society. Camargo even went so far as to contradict St. Thomas Aquinas, a supporter of the theater, insisting that a complete closure of the theaters would be the only resolution to the problem. Seeing the attack as a professional threat, Bances felt compelled to quickly write a response that was dignified, decorous, and civilized, qualities that also characterized his theatrical productions. Bances divided this comprehensive and methodical defense into four articles: a condemnation of classical theater, a statement of the immaculate nature of drama during the reign of Charles II, a response to Camargo's accusations, and a repudiation of the priest's works. Apparently, as court dramatist, Bances especially felt the barbs of the attack and the need to exonerate himself and the *comedia.* By citing the theories of Aristotle, Horace, Valdés, Torres Naharro, López-Pinciano, Cueva, Cascales and others—forty-three sources in the first version—Bances rooted his defense in antiquity, supported it with contemporary thought, and expanded dramatic theory to point towards the future.

In the introduction to the first version of the treatise, Bances acknowledges that Camargo is a notable theologian but an unqualified theater critic, whose citations are not well documented, adding that most priests do not have the experience or the

19. Attacks came from secular opponents—or competitors—too. One example is seen in a pamphlet criticizing the court poets directed at the Count of Clavijo: "Que decía mal de Candamo / siendo tan divino Yngenio / que como un Góngora escribe / pues casi escribe lo mismo" (qtd. in Sanz 145).

knowledge of the theater, so they should not enter into its criticism (3-4). Bances sees himself as the foremost authority of theater at the time, referring to present dramatic trends and doctrine, he states: "[e]n los presente, nunguno podrá tener más authoridad que yo, porque por las muchas que sé cómo son las comedias que oi se recitan, y por algunas que he escrito sé cómo deuen ser" (5). In the first article, Bances attempts to justify the morality of modern theater. His argumentation includes a history of classical theater, displaying its immorality and juxtaposing ancient pagan rituals with the Christian theater of the late-seventeenth century, to demonstrate the propriety of contemporary dramatic practice, or more accurately, the propriety of his own works.

The second article examines the history and evolution of the modern *comedia* and includes Bances's own ideas regarding theater, serving as a foundation for the subsequent versions of *Theatro*. He divides Golden Age theater into three distinct epochs: Renaissance, Primitive Baroque, and Modern Baroque. The section also offers commentary on good and bad dramaturgy, which, according to Moir, opens the door for modern criticism (prólogo 60). A brutally honest critic, Bances accuses Lope of writing indecorous and primitive plays, and elucidates his animosity towards his contemporary *calderonistas*, Moreto and Rojas Zorrilla; he even mentions that Calderón overstepped the bounds of decency in *De un castigo tres venganzas* (35-36). Regarding more classical theory, Bances does not mention Lope's *Arte nuevo* nor the *Fama póstuma*, but does note that Lope introduced Italian stagecraft and dramatic techniques to the stage after his visit to that country (29).[20] Bances credits Calderón with imposing the rules of decorum on the *comedia*, instilling the form with greatness and consequently perfecting the genre (28). Decorum forms the basis of Bances's dramatic theory; he asserts that decorum consists not of what someone is or can be but rather what he or she should be (35). In his dramatic treatise, Bances took the lead from Plato's *Republic,* Aristotle's *Ethics*, and Horace's *Ars poetica*, when

20. Such an oversight did not sit well with some critics, including W. Shaffer Jack, who thinks that Bances pales in comparison to Lope and Tirso, as he confuses in his treatise formal and technical norms with moral and ethical expectations (Moir, *prólogo* 82).

forming his concept of decorum as specific rules that governed moral conduct and modeled a perfect society. Furthermore, the insistence on decorum adds a more intellectual aspect to the drama and sets it apart from the earlier, more emotional theater.

In a struggle to uphold the decency and morality of the *comedia*, Bances continually focuses on the importance of maintaining decorum and exemplarity while remaining conscious of his goal to educate and entertain his royal audience. He notes that St. Thomas Aquinas did not see theater as intrinsically bad as long as it avoided including illicit materials (32). Furthermore, Bances refused to accept the blame for the public's misinterpretation of his works. He admits that many plays represent negative actions, but they serve as counterexamples of proper behavior; it is the responsibility of the public to actively interpret the message of the plays and recognize the lessons included in them: "no tendrá el Poeta ni la Comedia culpa alguna de que quien puede tomar lo bueno de el exemplo tome lo malo" (34), informing us of the playwright's expectation of the participation of the audience and the recognition of the public's role in the dramatic exchange.

Reminiscent of Torres Naharro, Bances regulates the subject matter of his plays by dividing the *comedia* into two categories: the *amatoria* and the *historial*, of which he primarily writes the latter (33); this distinction is not unique to Spain, as Castelvetro had categorized his plays in a similar manner during the Italian Renaissance. The didactic and exemplary *historiales* also include hagiographic plays; the fictitious *amatorias* are plays of pure invention divided into two subcategories: the *comedia de fábrica*, which deal with the unspecified noble figures, and the more specific *capa y espada*. Bances makes the following distinction:

> Las de capa y espada son aquéllas cuios personages son solo Caualleros particulares, como Don Juan, y Don Diego, etcetera, y los lances se reducen a duelos, a cellos, a esconderse el galán, a taparse la Dama, y, en fin, a aquellos sucesos más caseros de un galanteo. Las de Fábrica son aquéllas que llevan algún particular intento que probar con el suceso, y sos personages son Reies, Príncipes, Generales, Duques, etcétera, y personas preeminentes sin nombre

> determinado y conocido en las historias, cuio artificio consiste en varios acasos de la Fortuna, largas peregrinaciones, duelos de gran Fama, altas conquistas, eleuados Amores y, en fin, sucesos extraños, y más altos y peregrinos que aquéllos que suceden en los lances que, poco â, llamé caseros. (33)

This, according to Moir, is the first formal definition of the cloak-and-dagger play (prólogo 97), a form that, according to Bances, had lost popularity because it lacked didactic value, adding that only Calderón was capable of writing good ones (33). Bances also mentions another type of play, the *fábula*, which is characterized by extensive stage properties and music, deals with mythological themes, and provides a magnificent spectacle prepared for the courtly audience for their enjoyment during royal celebrations (36).

Bances never completed the last two articles of the first version of the treatise. Moir suggests that the playwright did not continue because of boredom or because he realized that Camargo's attack had posed no real threat to his art (prólogo 98). The importance of this first version lies in the precedent it set for the subsequent renderings of the treatise. In addition, Bances's erudition impresses the reader, as does his obstinate dedication to following the rules of decorum, which hint at the instructive nature of his dramatic expositions that follow. Though written hastily, the first draft incorporates effective argumentation and highlights Bances's logic and pragmatic sensibility in illustrating the role of the modern *comedia* as the representation of exemplary life.

In the second version of the treatise, the reader notes a less rushed style. Moir describes the tone as frank, calm, and authoritative, resulting in an even more contemplative document that includes additional information detailing literary history and dramatic precepts (prólogo 91). By not taking a defensive posture, Bances aspires to produce a dramatic treatise that provides models for other playwrights as he strives to instruct his contemporaries. He suggests that early playwrights mistakenly gave too much power to the *vulgo* when determining and establishing the trends that theatrical practice would follow; his predecessors were more interested in earning money than in preserving the good literary practices (49). Describing a playwright as the "maestro del pueblo"

(51), Bances implies that he writes to teach the commoner and not to learn from them, giving a distinctly different view from that of earlier playwrights who paid greater attention to the needs and tastes of their more democratic audiences. Of course, Bances's disqualification of the popular public does not mean that his audience did not influence the composition of his plays. Indeed, based on his statements that his role was to educate the nobility, it was a specific audience, Charles II, who inspired the production of the playwright's works.

Insisting on the intrinsic wholesomeness of the modern *comedia*'s subject matter, Bances criticizes the older, "primitive" plays, pointing out their inappropriate nature and unsuitable topics, but he notes that modern plays have generally rectified these shortcomings, making the *comedia* the highest form of literature because it portrays, perfects, and condenses realistic events (50, 53-55). It is the duty of the playwright to observe, not imitate, when composing a play. As such, the plays are difficult to write, but pleasant to hear (49). A confident man, Bances defines the contemporary *comedia* in flattering terms:

> Es oi la Commedia Española, en línea de Poema, vno de los más elleuados que en algún siglo se han conocido, lleno del más decoroso y remontado estilo del idioma, Castellano, de las más altas sentencias de la Philosophía moral, éthica y Pollitica, exornado de los más estraños succesos que ha representado la fortuna al gran theatro del mundo en sus varias scenas, abundante de todos los exemplares de la ida como la historia y aun mejore que ella.... (50)

Here, Bances underlines his experience as court playwright, legitimizing his views on what is considered good theater at the end of the seventeenth century.

When writing plays, Bances seeks equilibrium between historical veracity, beauty, and moral lessons. The goal of his theater, he states, is to instruct the king while he is relaxing:

> Son las Commedias de los reies vnas historias viuas que, sin hablar con ellos, les han de instruir con tal respecto que sea su misma razón quien de lo que ve tome las aduertencias, y no el Ingenio quien se las diga. (57)

He, therefore, has to gauge the potential reception of his work in order to compose a play that not only entertains but also advises. This proves no easy task, since normally the king and court are considered a more-educated public than the *vulgo*, though this may not be completely accurate in the case of Charles II, who was not known for his great intelligence. In fact, due to the king's perceived lack of intellectual facility, Bances may have felt a greater need to instruct his patron by means of his theater. Like in the *auto*, the didactic message of the court play is often presented in a grandiose and allegorical manner. Both dramatic forms identify the king as the most important audience member since it is expected that he will take advantage of the lessons learned from the examples in the plays to govern his kingdom in a righteous manner. Many of Bances's works represent *historia viva* (57) and offer lessons in the accessible form of particular historical events; although a useful teaching tool, history often needs to be presented in an amenable manner so that its lessons become apparent to the public. He states that his *comedias* are decorous and exemplary (58), and his works not only provide a perfect backdrop for the education of the king but also prove that theater could be—and was—reformed and perfected, at least in the eyes of the poet. Bances, as both playwright and theorist, does not attempt to defend how theater is, but rather to say how it should be (59).

The decisive third version was published shortly after the second and seemingly was meant to serve as a definitive guide for contemporary and future playwrights of the reformation of Spanish drama into a more decorous and proper form. In *Theatro*, Bances emphasizes the benefits of a authoritative document that outlines dramatic precepts (84). This prescriptive work is written in a straightforward manner since there is no room for artistic embellishment of the hard facts that drive the composition of dramatic poetry (88-89). Bances compiles and summarizes what he has written in previous renderings, but, like its predecessors, this version is incomplete. Four chapters still survive: the first is a compendium of the precepts found in versions one and two; the second, a poem, praises the divine nature of poetry; and the fourth and fifth–the third is missing–discuss classical theater. He tries to integrate the authority of scientific method into this treatise in an attempt to make his arguments more objective and persuasive.

According to Bances, experience and established traditions must be followed when composing dramatic poetry, adding an orderly and scientific aspect to his plays. This relates to writing *comedias*, he posits, because many playwrights do not follow the rules, choosing to be influenced by the caprices of the uneducated public in direct contradiction to Bances's goal of instructing the public and not being taught by them (77). He cites Pope John XXIII who stated that the farthest thing from the truth was the opinion of the audience, and that educated men should not have to play to the desires of the public (81).[21] Bances sees the position of the comic playwright as particularly precarious and challenging since he needs to know how to both entertain and please the *vulgo* without lowering standards of decency or ignoring the play's didactic purpose. His means of instruction is the *comedia*, which, compared to history, is the superior teaching tool:

> Imita la Commedia a la historia, copiando solo las acciones airosas de ella, ocultando las feas. Finalmente, la historia nos expone los sucesos de la vida como son, la comedia nos los exorna como deuían ser, añadiéndole a la verdad de la esperiencia mucha más perfección para la enseñanza. (82)

Following the lead of Cicero, Bances also insists on the scientific nature of poetry, and especially the *comedia*, since the playwright needs to understand, imitate, and evaluate all aspects of society (83).[22] Later in the document, he mentions how, according to López Pinciano, the study of hard science is little more than memorization. Bances continues by stating that the poet is superior to all because he has the ability to comprehend and express ideas that go beyond human understanding (94). His elitist attitude emerges in these statements, as he was not hesitant to place himself and his fellow playwrights above the rest of society.

---

21. According to Moir, Bances made a mistake when citing the source of this quote: it is not found in Count Manuel Tesauro's *Filosofía moral* but rather in Father Andrés Mendo's Document 78 in his 1662 book *Príncipe perfecto y ministros aiustados, documentos políticos y morales* (52).

22. Bances quotes Cicero in the text: "Esta tradicción tenemos de hombres grandes y eruditíssimos, que el Poeta debe constar de arte, y preceptos, y del estudio y ciencia de todas las demás cosas." (83)

By integrating philosophy, morals, ethics, and politics in its attempt to recreate history, the *comedia* actually strives to improve on original history. This new and improved account serves as a model that the audience can follow, since such a reworking illustrates how things should be; nevertheless, the implications of such an important tool demand prudence in its use. By recognizing the magnitude of teaching and entertaining his unique public, we see that Bances understood that there was more to a play than its didactic nature.

Theatro proves to be an important document on many levels. On the most basic, it is the last dramatic treatise of the Spanish Golden Age. The work expounds upon the evolution of Spanish theater and records its culmination at the end of the seventeenth century. It also recognizes the many factors at work in the production of a *comedia* and lays the groundwork for the reformation of the genre, portraying it as infallible and didactic in its purest form, as well as demonstrating that the value of a play lies in its entertainment and instructional values, two inseparable factors. In fact, the spectacle itself is a crucial step in the whole didactic process. Bances's obsession with the rules of decorum further evidences his preoccupation with reception, and he always had to consider his subject matter so as not to insult the courtly public. The document explains and defends what Bances sees as exemplary theater at the close of the seventeenth century. He highlights decorum as being fundamental to his theatrical output. His works are adorned with *culteranista* tendencies that target an educated and noble audience. The plays entertain the public with their great artifice while they simultaneously instruct the public by use of allegory and history. Bances successfully brought to fruition the notions of *decir sin decir* and *deleitar aprovechando*, which were also achieved by his predecessors, though perhaps by different means.

IV. *Decir sin decir*: the dramatic spectacle and didactic strategies seen in *Duelos de Ingenio y Fortuna*

Premiering in the Coliseo theater of the Buen Retiro in 1686, *Duelos de Ingenio y Fortuna* is a *fábula* written in celebration of the twenty-sixth birthday of Charles II. Because of its great critical success and popularity, the play enjoyed numerous performances, and, according to Moir, was the work that elevated Bances to the post of court dramatist (prólogo 27). The play exemplifies the *fiesta real* of the late seventeenth century with its complex scenery, storyline, and language, making clear that the court audience was generally well-educated and had high expectations regarding the spectacle. Although this dramatic piece may appear light-hearted due to the abundance of music and singing, these factors actually complement the development of the play's themes: the dominance of free will over destiny and the power of love to overcome adversity. As mentioned earlier, astute and relevant research on his so-called "political" plays (the final three written before he left Madrid) is plentiful, and these important studies invite us to take a closer look at some of the earlier and less-studied plays in the search for similar clues, which help to explain some of the factors that lie behind Bances's dramaturgy as a whole, as well as to discover the great extent to which all of his works formed the foundation of his profound and conclusive dramatic treatise. *Duelos* is an early example of how Bances integrates both entertainment and didactic agendas in a play's composition and performance. Following Arellano's cues, it is the intention of this analysis to examine the impact of *Duelos* with regard to its entertainment and didactic objectives, underlining how the play foresaw in its performance the later dramatic theory described in *Theatro*.

Like the play that follows it, the *loa* to *Duelos* introduces concepts important to Bances's dramatic theory. In it he presents the allegorical figures of Poetry (Poesía) and History (Historia), who argue about which of the two is more valuable to the didactic character of the play.[23] History contends that her value lies in the ability to recount true life events without invention or embellishment, to which Poetry replies that her idealization of life's events has more educational value:

HISTORIA. La Historia, que sin ficciones

---

23. See Roberto Castilla Pérez's and Miguel González Dengra's *La teatralización de la historia en el Siglo de Oro español*, a collection of essays that gives a general overview of the topic.

	quenta las hazañas todas
	como son.
POESÍA.	Y la Poesía
	enseña más, pues las forma,
	como deben ser: que aun es
	perfección mas rigurosa. (226 a)

Clearly, like many of his predecessors, Bances understands the didactic and dramatic potential offered by historical events. Their use on the Spanish stage dates back well into the sixteenth century and their appeal lies in the fact that the storyline is familiar and, most likely, interesting to the public by merit of its having been documented. At the same time, history is not always compatible with the ubiquitous goal of theater to entertain the public, so it often needs to be enhanced and made more amusing, which is where poetry plays its part. In the *loa*, Cupid (Cupido) resolves the argument by pronouncing that both work in unison in a drama:

CUPIDO.	Pues Historia, y Poesía,
	para tan festiva pompa,
	se unan.
HISTORIA.	Si haremos, supuesto,
	que la Historia, articifiosa
	Poesia es en las empresas.
POESÍA	Y la Poesía, heroyca
	en las hazañas que cuenta,
	es Historia numerosa.
APOLO.	Y de Historia, y Poesía
	la fábula se componga. (228 a)

The inclusion of Apollo (Apolo), the Greek god of Poetry, is important because it gives final authority to the decision that history and poetry are best combined in order to simultaneously teach and entertain. To fulfill his self-proclaimed duty to instruct the community, Bances wrote dramatic works with lessons that were accessible and appealing to all members of the public, but especially to the king. The allegorical debate in the *loa* perfectly explains the mutual relationship between poetry and history and their impact on one another: poetry idealizes history through its grandiose manner of expression, and history validates poetry with its description of heroic events. In theory, after seeing the aggrandizing of his noble feats, the king should feel compelled to repeat them. At the same time, the court would see these impressive events on stage in an embellished form, further raising their esteem for the king. In practice, however, neither consequence may have resulted. Nonetheless, when dealing with the reputation and image of the royal family, both history and poetry work in unison to help celebrate and honor the king. Bances's esteem for the royal family was evident long before he wrote *Theatro*.

Besides discussing how the combination of poetry and history makes for effective theater, this *loa* exemplifies the notion of *decir sin decir*. By explaining the goals and the results of blending history with poetry, the playwright demonstrates to the public—especially the king—the means by which he simultaneously teaches and entertains. In this *loa*, Bances underlines the didactic nature of the plays by explaining how he represents the lessons in his *comedias*. He also instructs the king on how to watch his plays, as well as what to expect and learn from the staged events. This introductory piece delineates the intentions and strategies of Bances's theater, details of which are later outlined in *Theatro*. The *loa* serves, therefore, as yet another example of how Bances's dramatic theory is manifested on the stage. It is an example in miniature of how *forma* and *fondo* produce an exemplary dramatic work. There is also the clear explanation of how a moralizing agenda is camouflaged in an interesting story.

The court dramas at the end of the seventeenth century can be described as nothing less than extravagant and sumptuous spectacles. Bances's *Duelos* is no exception, and by keeping in mind the ways in which performance and reception influenced the production of this play, we see how the combination of numerous artistic manifestations constitutes this exuberant dramatic celebration. An extensive and varied cast of twenty-three performs this complex play that includes mythological, allegorical, and fictitious characters, as well as seven choruses. The first act opens in Delphi with the protagonist, Himeneo, complaining about his unreciprocated love for Apollo's head priestess, Erictrea, whose portrait he acquired, igniting his desire. As the son of Apollo and Caliope, Himeneo has been raised in isolation by his mother and the other muses in an attempt to protect him from his fate: that love for a woman will cause his death. Hearing his son's pleas and lamentations, Apollo promises to protect him from Fortune (Fortuna). Fortune, with the help of Cupid, wages a battle with Apollo and Mars, who has joined forces with Apollo, thus giving the name to the play. Meanwhile, the king of Corinth, Periandro, is shipwrecked in Delphi after being chased by pirates and, as the original owner of the portrait, he, too, is in love with Erictrea. As the two men argue over who is the rightful owner of the portrait, Erictrea is struck with Cupid's arrow and falls in love with Himeneo, fulfilling the fatal premonition. Himeneo and Periandro continue to argue until Erictrea insists that Apollo will decide who will be her husband. Apollo then tells Erictrea and Himeneo to go to the House of Knowledge (Casa de las Ciencias) to consult Falsehood (Engaño) and Truth (Desengaño), who offer conflicting advice to the couple: Falsehood encourages their love and Truth warns against it. After a foiled plot to kidnap Erictrea, Periandro begins another duel with Himeneo, which is broken up by Apollo. The god reveals Himeneo's parentage and chooses his son to be Erictrea's husband, thereby defeating Fortune; but Fortune does not accept this loss lightly, and buries Himeneo alive in the ruins of his castle. Erictrea mourns the death of her beloved, not knowing that Apollo has saved his son's life. The play comes to an end with an exaggerated *deus ex machina*: a *Teatro de Gloria* and a chorus of gods appear, with Jupiter deciding that Himeneo will become the god of marriage, and Apollo finally wins the duel against Fortune. The play ends in a dance celebrating the king's birthday.

Duelos is an adaptation of a well-known Greek myth to which Bances adds further mythological and allegorical characters. Due to their exposure to other theatrical works and their common knowledge of mythology, the normal theater-going populace would be familiar with some of the more common figures: Apollo, Jupiter, and Cupid, to name a few, but other references would surely have escaped the uneducated. For example, when Himeneo and Erictrea go to the House of Knowledge for advice, both Truth and Falsehood utilize obscure mythological references to illustrate a point, clearly revealing that Bances took advantage of his erudition to reach out to his educated audience, emphasizing his message by means of less familiar but accurate analogies and references. To make up for possible gaps in knowledge of some of the public, the playwright includes a summary of the myth, told by Himeneo, at the beginning of the play. This strategy makes clear that Bances was concerned with the reception of the work. The message of the play would be lost if the story was not clear to the audience from the beginning. The intended result of using a familiar legend is that the public can spend more time contemplating and interpreting the themes of the play instead of struggling to navigate a complicated story, and the argument of *Duelos* is extremely complicated because of, among other factors, the huge cast of characters, constant scene changes, non-stop action, and complicated language.

The extravagance of the play assuredly pleased the audience, and the stage directions, which are included in the script, describe the lavish scenery and properties.[24] The proscenium stage of the Coliseo was deep, consisting of various levels to support the complicated plot and numerous scene changes that included sets and props being lowered from the ceiling as well as brought on stage from the sides.[25] The first act consists of six scene changes on the extravagant set: the play opens with the stage decorated with a forest, a mountain, and numerous characters, it then changes to the Temple of Apollo, where various gods appear flying in carts. The following stage directions illustrate the lavishness of the sets and their extensive changes with each scene:

> Passan los dos Carros, buela Apolo; hundese la Fortuna, desaparece el escollo, y mudase el Theatro hasta la mitad de, cuyo forro sera un Alcazár murado, que abiertas las puertas, se vera dentro el jardin, en que se vio recostado Himeneo, el qual saldra huyendo de las Musas que le siguen, y con ellas Sylvano, de jardinero rústico. (238)

---

24. See Ruano's "La escenografía del teatro cortesano" for more general details about the effect of perspective caused by the elaborate stages seen in court theater.

25. See Shergold for a detailed description of the staging of the play (*History* 350-52). Also, Kazimierz Sabik discusses Bances's mythological plays in "El teatro de tema mitológico en la corte de Carlos II" and "Dos fiestas teatrales en el ocaso del Siglo de Oro: 'La restauración de Buda' y 'Duelos de Ingenio y Fortuna' de Francisco Bances Candamo."

Such ornate scenery and props demonstrate the advanced state of stage technology at the end of the seventeenth century; the sparse sets so common to the *corral de comedias* did not suffice for the court dramas, and were replaced by sumptuous dramatic spaces. Of course, there is an economic factor to be considered since no expense was spared for the celebration of court holidays or birthdays. Also, because of their potential for fantastic stories and exotic, complicated scenery and mythological storylines were common. Although especially true in the case of the *fábulas*, all varieties of the court drama offered a spectacle that amazed and appealed to the public's senses and imagination, which may be seen as a reflection of the perceived greatness of the noble court and its decadent nature at the end of the seventeenth century.

Besides appealing to the visual desires of his audience, Bances's play also pleases their auditory appetite. The language he utilizes matches the scenery in terms of extravagance and intricacy, further demonstrating that he wrote for a generally educated audience. Bances emulates the elaborate use of language and rhetorical conventions common in the theater of Calderón, who he admired greatly. A *culteranista* style is prevalent throughout the work, one example being Himeneo's exaltation of Erictrea's beauty:

> [P]regunto: [¿]Qual es la Reyna
> de las flores? Quando halla,
> que entre esperezos purpureos,
> y entre bostezos de nacar,
> fragrancias son que suspira
> quantos alientos exala. Quien
> (quando la negra noche
> la vista dexa atezada,
> y va encendieno las sombras
> en las luzes que se apagan). (231 a)

Bances's use of clever conceits, in this case the metaphor of Erictrea's portrait as a venomous snake also riddle the play. The portrait has a great effect on Himeneo, who states:

> Dígalo el ver que aun en este
> retiro se vio assaltada

mi libertad de un retrato
tuyo, que acaso ocultavan
unas flores, colorido
aspid, que a la vida incauta,
que le piso con los ojos,
tan alevemente mata
que la vista es à quien muerde,
y es la que se muere el alma. (232 b)

A mere glance at Erictrea's portrait has imprisoned the heart of Himeneo, revealing the power that love has over her suitor. The reference to the portrait as a venomous asp whose bite poisons the soul, reminds us of the bittersweet effect of love.

A complex syntactical structure also is prevalent in the play, especially in those scenes of high tension. Here, Fortune urges Cupid to target Erictrea with his arrows in the hope that her love for Himeneo will ultimately lead the protagonist to fulfill his destiny:

Corre, corre, amor furioso,
batiendo à vengar mi injuria,
las alas que te tegieron
de tus harpones las plumas
que inconstantes dos ciegos, bien se
aúnan al celebre. (237 b-38 a)

This use of hyperbaton challenges the spectator to comprehend the complicated language while it augments the emotions invoked by the scenic action.

In *Duelos*, Bances combines the four elements, earth, wind, fire, and water, to represent disorder in the natural equilibrium of the world. The following sung dialogue between Fortune and Cupid occurs at the beginning of the second *jornada*, as preparations for the sacrifice of Arion to Apollo are being made. The scene is spectacular as both characters sweep down onto the stage; Cupid is riding on the back of a swan and Fortune on her winged wheel. Their appearance adds another layer of energy to the already vibrant scene:

CUPIDO. Puesto que baxa el amor à la tierra
de candido Cisne, moviendo las alas,
sudando el calor, en que el pecho se

(enciende
distilen los ojos oceanos de agua.

	(enciende distilen los ojos oceanos de agua.
CORO 2.	Agua, agua.
FORTUNA.	Pues oy la fortuna se suba à su Esfera que son los vagos Palacios del viento, despedidas las llamas del alma, lloren los ojos centellas de fuego.
CORO 2.	Fuego, fuego. (247)

The contrast formed by their association of the four elements, adds discord to the action. In *Duelos*, Bances clearly followed the example of Calderón in his use of complex language and imagery, which targeted the educated audience of the Hapsburg court. He did not, however, omit comic relief, a necessary element to such an action-packed play, but even his jokes were decorous in nature, and he never stooped to a base level of humor typical to earlier *comedias*.

The original use of language, however, is not restricted to the noble characters in *Duelos*. The pirate Pandion, for example, also speaks in a flamboyant manner. He describes his sinking ship in the following manner:

> Ya que la Nave, que apresar queria
> nos tragò con ansiosa hydropesia
> el mar, monstruo violento,
> que se sorbe sediento
> la rubia sangre, que quaxada encierra
> tanta palida vena de tierra. (248)

His words comprise a collection of rhetorical strategies, including hyperbaton, vivid imagery, and metaphor. On a lighter note, Silvano, Himeneo's lackey and the *gracioso* of the play, lightens the tone in numerous scenes with his sharp wit. For example, after witnessing Apollo's dramatic exit from the scene, Silvano is frightened and wants to flee, he states: "A esso de huir, yo sere / el primero, que jamás / fui tartamudo de pies" (262). This original manner to describe cowardice and fleetness of foot breaks the tension that built up by the thunder and lightning that accompanied Apollo's exit.

The lyric nature of the play made the dramatic experience more entertaining, as the abundance of choruses and singing called to mind classical dramatic traditions but also evoked the recently introduced two-act *zarzuela*, which was rapidly gaining popularity in early modern Spain. Although the versification of the text had always lent a musical aspect to the *comedia*, the use of so much music and song further highlighted the rhythm of the poetic verse and added to the entertainment value of the play, facilitating the concept of *deleitar aprovechando*.[26] The presence of seven choruses in the play stands out because it underlines the extravagance of the entire spectacle. In general, three primary purposes for song are identifiable in *Duelos*. First, the various choruses revived a similar role of their classic predecessor in ancient Greek drama, which was to serve as the voice of conventional wisdom. Second, the individual characters often broke into song during emotional situations. Singing, therefore, serves as a marker and an attention getter since it broke the rhythm of the recited—or spoken—lines. Third, song was used to emphasize the admonitions of the choruses throughout the play. Besides adding an obvious musical component to the production, the use of song broke the dramatic illusion and forced the public to pay attention to the message.

Duelos maintains the high standards of decorum that were so highly esteemed by Bances throughout his career as playwright and dramatic theorist. Typical to the concept of poetic justice and the *comedia* in general, in *Duelos*, good behavior is rewarded and frivolity is not. The action of the play is not inappropriate at any time and Himeneo's rational behavior is recognized and rewarded at the end of the play, when he is elevated to the status of the god of matrimony. On a thematic level, the importance of decorum is most clearly seen in the treatment of love in *Duelos*. The play clearly instructs against falling victim to the caprices of love. A person should be able to control their impulses. From the start of the play, the unfortunate horoscope of Himeneo reveals a negative attitude toward the effects that love has over mankind. Himeneo shows self-restraint as he leaves the safe haven offered by the muses and confronts the emotional challenges that confront him resulting from Erictrea's beauty, scorn, and, after being struck by Cupid's arrow, admiration. He maintains control of his emotions

26. See Sage, L.K. Stein, and Díez Borque.

and, in the House of Knowledge, follows the counsel of Truth. It is not until he succumbs to the power of love and enters the palace that he is put into danger, from which Apollo saves him. Of course, at the end of the play, when he is named the god of matrimony, love is esteemed, but it is a rational love, which Himeneo embodied throughout the play. Arión, too, is rewarded at the end of the play since the love he shared with Cintia, another priestess, was constant and sincere; in fact, Himeneo promises to bless their future nuptials. Thematically speaking, though, love is not the only topic examined in the play. As a whole, *Duelos* lauds decorous behavior and rational thought. Similar to the *loa*, in the *comedia*, Apollo expounds upon the irrefutable nature of science and to defend the infallibility of reason (262). This concept is later discussed in *Theatro*. Bances voices his ideas through Apollo to give them authority and to perhaps convince the public of their validity.

Reminiscent of Calderón's *La vida es sueño*, *Duelos* confronts the effects of destiny on a human life, demonstrating that one's actions and decisions, rather than predestination, determine the future. Spectators would have recognized the message not only through the performance and textual clues, but also because of similarities with Calderón's masterpiece. Himeneo speaks a soliloquy at the beginning of the play that echoes Segismundo's reflections in the first act of *La vida es sueño*; Bances not only emulates his master in terms of language, but also in theme and technique. Always a pragmatist, Bances uses the play to point out the benefits of reason and predominance of free will (266). Bances directs another message to the king, demonstrating the need to be a prudent ruler and not one who is overwhelmed by emotion like Periandro in *Duelos*, who, at the end, must return to his kingdom heartbroken and empty-handed. Finally, prudence is an underlying theme in the play. Apollo, for example, does not reveal the paternity of Himeneo until the end of the play in order to respect the honor of Caliope (276).

Departing from the metaphysical, Bances also addresses the question of loyalty to the king. In the third act, Arión, a nobleman, decides that he cannot help Himeneo in his quest for Erictrea, since it would be in direct opposition to his king, Periandro (266). Himeneo understands this conflict of interest and forgives his friend. Such a secondary theme also lends itself to the didactic message of the play in terms of the public's loyalty to Charles II. *Duelos* is a profound piece of work that contains moralizing themes that are to serve as lessons for the king and the rest of the noble public. By using a known mythological story as a framework, Bances was able to embellish the story and mold it to fit his didactic purpose. It was, therefore, entertaining in subject matter and educational through its use of allegory and symbols, all of which was placed in a contemporary context. The play exemplifies a dramatic work that is both *áulica* and *política*, which Bances describes later in *Theatro*.

Always keeping in mind his target audience, Bances was not overtly concerned with the needs of the popular public. Since he wrote his plays for courtly spectators, Bances confronted a different set of circumstances when writing a *comedia*: a homogeneous audience, an established form, and a plethora of stage properties and decorations. Bances's *Theatro* manifested itself in his plays, demonstrating in practice the technical principles he presented in the three versions of the treatise. His plays displayed equilibrium between artistic creation and historic representation. He took history and transformed it into the cultural expectations of the time, illustrating what A. Suárez calls the poetic functionality of history (39), which takes advantage of the didactic and entertaining characteristics of both. Bances clearly intended to teach responsibility and reason to the king, using his *comedias* as the vehicle to communicate his messages. Needless to say, he faced a great obstacle in Charles II, but he succeeded in exemplifying the ideal and he fulfilled his self-assigned role as educator and dramatist of the king serving as a bridge that helped span the gap between the dramatic epochs.

Both the *auto* and the court drama are indicative of theatrical trends at the close of the seventeenth century. The dramatic landscape had shifted from the *corrales de comedias* to more sumptuous performance spaces. The fact that money was essentially of no object in the production of these works tremendously impacted their composition, performance and reception. During this time, both the *auto* and the court drama demonstrated the advanced state of stage machinery and were written to include huge spectacle that impressed the public. These two forms took full advantage of the staging opportunities offered by embellishing mythological, biblical, and historical sources; contemporary issues and events were also commonly treated. These sources of inspiration brought a certain familiarity to obscure storylines as well as made well-known and often-represented plots current, new, and relevant. Furthermore, in both subgenres of theater, the rules of decorum dictated all aspects of the play, which is not surprising because of the didactic nature inherent to the styles.

Differences between the *auto* and the court play also existed. The most conspicuous divergence was the religious and secular contexts in which the plays were performed. The target audience was often different, too. Where the public of the *auto* was heterogeneous, that of the court play was more exclusive. Finally, the form and structure of the plays differed. The *auto*'s one-act structure was much shorter than the three-act *comedia*. This points to the fact that the religious play presented a profound message in an entertaining manner, and the secular works entertained in a didactic manner. Although both types of works conveyed important lessons to the public, the *auto* was more direct and the public entered the dramatic exchange knowing that they would come out with some religious teaching. The court play was more subtle in its teaching of the public—though no less effective—in this case the audience saw the play in a festive milieu without any real expectation of learning from it.

Both Calderón and Bances staged the theory that regulated their dramatic production. We see how both sets of poetics are either presented by the master, Calderón, or based on his achievements of arguably perfecting the theatrical forms in this case the *auto* and the court play. Calderón wrote numerous *autos* before documenting his theory in the prologue to the *Cuarta parte*. Throughout his career, in many of the *loas* he charted the path that the *auto* followed. In all of these works, he explained his vision of the *auto*. In the case of Bances, who used Calderon's exemplary works as a model and a point of departure, the playwright formulated a corpus of dramatic theory that was based on his experience as one of the court dramatists of Charles II. Bances recorded the virtues of Calderón's plays and attempted to elevate and reform the art of playwriting, resulting in decorous and educational plays. Like others before him, simply presenting the poetics on stage was not enough and he felt the need to document his work and cement his role as an educator of the king and the people.

Segunda esposa and *Duelos* take advantage of many of the same strategies in relation to performance and audience reception, revealing the impetus for the dramatic conventions that drove the dramatic production of Calderón and Bances, as well as other playwrights at the time. Spectacle comes to the forefront in both cases. We see in the stage directions that the scenery and machinery were opulent and complicated. While clearly included to awe the public, the playwrights had to be careful that the opulence of the background did not upstage the message of the plays, a preoccupation that Lope mentioned in the *Arte nuevo*. Music and song also played important roles in the productions of both plays and they added to the already great entertainment value of the play. While the music may seem distracting, the opposite is true. In both plays, the music complemented the messages embodied in the whole dramatic text in either implicit or explicit manners. Other strategies include the use of allegory, which was the favorite teaching strategy since it succeeds in presenting abstract notions in an impressive and clear manner. Although the *auto* and the court play are distinct theatrical forms, their similarities outweigh their differences. In both cases, the playwrights found innovative manners to deliver a profound message in an accessible manner.

CONCLUSION: FROM STAGE TO PAGE TO STAGE AGAIN

The title of this section suggests a circular structure that lends itself to the dynamic nature of theater as well as the poetics that drive its composition, performance, and reception. Dramatic conventions continually shift as a result of numerous factors, including artistic innovations, performance considerations, and public reception. Most often, change of any kind is difficult and conflictive and the fluid state of theater in early modern Spain was the subject of many literary, philosophical, and quite possibly, physical conflicts among the dramatic poets, scholars, and clergy of the time. In the interest of appeasing their personal artistic appetites and pleasing the public's hunger for innovation, the playwrights constantly strove to introduce new material on the boards, often at the expense of tradition. Of course, remnants of past conventions still existed in the new works, and it was the novel use of these recognizable forms and practice that ensured original productions. The six practitioner/theorists included in this study demonstrated their understanding of a need for innovation by staging new techniques and recording their successes not only on the page but also on the stage. Their dramatic treatises served as a point of departure for the theatrical output of contemporary and future playwrights. These men understood the importance and inevitability of change in the dramatic spectacle, as well as the factors that transformed their art. I specifically chose dramatic poets that documented these precepts because of their cognizance of all aspects of theatrical production, including the important role of dramatic theory. Their knowledge stems from years of experience of composing and contemplating plays that were in a continual state of change as a result of critical and popular demands.

In this study, the work of each playwright represents a critical time in the trajectory of early modern Spanish theater. Each man staged his nascent theory of dramatic conventions. For example, Torres's influence on Spanish theater is enormous although his works were never performed in the Iberian Peninsula. His introduction of dramatic theory to Spain sparked a long and vibrant tradition of recording and justifying precepts and practices. His notion of the *comedia a fantasia* cannot be overlooked because it added a new, creative dimension to playwriting with its focus on fiction and imagination. Later in the 1500s, although beginning his career as a follower of Neoclassical literary convention, Cueva eventually strayed from its strict rules, moving toward the tragicomic form that was to become so popular at the turn of the century. He had a keen dramatic intuition and his innovations on the stage were seen in later forms and performances. Lope was the literary giant of seventeenth-century Spain, and he had nothing to prove to anyone. All of his works, no matter the genre, enjoyed great success and admiration. He did, however, attempt to reach out to all sectors of the public to explain his rationale behind the composition of his literature. In his works, he highlighted the equal importance of the literary text, its performance, and its reception. Similarly, Tirso was an ardent supporter of literary innovation and variety. His defense of the *comedia* was simultaneously playful and stern. On the religious stage of the seventeenth century, Calderón took advantage of his unique genius and extensive experience of writing for secular audiences to produce the greatest *autos* in the history of Spanish theater. These works took performance to a new level, awing the spectators with lavish spectacle in order to guarantee that they understood the plays' dogmatic and allegorical message. Bances, too, wrote didactic theater, though his audience was distinct and much more exclusive. As the court playwright of Charles II, he shouldered the responsibility of educating the king in a subtle manner, which was no easy task. In all of these cases, the dramatic poets utilized their keen intuition to produce innovative and pleasing dramatic works.

Clearly, these playwrights/theorists grasped the connection between the composition, performance, and reception of dramatic works. It has been the intention of this study to reiterate and reflect upon the relationship shared between these three processes that make up the theatrical event. Benjamin Bennett states that "performance is what makes theater theater" (7), which is irrefutable. Of course, there also needs to be a text—written or not—that is always performed for an audience, whoever they may be: the actors, directors, or the actual spectators. When examining a play, it is imperative to treat the composition, performance and reception as equal parts. They work in unison to create the most vital and immediate art form, that is, theater. Differentiating between the reader and the theatergoer, B. Bennett notes that "[s]urely theatergoers are more likely than readers to be bewildered initially by the work of art, the performance, that bombards them with sensory stimuli at its own pace, leaving no room for readerly reflection" (3). His comment neatly sums up how composition, performance, and reception are linked, and it demonstrates the vitality of theater that we see not only in the theatrical trends of early modern Spain, but also in theater in general.

Indeed, the public impacts the success of a theatrical piece. This variable clearly drives the composition of the play text in addition to its performance. Innovation grows from the need to please the audience. All of the playwrights acknowledged this phenomenon as fact, though they viewed the different members of the public with varying attitudes. Tirso and Bances, for example, expressed the greatest dislike for the *vulgo*, refusing to cede the reins of creativity or laurels of change to the popular public. Tirso was not willing to admit that the populace held great sway over his work, though they arguably did. Bances asserted that the public did not teach him but rather he instructed them. Torres and Calderón are on the other end of the spectrum. The former felt a certain affiliation to the lower classes, though he never forgot about his duty to his patrons. When writing within the religious milieu, the Calderón strove to produce *autos* whose messages were intelligible to the heterogeneous public; he wrote for everyone in an attempt to reinforce their faith. Cueva and Lope are more ambivalent in their treatment of the *vulgo*. Cueva complains that they are not as refined and this has affected the composition of dramatic poetry. Lope, too, complains of the *vulgo*, but also recognizes their influence on both the production and the success of the *comedia*. In this last case, it is impossible to know to what degree Lope's words are ironic, especially since he wrote his treatise for an entirely different audience who disparaged the popular classes; yet another example of the importance of reception on composition.

This book is not meant to close the door on a discussion that has been going on since the seventeenth century. Instead, it strives to open another door leading to a further examination of a wide variety of theatrical traditions and styles since the impact of performance and reception is basic to all forms of drama. Indeed, there are many doors to open and pass through. Within the context of early modern Spanish theater studies, this research can be expanded to look at the entire dramatic spectacle on the secular stage, that is, both the principal work and the short dramatic pieces intercalated between its acts. Within the religious milieu, further examination of the *auto* and other liturgical dramatic pieces would prove useful. Expanding the number of playwright-theorists studied and including a similar examination of how the more classically inspired playwrights staged their dramatic theory would be fruitful.

Of course, the observations here are not limited to Spanish drama and a similar survey of other time periods, countries, and dramatic styles could benefit from an analysis from the perspective of performance and reception, revealing new information about the creative process that cannot be deduced simply from the text. One clear example would be the case of French playwright Pierre Corneille's dramatic works and defense of his theatrical innovations to the French Academy, especially when compared to his Spanish contemporaries, who included Lope, Tirso, and Calderón. Also, a side-by-side analysis of Ben Johnson's dramatic treatises and plays might draw parallels to the similar circumstances found in early modern England and Spain.

By examining the dramatic precepts of several major playwrights of sixteenth- and seventeenth-century Spain from a perspective that looks away from the tangible clues provided by the script and moves toward the more subjective aspects of its performance and subsequent audience response, we see that practice impacts theory just as theory influences practice. The majority of early modern Spanish playwrights-drama theorists wrote their theoretical treatises after years of successfully writing and staging plays, underlining the importance of experience to the creative process and underlining an *a posteriori* characteristic of dramatic theory. Furthermore, by using as a point of departure recent theoretical approaches based on audience response and performance theories, we experience a shift of textual authority that places the representation of the script and its subsequent reception on the same plane as the written script, not only reiterating the vivacity of theater, but also broadening theater studies and further illustrating the interrelation between the dramatic spectacle, the message, its reception, and the resultant theory governing the theater of Golden Age Spain.

BIBLIOGRAPHY

Agheana, Ion T. *The Situational Drama of Tirso de Molina.* Madrid: Playor, 1973.

Aitken, Maria. *Style: Acting in High Comedy.* New York: Applause, 1996.

Albrecht, Jane White. *Irony and Theatricality in Tirso de Molina.* Ottawa: Dovehouse, 1994.

---. *The Playgoing Public of Madrid in the Time of Tirso de Molina.* New Orleans: UP of the South, 2001.

Alcázar, José. *Ortografía castellana. Ensayo de una biblioteca española de libros raros y curiosos.* Ed. Bartolomé José Gallardo. 4 vols. Madrid: Gredos, 1968.

Alegre Peyrón, José María. "La censura literaria en España en el siglo XVI." *Revue Romane* 25.2 (1990): 428-41.

[Alfonso X.] *Las siete partidas del Rey Don Alfonso el Sabio.* Vol. 1. Ed. Real Academia de la Historia. Madrid: Imprenta Real, 1807.

Allen, John J. "Documenting the History of Spanish Theatre: *Fuentes para la historia del teatro en España.*" *MLR* 93 (1998): 997-1006.

---. *The Reconstruction of a Spanish Golden Age Playhouse: el corral del Príncipe, 1583-1744.* Gainesville: U of Florida P, 1983.

---. "The World of the *Comedia.*" *Comedia Performance* 4.1 (2007): 15-34.

Álvarez-Pelliteros, Ana María. *Teatro medieval.* Madrid: Espasa-Calpe, 1990.

Amezúa, Agustín G. de. *Lope de Vega en sus cartas.* 4 vols. Madrid: Escelicer, 1935-1943.

Antonio, Nicolás. *Biblioteca hispana nova, sive hispanorum scriptorum qu ab anno MD ad MDCLXXXIV floruere notitia.* Alicante: Bilblioteca Virtual Miguel de Cervantes,2006.<http://www.cervantesvirtual.com/FichaObra.html?Ref=21138>. 29 Aug. 2009.

Arellano, Ignacio. "Bances Candamo, poeta áulico. Teoría y práctica en el teatro cortesano del postrer Siglo de Oro." *Iberoromania* 27/28 (1988): 42-60.

---. *Convención y recepción: Estudios sobre el teatro del Siglo de Oro.* Madrid: Gredos, 1999.

---. *Diccionario de los autos sacramentales de Calderón.* Kassel: Reichenberger, 2000.

---. *Estructuras dramáticas y alegóricas en los autos de Calderón.* Kassel: Reichenberger, 2001.

---. *Historia del teatro español del siglo XVII.* Madrid: Cátedra, 1995.

---. "Presencia de Góngora en Bances Candamo, poeta oficial de Carlos II." *RLit* 53.106 (1991): 619-30.

---. "Teoría dramática y práctica teatral sobre el teatro áulico y político de Bances Candamo." *Criticón* 42 (1988): 169-93.

Arellano, Ignacio, Kurt Spang, and M. Carmen Pinillos eds. *Apuntes sobre la loa sacramental y cortesana.* Kassel: Reichenberger, 1994.

Aristotle. *Poetics. Dramatic Theory and Criticism.* Ed. Bernard F. Dukore. New York: Harcourt, Brace, Jovanovich, 1974. 31-55.

Arróniz, Othón. *La influencia italiana en el nacimiento de la comedia española.* Madrid: Gredos, 1969.

Association for Hispanic Classical Theater. Ed. Laura Vidler. 27 Aug. 2009. <http://www.comedias.org>.

Ayala, Francisco de. Introducción. *El vergonzoso en palacio.* By Tirso de Molina. Madrid: Castalia, 1971.

Bances Candamo, Francisco Antonio. *Duelos de Ingenio y Fortuna. Poesias cómicas, obras pósthumas de don Francisco Banzes Candamo. Tomo I.* Madrid: Blás de Villa-Nueva, 1722. 229-83.

---. Loa. *Duelos de Ingenio y Fortuna. Poesias cómicas, obras posthumas de don Francisco Banzes Candamo. Tomo I.* Madrid: Blás de Villa-Nueva, 1722. 224-28.

---. *Theatro de los theatros de los passados y presentes siglos.* Ed. Duncan Moir. London: Tamesis, 1970.

Barceló Jiménez, Juan. "La epístola de Cascales a Lope de Vega." *Segismundo* 1.2 (1965): 227-45.

Bass, Laura R. and Margaret R. Greer. *Approaches to Teaching Early Modern Spanish Drama.* New York: MLA, 2006

Bataillon, Marcel. "Ensayo de explicación del <<auto sacramental>>." *Calderón y la crítica: historia y antología.* Ed. Manuel Durán and Roberto González Echevarría. Madrid: Gredos, 1976. 455-80.

---. *Varia lección de clásicos españoles.* Trans. José Pérez Riesco. Madrid: Gredos, 1964.

Benabu, Isaac. "Interpreting the *Comedia* in the Absence of a Performance Tradition: Gutierre in Calderón's *El médico de su honra.*" *Prologue to Performance.* Ed. Louise and Peter Fothergill-Payne. Lewisburg, PA: Bucknell UP, 1991. 23-35.

Bennett, Benjamin. *All Theater is Revolutionary Theater.* Ithaca, NY: Cornell UP, 2005.

Bennett, Susan. *Theatre Audiences: A Theory of Production and Reception.* 2nd ed. New York: Routledge, 1997.

Blau, Herbert. *The Audience.* Baltimore: Johns Hopkins UP, 1990.

---. *The Eye of Prey.* Bloomington, IN: Indiana UP, 1987.

---. "Ideology and Performance." *TJ* 35.4 (1983): 441-60.

---. *To All Appearances: Ideology and Performance.* New York: Routledge, 1992.

Botrel, Jean François, ed. *Creación y público en la literatura española.* Madrid: Castalia, 1974.

Brook, Peter. *The Empty Space.* New York: Atheneum, 1968.

Burton, David G. "The Historical Dramas of Juan de la Cueva." *Crítica Hispánica* 12.1-2 (1990): 5-13.

---. *The Legend of Bernardo del Carpio From Chronicle to Drama.* Potomac, MD: Scripta Humanistica, 1988.

---. "Virtue Triumphant in Cueva's *La libertad de España por Bernardo del Carpio.*" *BCom* 38.2 (1986): 219-29.

Burningham, Bruce R. "Barbarians at the Gates: The Invasive Discourse of Medieval Performance in Lope's *Arte nuevo.*" *TJ* 50.3 (1998): 289-302.

---. *Radical Theatricality: Jongleuresque Performance on the Early Spanish Stage.* West Lafayette, IN: Purdue UP, 2007.

Bushee, Alice H. "The Greatest Spanish Dramatists." *Hispania* 17.1 (1934): 51-58.

Butcher, Samuel Henry. *Aristotle's Theory of Poetry and Fine Art.* New York: Dover, 1951.

Calderón de la Barca, Pedro. *La segunda esposa y triunfar muriendo. Obras completas.* Ed. Ángel Valbuena Prat. 3 vols. Madrid: Aguilar, 1960-67. 428-47.

---. Loa. *La segunda esposa y triunfar muriendo. Obras completas.* Ed. Ángel Valbuena Prat. 3 vols. Madrid: Aguilar, 1960-67. 425-27.

---. *Obras completas.* Ed. Ángel Valbuena Prat. 3 vols. Madrid: Aguilar, 1960-67.

---. Prólogo. *Obras completas.* Ed. Ángel Valbuena Prat. 3 vols. Madrid: Aguilar, 1960-67. 41-42.

Cammarata, Joan F., ed. *Women in the Discourse of Early Modern Spain.* Gainesville: U of Florida P, 2003.

Cameron, Kenneth M., and Theodore J. C. Hoffman. *The Theatrical Response*. London. Macmillan, 1969.

Canavaggio, Jean. "Las reflexiones de Marcel Bataillon sobre Juan de la Cueva, sesenta años después." *España y América en una perspectiva humanista. Homenaje a Marcel Bataillon*. Ed. Joseph Pérez. Madrid: Casa de Velázquez, 1998. 35-44.

---. "Nuevas reflexiones sobre Juan de la Cueva." *EdO* 16 (1997): 99-108.

Carlson, Marvin. *Places of Performance: The Semiotics of Theatre Architecture*. Ithaca: Cornell UP, 1989.

---. *Theatre Semiotics: Signs of Life*. Bloomington, IN: Indiana UP, 1990.

---. "Theatrical Performance." *TJ* 37.1 (1985): 5-12.

---. *Theories of the Theatre*. Ithaca, NY: Cornell UP, 1993.

Caro, Rodrigo. *Varones insignes en letras naturales de la ilustrísima ciudad de Sevilla*. Ed. L. Gómez Canseco. Seville: Excma. Diputación Provincial de Sevilla, 1992.

Carvalho, Susan de. "The Legend of the *Siete infantes de Lara* and its Theatrical Representation by Cueva and Lope." *BCom* 40.1 (1988): 85-102.

Carvallo, Luis Alfonso. *Cisne de Apolo*. Ed. Alberto Porqueras Mayo. Kassel: Reichenberger, 1997.

Casalduero. Joaquín. "Sentido y forma de *El vergonzoso en palacio*." *NRFH* 15 (1961): 198-216.

Cascales, Francisco. *Tablas Poéticas*. Ed. Benito Brancaforte. Madrid: Espasa-Calpe, 1975.

---. *Cartas filológicas*. Ed. Justo Garcia Soriano. 2 vols. Madrid: Espasa Calpe, 1951.

Cascardi, Anthony J. "Lope de Vega, Juan de la Cueva, Giraldi Cinthio, and Spanish Poetics." *RHM* 39.1-2 (1976-77): 150-55.

Caso González, José M. Introducción. *Comedia del Infamador*. Salamanca: Anaya, 1965.

---. "Las obras de tema contemporáneo en el teatro de Juan de la Cueva." *AO* 19 (1969): 127-47.

Castilla Pérez, Roberto, and Miguel González Dengra, eds. *La teatralización de la historia en el Siglo de Oro español*." Granada: U of Granada P, 2001.

Castro, Américo, and Hugo A. Rennert. *Vida de Lope de Vega (1562-1635)*. Madrid: Anaya 1968.

Castro Caridad, Eva. *Introducción al teatro latino medieval*. Santiago de Compostela: U of Santiago de Compostela P, 1996.

--- *Tropos y troparios hispánicas*. Santiago de Compostela: U of Santiago de Compostela P, 1991.

Castro, Guillén de. *El curioso impertinente*. Ed. Cristiane Faliu-Lacourt and María Luisa Lobato. Kassel: Reichenberger, 1991.

Cebrián, José. *Estudios sobre Juan de la Cueva*. Seville: U of Seville P, 1991.

Cervantes, Miguel de. *Don Quijote de la Mancha*. Ed. Tom Lathrop. Newark, DE: Juan de la Cuesta, 2000.

---. Prólogo. *Ocho comedias y ocho entremeses nuevos nunca representados. Obras completas de Miguel de Cervantes: Comedias y entremeses Tomo I*. Ed. Rodolfo Schevill and Adolfo Bonilla. Madrid: Bernardo Rodríguez, 1915. 5-10.

---. *Obras completas*. Ed. Ángel Valbuena Prat. 7th ed. Madrid: Aguilar, 1946.

---. *El rufián dichoso*. Ed. Edward Nagy. Madrid, Cátedra, 1975.

Cioranescu, Alexandre. "Tirso de Molina y Lope de Vega." *Homenaje a William L. Fichter: Estudios sobre el teatro antiguo hispánico y otros ensayos*. Ed. A. David Kosoff et al. Madrid: Castalia, 1971. 151-60.

Cilvetti, Ángel L. "El auto sacramental de Calderón y la continuidad cultural." *Divinas y humanas letras. Doctrina y poesía en los autos sacramentales de Calderón*. Ed. Ignacio Arellano, et al. Kassel: Reichenberger, 1997. 45-72.

Cilvetti, Ángel, and Ignacio Arellano. *Bibliografía crítica sobre el auto sacramental.* Kassel: Reichenberger, 1994.

Close, Anthony. "Lo cómico y la censura en el Siglo de Oro, II." *BH* 2 (2003): 271-301.

Compte, Deborah. "A Cry in the Wilderness: Pastoral Female Discourse in María de Zayas." *Women in the Discourse of Early Modern Spain.* Ed. Joan F. Cammarata. Gainesville: U of Florida P, 2003. 235-52.

Connor, Catherine. "Hacia una teoría sociocultural del espectador aurisecular." *El texto puesto en escena: Estudios sobre la comedia del siglo de oro en honor a Everett W. Hesse.* Ed. Barbara Mujica and Anita K. Stoll. London: Tamesis, 2000. 3-13.

Corbató, Hermengildo. *Los Misterios del corpus de Valencia.* Berkeley: U of CA P, 1932.

---. "Notas sobre el misterio de Elche y otros dramas sagrados de Valencia." *Hispania* 15.2 (1932): 103-08.

---. "Some Outstanding and Recurring Themes in Valencian Literature." *Hispania* 14.3 (1931): 167-82.

Cotarelo y Mori, Emilio. *Bibliografía de las controversias sobre la licitud del teatro en España.* Granada: U of Granada P, 1997.

---. *Colección de entremeses, loas, bailes, jácaras y mojigangas.* Madrid: Bailly y Bailliére, 1911.

Cox Davis, Nina. "Torres Naharro's Comic Speakers." *HR* 56.2 (1988): 139-55.

Crawford, J. P. Wickersham. *Spanish Drama Before Lope de Vega.* Rev. and reprinted ed. Philadelphia: U of Pennsylvania P, 1968.

---. "The Braggart Soldier in Spanish Drama." *RR* 2 (1911): 186-208.

Cubillo de Aragón, Álvaro. *El enano de las musas.* Ed. Guido Mancini. New York: Georg Olms Verlag, 1971.

Cuervo-Arango, Francisco. *Don Francisco Antonio de Bances y López-Candamo.* Madrid: Hijos de M. G. Hernández, 1916.

Cueva, Juan de la. *Comedia de la muerte del Rey Don Sancho. Comedias y tragedias de Juan de la Cueva.* Vol. 1. Ed. Francisco A. de Icaza. Madrid: Imprenta Ibérica, 1917. 11-53.

---. *Comedia otava, del Viejo enamorado. Primera parte de las comedias y tragedias de Juan de la Cueva.* Seville: Joan de León, 1588. 242 v.-276 r.

---. *Comedia sexta, de la constancia de Arcelina. Primera parte de las comedias y tragedias de Juan de la Cueva.* Seville: Joan de León, 1588. 137 r.-164 v.

---. *Comedias y tragedias de Juan de la Cueva.* 2 vols. Ed. Francisco A. de Icaza. Madrid: Imprenta Ibérica, 1917.

---. "Epístola dedicatoria a Momo." *Comedias y tragedias de Juan de la Cueva.* 2 vols. Ed. Francisco A. de Icaza. Madrid: Imprenta Ibérica, 1917. 5-8.

---. *Exemplar poético.* Ed. José María Reyes Cano. Sevilla: Ediciones Alfar, 1986.

---. *Los cuatro Libros de Juan de la Cueva, De los Ynventores de las Cossas.* Ms. 10182 (3) Biblioteca Nacional. Ff. 61 r.-122 v.

---. *Tragedia de Ayax Telamon. Comedias y tragedias de Juan de la Cueva.* Vol. 1. Ed. Francisco A. de Icaza. Madrid: Imprenta Ibérica, 1917. 278-327.

---. *Tragedia de la muerte de Virginia y Appio Claudio. Primera parte de las comedias y tragedias de Juan de la Cueva.* Seville: Joan de León, 1588. 164 v.-186 v.

---. *Tragedia de los siete Infantes de Lara. Comedias y tragedias de Juan de la Cueva.* Vol. 1. Ed. Francisco A. de Icaza. Madrid: Imprenta Ibérica, 1917. 100-150.

---. *Viaje de Sannio.* Ed. José Cebrián. Madrid: Miraguano, 1990.

Darst. David H. *The Comic Art of Tirso de Molina.* Madrid: Castalia, 1974.

De Armas, Frederick A. "Dreams, Voices, Signatures: Deciphering Woman's Desires in

Angela de Azevedo's *Dicha y desdicha del juego*." *Women in the Discourse of Early Modern Spain*. Ed. Joan F. Cammarata. Gainesville: U of Florida P, 2003. 146-59.

---. *Ekprhasis in the Age of Cervantes*. Lewisburg, PA: Bucknell UP, 2005.

Deleito y Piñuela, José. *El declinar de la monarquía Española*. 4 ed. Madrid: Espasa Calpe, 1966.

Delgado, Manuel, ed. Introduction. *The Calderonian Stage*. Lewisburg, PA: Bucknell UP, 1997. 13-24.

Delicado, Francisco. *La lozana andaluza*. Ed. Bruno Damiani. Madrid: Castalia, 1969.

Deyermond, Alan D. *Historia de la literatura española*. Madrid: Ariel, 1998.

---. *Historia y crítica de la literatura española*. Barcelona: Crítica, 1979.

Diago, Manuel V., and Teresa Ferrer, eds. *Comedias y comediantes: Estudios sobre el teatro clásico español*. Valencia: U of Valencia P, 1989.

Diamond, Elin, ed. *Performance and Cultural Politics*. London: Routledge, 1996.

Díaz Balsera, Viviana. *Calderón y las quimeras de la culpa*. West Lafayette, IN: Purdue UP, 1997.

Díaz-Castañón, Carmen. "Bances Candamo y su teatro político." *Los Cuadernos del Norte* 5 (1981): 74-82.

---. "La teoría dramática de Bances Candamo y la crítica teatral dieciochesca en España." *Studies on Voltaire and the Eighteenth Century* 265 (1989): 1362-1363.

Dietz, Donald T. "Conflict in Calderón's *Autos Sacramentales*." *Approaches to the Theater of Calderón*. Ed. Michael McGaha. Washington, DC: UP of America, 1982. 175-86.

---. "Theology and the Stage: The God Figure in Calderón's *Autos Sacramentales*." *Bcom* 34.1 (1982): 97-105.

---. "Toward Understanding Calderón's Evolution as an *Auto* Dramatist: A Study in Dramatic Structure." *Studies in Honor of Ruth Lee Kennedy*. Ed. Vern G. Williamsen, et al. Chapel Hill: *Hispanófila*, 1977. 45-55.

Díez Borque, José María. *Actor y técnica de representación del teatro clásico español*. London: Tamesis, 1989.

---. *La sociedad española y los viajeros del siglo XVIII*. Madrid: Sociedad General Española de Librería, 1975.

---. "Teatro y fiesta en el Barroco español: El auto sacramental de Calderón y el público. Funciones del texto cantado." *Estudios sobre Calderón*. Ed. Javier Aparicio Maydeu. Madrid: Istmo, 2000. 135-83.

---. *Una fiesta sacramental barroca*. Madrid: Taurus, 1984.

---. *La vida española en el Siglo de Oro según los extranjeros*. Barcelona: Serbal, 1990.

Diccionario de la Real Academia Española. 22 ed. Madrid: RAE, 2001.

Dixon, Victor. "*Lo fingido verdadero* y sus espectadores." *Diablotexto* 4-5 (1997-98): 97-114.

---. "<<Ya tienes la comedia prevenida...la imagen de la vida>>: *Lo fingido verdadero*." *Doce comedias buscan un tablado*. Ed. Felipe B. Pedraza Jiménez. Madrid: Teatro Clásico, 1999.

Donovan, Richard B. *The Liturgical Drama in Medieval Spain*. Toronto: Pontifical Institute of Medieval Studies. 1958

Durán, Manuel, and Roberto González Echevarría. *Calderón y la crítica: Historia y Antología*. 2 vols. Madrid: Gredos, 1976.

Elizalde, Ignacio. "Teoría del teatro de F. A. Bances Candamo." *Diálogos Hispánicos de Amsterdam*. 8.2 (1989): 219-231.

Encina, Juan del. *Égloga de Plácida y Victoriano. Teatro completo*. Ed. Miguel Ángel Pérez Priego. Madrid: Cátedra, 1991. 287-371,

Enríquez de Guzmán, Feliciana. *The Dramatic Works of Feliciana Enríquez de Guzmán*.

Ed. Louis C. Pérez. Valencia: Albatros, 1988.
Entrambasaguas, Joaquín. *Estudios y ensayos sobre Góngora y el Barroco*. Madrid: Nacional, 1975.
---. *Lope de Vega: Símbolo del temperamento estético español*. Murcia: U of Murcia P, 1936.
---. "Una guerra literaria del Siglo de Oro. Lope de Vega y los preceptistas aristotélicos." *Estudios sobre Lope de Vega*. 2 ed. 2 vols. Madrid: CSIC, 1967.
---. *Vida de Lope de Vega*. Madrid: Labor, 1936.
Falconieri, John V. "La situación de Torres Naharro en la historia literaria." *Hispanófila* 1 (1957): 32-39.
Farré Vidal, Judith, ed. *Teatro y poder en la época de Carlos II: Fiestas en tono a reyes y virreyes*. Madrid: Iberoamericana, 2007.
Féral, Josette. "Performance and Theatricality: The Subject Demystified." Trans. Terese Lyons. *Modern Drama*. 25:1 (1982): 171-81.
Fernández de Moratín, Leandro. *Orígenes del teatro español*. Madrid, 1830.
Fischer, Susan L. "Lope's *Lo fingido verdadero* and the Dramatization of the Theatrical Experience." *RHM* 39:1-2 (1976-77): 156-66.
Fish, Stanley L. *Is There a Text in This Class? The Authority of Interpretive Communities*. Cambridge, MA: Harvard UP, 1980.
Flasche, Hans. "El acto de mostrar en el teatro calderoniano." *Studien Zur Romanischen Wortgeschichte*. Ed. Gerhard Ernst and Arnulf Stefenelli. Stuttgart: Steiner, 1989. 82-91.
---, ed. *Hacia Calderón*. Berlin: Walter de Gruyter, 1973.
Florit Duran, Francisco. *Tirso de Molina ante la comedia nueva*. Madrid: Estudios, 1986.
Fortier, Mark. *Theory/Theatre*. London: Routledge, 1997.
Fothergill-Payne, Louise. *La alegoría en los autos y farsas anteriores a Calderón*. London: Tamesis, 1977.
Fothergill-Payne, Louise, and Peter Fothergill-Payne, eds. *Prologue to Performance: Spanish Classical Theater Today*. Lewisburg, PA: Bucknell UP, 1991.
Frenk, Margit. "*El vergonzoso en palacio:* duplicaciones y multiplicaciones." *NRFH* 42 (1994): 77-86.
Friedman, Edward H. "Resisting Theory: Rhetoric and Reason in Lope de Vega's *Arte nuevo*." *Neophilologus* 75.1 (1991): 86-93.
Froldi, Rinaldo. *Lope de Vega y la formación de la comedia*. Rev. ed. Madrid: Anaya, 1968.
Ganelin, Charles. "Peter Brook: Performance Theory and the *Comedia*." *BCom* 43.1 (1991): 101-09.
Ganelin, Charles and Howard Mancing, eds. *The Golden Age* Comedia*: Text, Theory, and Performance*. West Lafayette: Purdue UP, 1994.
García-Castañón, Santiago. "Algunas consideraciones sobre la poesía de Bances Candamo." *Boletín del Real Instituto de Estudios Asturianos* 136 (1990): 707-16.
---. "La historia como pre-texto: el caso de *Por su rey y por su dama*, de Bances Candamo." *Boletín del Real Instituto de Estudios Asturianos* 141 (1993): 151-55.
---. "La presencia del ideario de Saavedra Fajardo en Bances Candamo." *BCom* 50.2 (1998): 405-17.
García Mercadal, José. *Viajes de Extranjeros por España y Portugal*. Madrid: Aguilar, 1959
García Ruiz, Víctor. "Algunas notas filológicas sobre el auto de Calderón *La segunda esposa y triunfar muriendo*." *Homenaje a Alberto Navarro González*. Ed. Víctor García de la Concha, et al. Kassel: Reichenberger, 1990. 185-220.

Garrido, José Lara ed. *El mundo como teatro. Estudios sobre Calderón de la Barca.* Málaga: U of Málaga P, 2003.

George, David. "On Ambiguity." *ThR* 14:1 (1989): 71-85.

Gilbert, Donald. "Playing to the Masses: Economic Rationalism in Lope de Vega's *Arte nuevo de hacer comedias en este tiempo*." *Comitatus* 31 (2000): 109-36.

Gillet, Joseph E. "Cueva's *Comedia del infamador* and the Don Juan Legend." *MLN* 37 (1922): 206-12.

---. "Torres Naharro and the Spanish Drama of the 16th Century." *Estudios eruditos in memoriam de Adolfo Bonillas San Martín.* 2 vols. Madrid: Viuda e hijos de Jaime Ratés, 1930. 437-68.

---. "Torres Naharro and the Spanish Drama of the 16th Century II." *HR* 5.3 (1937): 193-207.

Gladhart, Amalia. *The Leper in Blue.* Chapel Hill, NC: U of North Carolina P, 2000.

Glenn, Richard F. "Disguises and Masquerades in Tirso's *El vergonzoso en palacio*." *BCom* 17.1 (1965): 16-22.

---. *Juan de la Cueva*. New York: Twayne, 1973.

Gómez Moreno, Ángel. *El teatro medieval castellano en su marco románico*. Madrid: Taurus, 1991.

Góngora y Argote, Luis de. *Sonetos*. Ed. Biruté Ciplijauskaité. Madison, WI: The Hispanic Seminary of Medieval Studies, 1981.

González de Salas, Juseppe Antonio. *Nueva idea de la tragedia antigua*. Madrid: Antonio de Sancha, 1778.

Green, Otis H. "Imaginative Authority in Spanish Literature." *PMLA* 84 (1969): 209-16.

---. "On the Attitude toward the *Vulgo* in the Spanish *Siglo de Oro*." *Studies in the Renaissance* 4 (1957): 190-200.

Greer, Margaret Rich. "Art and Power in the Spectacle Plays of Calderón de la Barca." *PMLA* 104.3 (1989): 329-39.

---. *The Play of Power: Mythological Court Dramas of Calderón de la Barca*. Princeton: Princeton UP, 1991.

Greer, Margaret Rich, and J. E. Varey. *El teatro palaciego en Madrid: 1586 – 1707. Estudio y documentos*. London: Tamesis, 1997.

Grigely, Joseph. *Textualterity: Arte, Theory, and Textual Criticism.* Ann Arbor: U of Michigan P, 1995.

Grismer, Raymond Leonard. *The Influence of Plautus in Spain before Lope de Vega.* New York, Hispanic Institute, 1944.

Grubbs, Anthony J. "The Dramatization of the *Arte nuevo*: Revisiting *Lo fingido verdadero*." *BCom* 58.2 (2006): 341-57.

---. "Major Change in 'Minor' Theater: Luis Quiñones de Benavente's Dramatization of Dramatic Theory and its Effects on the Interlude in Early Modern Spain." *Hispanófila* 151 (2007): 1-20.

Guerra y Ribera, Manuel. "*Aprobación de la Verdadera Quinta Parte de Comedias de don Pedro Calderón* (1682)." Ed. Carine Herzig. *Criticón* 93 (2005): 95-154.

Guerrieri Crocetti, Camillo. *Juan de la Cueva e le origini del teatro nazionale spagnuolo.* Torino: Giuseppe Gambino, 1936.

Halkhoree, P. R. K. *Social and Literary Satire in the comedies of Tirso de Molina.* Ed. José M. Ruano de la Haza and Henry W. Sullivan. Ottawa: Dovehouse, 1989.

Heiple, Daniel. "Profeminist Reactions to Huarte's Misogyny in Lope de Vega's *La prueba de los ingenios* and María de Zayas's *Novelas amorosas y ejemplares. The Perception of Women in the Spanish* Comedia. Ed. Anita K. Stoll and Dawn L. Smith. Lewisburg, PA: Bucknell UP, 1991. 121-34.

Hermenegildo, Alfredo. *Juegos dramáticos de la locura festiva.* Palma de Mallorca: Olañeta, 1995.

Herrick, Marvin T. *Comic Theory in the Sixteenth Century*. Urbana, IL: U of Illinois P, 1964.

Hesse, Everett W. *Calderón de la Barca*. New York: Twayne, 1967.

---. "Courtly Allusions in the Plays of Calderón." *PMLA* 65.4 (1950): 531-49.

---. "The First and Second Editions of Calderón's *Cuarta Parte*." *HR* 16.3 (1948): 209-37.

---. "The Publication of Calderón's Plays in the Seventeenth Century." *Philological Quarterly* 27 (1948): 37-51.

Hesse, José. *Vida teatral en el Siglo de Oro*. Madrid: Taurus, 1965.

Hillach, Ansgar. "El auto sacramental calderoniano considerado en un relieve histórico-filosófico." *Haciá Calderón Quinto Coloquio Anglogermano Oxford 1978*. Ed. Hans Flasche and Robert D. F. Pring-Mill. Weisbaden: Steiner, 1978. 20-29.

Horace. *The Art of Poetry. Dramatic Theory and Criticism*. Ed. Bernard F. Dukore. New York: Harcourt, 1974. 67-76.

Huerta Calvo, Harm den Boer, and Fermín Sierra Martínez, eds. *Diálogos hispánicos de Amsterdam*. 3 vols. Amsterdam: Rodopi, 1989.

Icaza, Francisco A. de. Introduction. *Comedias y tragedias de Juan de la Cueva*. By Juan de la Cueva. 2 vols. Madrid: Imprenta Ibérica, 1917.

Impola, Richard A. *The Philosophia Antigua Poética of Alonzo López Pinciano. Translated with an Introduction and Annotations*. Diss. Columbia University, 1972.

Iser, Wolfgang. *The Act of Reading: A Theory of Aesthetic Response*. Baltimore: Johns Hopkins UP, 1978.

Jauss, Hans Robert. *Toward an Aesthetic of Reception*. Trans. Timothy Bahti. Minneapolis, U of Minnesota P, 1982.

---. "Tradition, Innovation and Aesthetic Experience." *Journal of Aesthetics and Art Criticism* 46.3 (1988): 375-87.

Jehenson, Yvonne, and Marcia L. Welles. "María de Zayas's Wounded Women: A Semiotics of Violence." *Gender, Identity, and Representation in Spain's Golden Age*. Ed. Dawn L. Smith and Anita K. Stoll. Lewisburg, PA: Bucknell UP, 2000. 178-202.

Juliá Martínez, Eduardo. *Lope de Vega y Valencia*. Madrid: Bermejo, 1935.

Kamen, Henry. *Spain in the Later Seventeenth Century, 1665-1700*. London: Longman, 1980.

Kelemen, Erick. "Drama in Sermons: Quotation, Performativity, and Conversion in a Middle English Sermon on the Prodigal Son in a *Tretise of Miraclis Pleyinge*." *ELH* 69.1 (2002): 1-19.

Kennedy, Ruth Lee. "A Reappraisal of Tirso's Relations to Lope and his Theater." *Bcom* 17 (1965): 23-34.

---. "A Reappraisal of Tirso's Relations to Lope and his Theater (Continued)." *Bcom* 18 (1966) 1-13.

---. *Studies in Tirso, I: The Dramatist and his Competitors,* 1620-26. Chapel Hill, NC: U of North Carolina P, 1974.

Kirschner, Teresa J. *Técnicas de representación en Lope de Vega*. London: Tamesis, 1998.

Kurtz, Barbara E. "Calderón de la Barca contra la Inquisición: *Las órdenes militares* como proceso y como pieza." *Encuentros y desencuentros de culturas: desde la edad media al siglo XVIII*. Ed. Juan Villegas. 5 vols. Irvine, CA: U of California P, 1992. 146-54.

---. "Defining Allegory, or Troping through Calderón's *Autos*." *HR* 58.2 (1990): 227-43.

---. "Guilty Pleasure: The Comic, the Sacred, and *Placer(es)* in the *Autos Sacramentales* of Calderón de la Barca." *Play, Literature, Religion: Essays in Cultural Intertextuality*. Ed. Virgil Nemoiano and Robert Royal. Albany: SUNY P, 1992. 61-75.

---. "Illusions of Power: Calderón de la Barca, the Spanish Inquisition, and the Prohibition of *Las órdenes militares* (1662-1671). *RCEH* 18.2 (1994): 189-218.

---. *The Play of Allegory in the* Autos Sacramentales *of Pedro Calderón de la Barca*. Washington D.C.: Catholic U of America P, 1991.

Larson, Catherine. *Language and the* Comedia: *Theory and Practice*. Lewisburg: Bucknell UP, 1991. 204-21.

---. "Metatheater and the *Comedia*: Past, Present, and Future." *The Golden Age* Comedia*: Text, Theory, and Performance*. Ed. Charles Ganelin and Howard Mancing. West Lafayette, IN: Purdue UP, 1994.

---. "Test–Driving the *Comedia*: Transmission, Filters, and Brakes." *Texto y espectáculo: Nuevas dimensiones críticas de la comedia*. Ed. Arturo Pérez–Pisonero. El Paso: U of Texas P, 1990. 73–80.

---. "You Can't Always Get What You Want: Gender, Voice, and Identity in Women-Authored *Comedias*." *Gender, Identity, and Representation in Spain's Golden Age*. Ed. Dawn L. Smith and Anita K. Stoll. Lewisburg, PA: Bucknell UP, 2000. 127-41.

Lauer, A. Robert. "The *Comedia* and Its Modes." *HR* 63.2 (1995): 157-78.

---. "The Use and Abuse of History in Spanish Theater of the Golden Age: The Regicide of Sancho II as Treated by Juan de la Cueva, Guillen de Castro, and Lope de Vega." *HR* 56.1 (1988): 17-37.

Leoni, Monica. "Silence Is/As Golden...Age Device: Ana Caro's Eloquent Reticence in *Valor, agravio y mujer*." *Women in the Discourse of Early Modern Spain*. Ed. Joan F. Cammarata. Gainesville: U of Florida P, 2003. 192-212.

Levy, Kurt, Jesús Ara, and Gethin Hughes. *Calderón and the Baroque Tradition*. Waterloo: Wilfrid Laurier UP, 1985.

Lihani, John. *Bartolomé de Torres Naharro*. Boston: Twayne, 1979.

---. *El lenguaje de Lucas Fernández*. Bogotá: Caro y Cuervo, 1973.

---. "La técnica de recapitulación auténtica en el teatro del siglo XVI." *Lope de Vega y los orígenes del teatro español. Actas del I Congreso Internacional sobre Lope de Vega*. Ed. Manuel Criado de Val. Madrid: EDI-6, 1981. 303-09.

---. "New Biographical Ideas on Bartolomé Torres Naharro." *Hispania* 54.4 (1971): 828-35.

---. "Play-Audience Relationship in Bartolomé Torres Naharro." *BCom* 31.2 (1979): 95-102.

Lipmann, Stephen. "'Metatheater' and the Criticism of the *Comedia*." *MLN* 91.2 (1976), 231-46.

López de Vega, Antonio. *Paradoxas racionales*. Ed. Erasmo Buceta. Madrid: Hernando, 1935.

López Morales, Humberto. *Tradición y creación en los orígenes del teatro castellano*. Madrid: Alcalá, 1968.

López Pinciano, Alonso. *Philosophia Antigua Poética*. Ed. Alfredo Carballo. 3 vols. Picazo. Madrid: Marsiega, 1953.

Luján de Sayavedra, Mateo. *Segunda parte de la vida del pícaro Guzmán de Alfarache*. Ed. Enrique Suárez Figaredo. 27 Aug. 2009. <users.ipfw.edu /JEHLE/CERVANTE/.../Guzman_Apocrifo.PDF>.

Maior, Aguilar. *Vida y reinado de Carlos II*. Madrid: Aguilar, 1990.

Malinak, Edward. "Torres Naharro's Innovative Dramaturgic Contributions to the Spanish Theater." *Estudios Alfonsinos y Otros Escritos en Homenaje a John Esten Keller y a Anibal A. Biglieri.* Ed. Nicolás Toscano Liria. New York: NEH, 1991. 140-48.

Maravall, José Antonio. *Teatro y literatura en la sociedad barroca.* Ed. Francisco Abad. Barcelona: Crítica, 1990.

---. *The Culture of the Baroque.* Minneapolis: U of Minnesota P, 1986.

Marbán, Edilberto. *El teatro español medieval y del renacimiento.* New York: Las Américas, 1971.

Martin, Vincent. *El concepto de <<representación>> en los autos sacramentales de Calderón.* Kassel: Reichenberger, 2002.

Mártir Rizo, Juan Pablo. *Poética de Aristóteles traducida de latín.* Ed. Margaret Newels. Westfalen: Westdeutscher Verlag, Köln und Opladen, 1965.

Mathias, Julio. *Moratín.* Madrid: Compañía Bibliográfica Española, 1964.

Mas, Pascual. *La práctica escénica del Barroco tardío: Alejandro Arboreda.* Valencia: Institució Valenciana D'Estudis I Investigació, 1987.

McGaha, Michael. Introduction. *Acting is Believing.* Trans. Michael McGaha. San Antonio: Trinity UP, 1986. 3-36.

McGinniss, Cecilia. "Legitimando lo imaginado: dimensiones ocultas de las leyendas de San Ginés de Pedro de Rivadeneira, S. J. (1599) y de *Lo fingido verdadero* de Lope de Vega (1607-1608)." *El texto puesto en escena: Estudios sobre la comedia del siglo de oro en honor a Everett W. Hesse.* Ed. Barbara Mujica and Anita K. Stoll. Madrid: Tamesis, 2000. 104-12.

McGrady, Donald. "Italian Influences upon Torres Naharro's *Comedia Calamita.*" *BCom* 35.2 (1983): 181-87.

McKendrick, Melveena. *Theatre in Spain: 1499-1700.* Cambridge: Cambridge UP, 1992.

Mena, José María de. *Tradiciones y leyendas sevillanas.* Barcelona: Random House, 1999.

Ménendez y Pelayo, Marcelino. *Calderón y su teatro.* Buenos Aires: Emecé, 1946.

---. *Estudios sobre el teatro de Lope de Vega.* Ed. Enrique Sánchez Reyes. 6 vols. Santander: CSIC, 1949.

---. *Historia de las ideas estéticas.* 2 Vols. 4th ed. Madrid: CSIC, 1974.

Mérimée, Henri. *El arte dramático en Valencia.* Trans. Octavio Pellissa Safont. 2 vols. Valencia: Institució Alfons el Magnanim, 1985.

Mesonero Romanos, Ramón de. *Dramáticos posteriores a Lope de Vega.* Madrid: Rivadeneyra, 1858.

Metford, J. C. J. "The Enemies of the Theatre in the Golden Age." *BHS* 28 (1951): 76-92.

Miller, Jonathan. *The Afterlife of Plays.* San Diego: San Diego State UP, 1992.

Minich Brewer, Maria. "Performing Theory." *TJ* 37.1 (1985): 13-30.

Moir, Duncan. Prólogo. *Theatro de los theatros de los passados y presentes siglos.* By Francisco Antonio Bances Candamo. London: Tamesis, 1970. xi-cii.

Moir, Duncan, and Edward W. Wilson. *The Golden Age: Drama 1492-1700, A Literary History.* Vol. 3. London: Ernest Benn, 1971.

Montesinos, José F. *Estudios sobre Lope de Vega.* Madrid: Anaya, 1967.

Montoto, Santiago. *Ingenios sevillanos del Siglo de Oro que vivieron en América.* Madrid: Ibero-Americano, 1929.

Morby, Edwin S. "The Influence of Senecan Tragedy in the Plays of Juan de la Cueva." *SP* 34.3 (1937): 383-91.

---. "Notes on Juan de la Cueva: Versification and Dramatic Theory." *HR* 8.3 (1940): 213-18.

---. "The Plays of Juan de la Cueva." Diss. University of California, 1936.

Morel-Fatio, Alfred. *La Comedia espagnole du XVIIe siècle*. 2nd ed. Paris: Champion, 1923.

---. "Notes on Juan de la Cueva: Versification and Dramatic Theory." *HR* 8.3 (1940): 213-18.

Morley, S. Griswold, and Courtney Bruerton. *Cronología de las comedias de Lope de Vega con un examen de las atribuciones dudosas, basado todo ello en un estudio de su versificación estrófica*. Trans. María Rosa Cartes. Madrid: Gredos, 1968.

Morón Arroyo, Ciriaco. "Semiótica del texto y semiótica de la representación." *Teatro del Siglo de Oro: Homenaje a Alberto Navarro González*. Ed. Jean Canavaggio, et al. Kassel: Edition Reichenberger, 1990. 436-54.

Mujica, Bárbara, and Anita K. Stoll, eds. *El texto puesto en escena: estudios sobre la comedia del Siglo de Oro en honor a Everett W. Hesse*. Woodbridge, UK: Tamesis, 2000.

Neumeister, Sebastián. "Las bodas de España: alegoría y política en el auto sacramental." *Haciá Calderón Quinto Coloquio Anglogermano Oxford 1978*. Ed. Hans Flasche and Robert D. F. Pring-Mill. Weisbaden: Steiner, 1978. 30-41.

Nigro, Kirsten F. "Apuntes para una lectura del texto dramático." *La palabra y el hombre* 38-39 (1981): 121-27.

Nougué, André. *L'oeuvre en prose de Tirso de Molina*. Toulouse: Librairie des Facultés, 1962.

O'Connor, Thomas Austin. "Is the Spanish *Comedia* a Metatheater?" *HR* 43.3 (1975): 275-89.

Oleza, Juan. "Hipótesis sobre la génesis de la comedia barroca." *Cuadernos de Filología. Literaturas: Análisis* 3.1-2 (1981): 9-44.

Olid, Juan de, Diego de Gámez, and Pedro de Escavias. *Hechos del condestable don Miguel Lúcas de Iranzo*. Ed. Juan de Mata Carriaza. Madrid: Espasa-Calpe, 1940.

Orozco Díaz, Emilio. *Lope y Góngora frente a frente*. Madrid: Gredos, 1973.

---. "Sobre la actitud de Góngora ante el teatro de Lope." *Studia hispánica in honorem R. Lapesa II*. 3 vols. Madrid: Cátedra, 1974.

Palomo, María del Pilar. "Proceso de comunicación en *Lo fingido verdadero*." El castigo sin venganza *y el teatro de Lope de Vega*. Ed. Ricardo Doménech. Madrid: Cátedra, 1987. 79-98.

Parker, Alexander A. *The Allegorical Drama of Calderón*. Oxford: Dolphin, 1943.

---. "Tirso de Molina, Defensor de la Comedia Nueva." *Universidad de San Carlos (Guatemala)*. 12 (1950): 39-48.

Parker, Mary. *Spanish Dramatists of the Golden Age*. Westport, CT: Greenwood, 1998.

Paun de García, Susan. "Zayas's Ideal of the Masculine: Clothes Make the Man." *Women in the Discourse of Early Modern Spain*. Ed. Joan F. Cammarata. Gainesville: U of Florida P, 2003. 253-71.

Paun de García, and Donald R. Larson, eds. *The* Comedia *in English: Translation and Performance*. Woodbridge, UK: Tamesis, 2008.

Pavia, Mario N. *Drama of the Siglo de Oro: A Study of Magic, Witchcraft and Other Occult Beliefs*. New York: Hispanic Institute, 1959.

Pedraza, Pilar. *Barroco efímero en Valencia*. Valencia: Ayuntamiento de Valencia, 1982.

Pellicer, Casiano. *Tratado histórico sobre el origen y progreso del la comedia y del histrionismo en España*. Ed. José María Díez Borque. Barcelona: Labor, 1975.

Penzol, Pedro. *Francisco Bances Candamo de la comedia a la zarzuela*. Madrid: Velasco, 1932.

Pérez, Luis C., and Federico Sánchez Escribano. *Afirmaciones de Lope de Vega sobre preceptiva dramática a base de cien comedias*. Madrid: CSIC, 1961.

Pérez Feliu, José J. *Autos sactramentales de Francisco Bances Candamo*. Oviedo: Instituto de estudios asturianos, 1975.

Pérez-Magallón. Jesús. "Del *Arte Nuevo* de Lope al arte 'reformado' de Bances: Algunas cuestiones de poética dramática." *Edad de Oro* 19 (2000): 207-22.

Pérez-Priego, Miguel Ángel, ed. *Cuatro comedias celestinescas*. Madrid: UNED P, 1993.

---. Introducción. *Teatro Renacentista*. Barcelona: Plaza & Janés, 1986. 17-28.

Pfandl, Ludwig. *Geschichte der spanischen Nationalliteratur in ihrer Blütezeit*. Freiburg: Herder, 1929.

---. *Historia de la literatura nacional española en la Edad de Oro*. Trans. Jorge Rubió Balaguer. Barcelona: Gustavo Gili, 1952.

Pinta Llorente, Miguel de la. *La inquisición española y los problemas de la culture y de la intolerancia*. 2 vols. Madrid: Cultura Hispánica, 1953.

Pinto, Virgilio. "Pensamiento, vida intelectual y censura en la España de los siglos XVI y XVII." *EdO* 8 (1989): 181-92.

Pollin, Alice M. "Calderón de la Barca and Music: Theory and Examples in the *Autos* (1675-1681)." *HR* 41.2 (1973): 362-70.

Polo de Medina, Jacinto. *Poesía*. Ed. Francisco J. Díez de Revenga. Madrid: Cátedra, 1987.

Porqueras-Mayo, Alberto. "El *Arte nuevo* de Lope de Vega o la loa dramática a su teatro." *HR* 53.4 (1985): 399-414.

---. "Classical Patterns in the Spanish Prologues of the Mannerist Period." *Classical Models in Literature*. Ed. Warren Anderson et al. Innsbruck: U of Innsbruck P, 1981. 225-31.

---. *El prólogo en el renacimiento español*. Madrid: CSIC, 1965.

Porrata, Francisco E. *Incorporación del romancero a la temática de la comedia española*. Madrid: Playor, 1973.

Portes, Francisco. "Reflexiones sobre el actor." *Del texto al espectáculo: Homenaje a Francisco Portes*. Ed. Ysla Campbell. Ciudad Juárez: Universidad Autónoma de Ciudad Juárez Press, 2008. 29-33.

Poteet-Bussard, Lavonne C. "Algunas perspectivas sobre la primera época de Lope de Vega." *Lope de Vega y los orígenes del teatro español*. Ed. Manuel Criado de Val. Madrid: EDI-6, 1981. 341-54.

Prades, Juana de José, ed. Estudio preliminar. *El arte nuevo de hacer comedias en este tiempo*. By Félix Lope de Vega . Madrid: Clásicos Hispánicos, 1971. 1-278.

Pratt, Dale J. "*Felix Culpa*: Allegory and Play in Calderón's *Autos*." *BCom* 51.1 & 2 (1999): 37-53.

Prieto Martín, Antonio. "Con los autos sacramentales de Calderón." *AnMal* 47 (2002): 83-101.

Quintero, María Cristina. "Monarchy and the Limits of Exemplarity in the *Teatro palaciego* of Francisco Bances Candamo." *HR* 66.3 (1998): 309-29.

---. "Political Intentionality and Dramatic Convention in the *Teatro Palaciego* of Francisco Bances Candamo." *REH* 20.3 (1986): 37-53.

Reinelt, Janelle G., and Joseph R. Roach, eds. *Critical Theory and Performance*. Ann Arbor: U of Michigan P, 1999.

Rennert, Hugo Albert. *The Spanish Stage in the Time of Lope de Vega*. New York: Dover, 1963.

Rey de Artieda, Andrés. *Discursos, epistolas y epigramas de Artemidoro*. Ed. Antonio Vilanova. Barcelona: García Rico, 1956.

---. *Los amantes*. Ed. Carmen Iranzo. Madrid: Taurus, 1971.

Riley, Edward W. "The Dramatic Theories of Don Jusepe Antonio González de Salas." *HR* 19.3 (1951): 183-203.

Robertellus, Franciscus. *On Comedy. Comic Theory in the Sixteenth Century*. Ed. Marvin

T. Herrick. Urbana, IL: U of Illinois P, 1964. 227-39.
Rodríguez López-Vázquez, Alfredo. Introduction. *El burlador de Sevilla*. By Tirso de Molina. Madrid: Cátedra, 1994.
Rodríguez Sánchez de León, María José. *La crítica ante el teatro barroco español*. Salamanca: Almar, 2000.
Rojas, Fernande de. *La Celestina*. Ed. Dorothy S. Severin. Madrid: Cátedra, 1995.
Romera-Navarro, Miguel. "Estudio de la *Comedia Himenea* de Torres Naharro." *RR* 12 (1921): 50-72.
---. *La preceptiva dramática de Lope de Vega*. Madrid: Yunque, 1935.
Romeu Figueras, Joseph, ed. *Teatre Hagiogràfic*. 4 vols. Barcelona: Barcino, 1957.
Royano-Gutiérrez, Lourdes. "La teoría de la recepción en las literaturas española y francesa." *Ensayos de literatura europea e hispanoamericana*. Ed. Félix Menchacatorre. San Sebastián: U del País Vasco P, 1990. 477-86.
Rozas, J. M. *Estudios sobre Lope de Vega*. Ed. Jesús Cañas Murillo. Madrid: Cátedra, 1990.
---. "La licitud del teatro y otras cuestiones en Bances Candamo, escritor límite." *Segismundo* 1.2 (1965): 247-73.
---. *Significado y doctrina del* Arte nuevo *de Lope de Vega*. Madrid: S.G.E.L., 1976.
Rozik, Eli. "Framing, Decoding and Interpretation: On the Spectator's Vital Role in Creating Theatrical Meaning." *Gestos* 34 (2002): 9-27.
---. "Theatrical Experience as Metaphor." *Semiotica* 149 (2004): 277-96.
Ruano de la Haza, José M. "Los carros de los autos sacramentales de Calderón (1659-1681)." *BHS* 77 (2000): 317-39.
---. "Dos censores de comedias de mediados del siglo XVII." *Estudios sobre Calderón y el teatro de la edad de oro: Homenaje a Roswitha Reichenberger*. Ed. Francisco Mundi Pedret. Barcelona: PPU, 1989.
---."La escenografía calderoniana." *Teatro cortesano en la España de los Austrias*. Ed. José María Díez Borque. Madrid: Teatro Clásico, 1998. 137-67.
Ruiz Ramón, Francisco. *Historia del Teatro Español: Desde sus orígenes hasta 1900*. Madrid: Cátedra, 1988.
Sabik, Kazimierz. "Dos fiestas teatrales en el ocaso Siglo de Oro: *La restauración de Buda* y *Duelos de Ingenio y Fortuna* de Francisco Bances Candamo." *Teatro del Siglo de Oro: Homenaje a Alberto Navarro González*. Ed. Jean Canavaggio, et al. Kassel: Reichenberger, 1990. 577-95.
---. "El teatro de tema mitológico en la corte de Carlos II: Texto y escenografía." *Diálogos Hispánicos de Amsterdam*, 8.3 (1989): 775-91.
Sage, Jack. "Calderón y la música teatral." *Bulletin Hispanique* 58 (1957): 275-300.
Salvi, Marcella. "La *Soldadesca* de Bartolomé Torres Naharro: 'Hibridismo' en la Italia española del Renacimiento." *BCom* 54.1 (2002): 11-31.
Sánchez, José. *Academias literarias del Siglo de Oro español*. Madrid: Gredos, 1961.
Sánchez Albornoz, Claudio. *España, un enigma histórico*. 2 vols. Barcelona: Edhasa, 2000.
Sánchez Belén, Juan A. "La educación del príncipe en el teatro de Bances Candamo: *El esclavo en grillos de oro*." *Revista de literatura* 49 (1987): 73-93.
Sánchez de León, María José, ed. *La crítica ante el teatro barroco español*. Colección Patio de Escuelas 6. Salamanca: Airear, 2000.
Sánchez Escribano, Federico, and Alberto Porqueras Mayo. *Preceptiva dramática española del Renacimiento y el Barroco*. 2nd ed. Madrid: Gredos, 1972.
Sanz Ayán, Carmen. *Pedagogía de reyes: el teatro palaciego en el reinado de Carlos II*. Madrid: Taravilla, 2006.
Sauter, Willmar, ed. *New Directions in Audience Reception*. Stockholm: International Committee for Reception and Audience Research, 1988.

Schechner, Richard. *Performance Studies: An Introduction*. London: Routledge, 2002.
---. *Performance Theory*. London: Routledge, 1988.
Sentaurens, Jean. "Sobre el público de los *corrales* sevillanos en el Siglo de Oro." *Creación y público en la literatura española*. Ed. J. F. Botrel and S. Salaün. Madrid: Castalia, 1974. 56-92.
Sepúlveda, Lorenzo de. *Comedia de Sepúlveda*. Ed. Emilio Cotarelo y Mori. Madrid: Revista Española, 1901.
Shaffer, Jack W. "Bances Candamo and the Calderonian Decadents." *PMLA* 44.4 (1929): 1079-89.
---. "Development of the 'entremés' before Lope de Rueda." *PMLA* 37.2 (1922): 187-207.
Shergold, N. D. *A History of the Spanish Stage*. Oxford: Clarendon, 1967.
---. "Juan de la Cueva and the Early Theatres of Seville." *BHS* 32.1 (1955): 1-7.
Shergold, N. D., and J. E. Varey. *Representaciones palaciegas: 1603-1699: estudio y documentos*. London: Tamesis, 1982.
---. *Los autos sacramentales en Madrid en la época de Calderón: 1637-1681: estudio y documentos*. Madrid: Ediciones de Historia, Geografía y Arte, 1961.
Shepard, Sanford. *El Pinciano y las teorías literarias del Siglo de Oro*. Madrid: Gredos, 1970.
Shoemaker, William H. The Multiple Stage in Spain during the Fifteenth and Sixteenth Centuries. Westport, CT: Greenwood, 1973.
---. "Windows on the Spanish Stage." *HR* 2.4 (1954): 303-18.
Sieber, Harry. "Unity of Action in Juan de la Cueva's *Los siete infantes de Lara*." *MLN* 88.2 (1973): 215-32.
Silveira, Jorge A. "El *Romancero* y el teatro nacional español: De Juan de la Cueva a Lope de Vega." *Lope de Vega y los orígenes del teatro español. Actas del I Congreso Internacional sobre Lope de Vega*. Ed. Manuel Criado de Val. Madrid: EDI-6, 1981. 73-81.
Smith, Dawn L. "*El vergonzoso en palacio*: A play for actors." *Tirso de Molina: His Originality Then and Now*. Ed. Henry W. Sullivan and Raúl A. Galoppe. Ottawa: Dovehouse, 1996. 80-101.
Smith, Dawn L. And Anita K. Stoll, eds. *Gender, Identity, and Representation in Spain's Golden Age*. Lewisburg, PA: Bucknell UP, 2000.
Soufas, Teresa. "The Absence of Desire in Leonor de la Cueva's *la firmeza en la ausencia* [*Loyalty in Absence*]." *Gender, Identity, and Representation in Spain's Golden Age*. Ed. Dawn L. Smith and Anita K. Stoll. Lewisburg, PA: Bucknell UP, 2000. 142-55.
---. "Ana Caro's Re-evaluation of the *Mujer varonil* and Her Theatrics in *Valor, agravio y mujer*." *The Perception of Women in the Spanish* Comedia. Ed. Anita K. Stoll and Dawn L. Smith. Lewisburg, PA: Bucknell UP, 1991. 85-106.
---. *Dramas of Distinction*. Lexington, KY: U of Kentucky P, 1997.
Spang, Kurt. "El auto sacramental como género literario." *Divinas y humanas letras. Doctrina y poesía en los autos sacramentales de Calderón*. Ed. I. Arellano, et al. Pamplona: U of Navarra P, 1997. 469-505.
---. *Teoría del drama*. Pamplona: U of Pamplona P: 1991.
Stern, Charlotte. "Lope de Vega, Propagandist?" *BCom* 34 (1983): 1-36.
---. "Sayago and Sayagüés in Spanish History and Literature." *HR* 29.3 (1961): 217-37.
Stoll, Anita K. and Dawn L. Smith, eds. *The Perception of Women in the Spanish* Comedia. Lewisburg, PA: Bucknell UP, 1991.
Storey, John. *Cultural Theory and Popular Culture: An Introduction*. 3 ed. London: Prentice Hall, 2001.

Suárez, Ana. "Bances Candamo: hacia un teatro ilustrado y polémico." *RLit* 60.109 (1993): 5-53.

Suárez-Galbán, Eugenio. Introducción. *Antología del teatro del Siglo de Oro*. Madrid: Orígenes, 1989. 9-23.

States, Bert O. "Performance as Metaphor." *TJ* 48.1 (1996): 1-26.

Stein, Louise K. "Eros, Erato, Terpsíchore and the Hearing of Music in Early Modern Spain." *Music Quarterly* 82.3-4 (1998): 654-77.

---. *Songs of Mortals, Dialogues of the Gods: Music and Theatre in Seventeenth-Century Spain*. Oxford: Clarendon, 1993.

Stroud, Matthew D. "Defining the *Comedia*: On Generalizations Once Widely Accepted That Are No Longer Accepted So Widely." *Bcom* 58.2 (2006): 285-306.

---. *Fatal Union: A Pluralistic Approach to Spanish Wife-Murder* Comedias. Lewisburg, PA: Bucknell UP, 1990.

---. "Some Practical Thoughts on Producing Calderón's Court Plays." *BCom* 36.1 (1984): 33-41.

Suárez de Figueroa, Cristóbal. *El pasajero.* Ed. M. A. López Bascuñana. 2 vols. Barcelona: Promociones y Publicaciones Universitarias, 1988.

---. *Plaza universal de todas ciencias, y artes.* Madrid: n.p., 1733.

Sullivan, Henry W. *Calderón in the German Lands and the Low Countries: His Reception and Influence, 1654-1980.* Cambridge: Cambridge UP, 1983.

---. *Tirso de Molina and the Drama of the Counter Reformation.* Amsterdam: Rodopi, 1981.

Sullivan, Henry W. and Raúl Galoppe. *Tirso de Molina: His Originality Then and Now.* Ottawa: Dovehouse, 1996.

Surtz, Ronald E. *The Birth of a Theater.* Madrid: Castalia, 1979.

Taylor, Diana. "Negotiating Performance." *LATR* 26.2 (1993): 49-58.

Ter Horst, Robert. "A New Literary History of Don Pedro Calderón." *Approaches to the Theater of Calderón.* Ed. Michael McGaha. Washington D.C.: UP of America, 1982. 33-51.

Téllez, Gabriel. *Los cigarrales de Toledo.* Ed. Luis Vázquez Fernández. Madrid: Castalia, 1996.

---. *El vergonzoso en palacio.* Ed. Francisco Ayala. Madrid: Castalia, 1971.

---. *El vergonzoso en palacio.* Ed. Everett W. Hesse. Madrid: Cátedra, 1976.

Thacker, Jonathan. *A Companion to Golden Age Theatre*. Woodbridge, UK: Tamesis, 2007.

Tietz, Manfred. "El 'espectador implícito' de los autos sacramentales de Pedro Calderón de la Barca." *La dramaturgia de Calderón: t´cnicas y estructuras: homenaje a Jesús Sepúlveda.* Ed. Ignacio Arellano y Enrique Canciliere. Madrid: Iberoamericana, 2006. 561-86.

Timoneda, Juan de. *Obras completas de Juan de Timoneda*. Ed. M. Menéndez y Pelayo. Valencia: Sociedad de Bibliófilos Valencianos, 1911.

Torres Naharro, Bartolomé de. *Comedia Serafina. Propalladia*. Ed. Joseph Gillett. Vol. 2. Bryn Mawr UP: Banta, 1946. 1-80.

---. *Comedia Soldadesca. Propalladia*. Ed. Joseph Gillett. Vol. 2. Bryn Mawr UP: Banta, 1946. 139-86.

---. *Comedia Tinellaria. Propalladia*. Ed. Joseph Gillett. Vol. 2. Bryn Mawr UP: Banta, 1946. 187-268.

---. *Comedia Trophea. Propalladia*. Ed. Joseph Gillett. Vol. 2. Bryn Mawr UP: Banta, 1946. 81-138.

---. *Comedia Ymenea. Propalladia*. Ed. Joseph Gillett. Vol. 2. Bryn Mawr UP: Banta, 1946. 269-322.

---. *Prohemio. Propalladia*. Ed. Joseph Gillett. Vol. 1. Bryn Mawr UP: Banta, 1946. 141-

43.
---. *Propalladia*. Ed. Joseph Gillett. 4 vols. Bryn Mawr UP: Banta, 1946.
Torroja Menéndez, Carmen, and María Rivas Palá. *Teatro en Toledo en el siglo XV:* Auto de la Pasión *de Alonso del Campo*. Madrid: Aguirre, 1977.
Trancón, Santiago. Teoría de teatro. Madrid: Fundamentos, 2006.
Turia, Ricardo de. *Apologético de las comedias españolas*. Valencia: Impr. De Felipe Mey, 1616.
---. *Loa. La burladora burlada*. Biblioteca Virtual Miguel de Cervantes. <<http://www.cervantesvirtual.com/servlet/SirveObras/01048185985697257448813/017865_6.pdf>>. 7 July 2006. 417-22.
Trueblood, Alan S. "Role-Playing and the Sense of Illusion in Lope de Vega." *HR* 32.4 (1964): 305-18.
Valbuena Prat, Ángel. *Calderón: su personalidad, su arte dramático, su estilo y sus obras*. Barcelona: Juventud, 1941.
---. *Historia de la literatura española*. 2 vols. Barcelona: Gustavo Gili, 1937.
---. Introducción. *Obras completas*. By Pedro Calderón de la Barca. 3 vols. Madrid: Aguilar, 1960-67. III 9-37.
---. Notas preliminarias. *La segunda esposa y triunfar muriendo. Obras completas*. By Pedro Calderón de la Barca. 3 vols. Madrid: Aguilar, 1960-67. 425-27.
Valdés, Juan de. *Diálogo de la lengua*. Ed. Cristina Barbolani. Madrid: Cátedra, 1995.
Vargas-Hidalgo, Rafael. "Censura teatral en la España de 1600." *Revista de literatura* 117 (1997): 129-36.
Varey, J. E. "A Further Note on the Actor/Audience Relationship in Spanish Court Plays of the Seventeenth Century." *Arts du spectacle et histoire des idées*. Tours: Centre d'Études Superieures de la Renaissance, 1984. 177-82.
---. "The Audience and the Play at Court Spectacles: The Role of the King." *BHS* 61.3 (1984): 399-406.
---. "Carros y corrales." *Divinas y humanas letras. Doctrina y poesía en los autos sacramentales de Calderón*. Ed. Ignacio Arellano, et al. Kassel: Reichenberger, 1997. 553-64.
---. *Cosmovisión y escenografía*. Madrid: Castalia, 1987.
Varey, J. E. and N. D. Shergold. *Comedias en Madrid: 1609-1709. Repertorio y estudio bibliográfico*. London: Tamesis, 1989.
---. *Teatros y comedias en Madrid: 1666-1687. Estudio y documentos*. London: Tamesis, 1975.
Vázquez Fernández, Luis. Introducción. *Cigarrales de Toledo*. By Tirso de Molina. Madrid: Castalia, 1996. 9-88.
Vega, María José. *La formación de la teoría de la comedia*. Cáceres, Spain: U of Extremadura P, 1997.
Vega Carpio, Félix Lope de. *Acting is Believing*. Trans. Michael McGaha. San Antonio: Trinity UP, 1986.
---. "Al Duque de Sessa." May (?) 1612. Letter 89 of *Lope de Vega en sus cartas*. Ed. Agustín G. de Amezúa. Vol. 3. Madrid: Escelicer, 1940. 104.
---. *Arte nuevo de hacer comedias en este tiempo*. Appendix. *Significado y doctrina del* Arte nuevo *de Lope de Vega*. By Juan Manuel Rozas. Madrid: S.G.E.L., 1976. 181-94.
---. *Comedias escogidas de frey Lope Félix de Vega Carpio; juntas en colección y ordenadas por Juan Eugenio Hartzenbusch*. 4 vols. Ed. Juan Eugenio Hartzenbusch. Madrid: Hernando, 1925-28.
---. *El arte nuevo de hacer comedias en este tiempo*. Ed. Juana de José Prades. Madrid: Clásicos Hispánicos, 1971.

---. "Epístola a Antonio Hurtado de Mendoza." *Boletín de la Real Academia Española.* 38 (1915): 400-02.

---. *Laurel de Apolo*. Ed. Antonio Carreño. Madrid: Cátedra, 2007.

---. *Lo fingido verdadero. Obras de Lope de Vega.* 13 vols. Madrid, 1894. 41-79.

---. *Lo fingido verdadero*. Ed. María Teresa Cattaneo. Rome: Bulzoni, 1992.

Villalón, Cristóbal. *Ingeniosa comparación entre lo antiguo y lo presente*. Madrid: Viuda e hijos de Tello, 1898.

Villegas, Esteban Manuel de. *Eróticas o amatorias*. Ed. Narciso Alonso Cortés. Madrid: Espasa-Calpe, 1956.

Vitse, Marc. *Éléments pour une théorie du téâtre espagnol du XVII siècle*. Toulouse: Université de Toulouse-Le Mirail, 1988.

Vollendorf, Lisa. "Desire Unbound: Women's Theater of Spain's Golden Age." *Women in the Discourse of Early Modern Spain*. Ed. Joan F. Cammarata. Gainesville: U of Florida P, 2003. 272-91.

Voros, Sharon D. "Fashioning Feminine Wit in María de Zayas, Ana Caro, and Leonor de la Cueva." *Gender, Identity, and Representation in Spain's Golden Age*. Ed. Dawn L. Smith and Anita K. Stoll. Lewisburg, PA: Bucknell UP, 2000. 156-77.

Vossler, Karl. *Lecciones sobre Tirso de Molina*. Madrid: Taurus, 1965.

---. *Lope de Vega y su tiempo.* 2 ed. Madrid: Revista de Occidente, 1940.

Wade, Gerald E. *Juan de la Cueva*. New York: Twayne, 1973.

---. "Tirso de Molina, Priest-Playwright." *BCom* 38.1 (1986): 117-35.

Walberg, E. "L'auto sacramental de *Las órdenes militares* de D. Pedro Calderón de la Barca." *BH* 5 (1903): 383-408.

Wardropper, Bruce W. "The Implicit Craft of the Spanish *Comedia*." *Studies in Spanish Literature of the Golden Age*. Ed. R. O. Jones. London: Tamesis, 1973.

---. "Juan de Cueva y el drama histórico." *NRFH* 10.1 (1955):149-56.

Warnke, Frank J. *Versions of Baroque*. New Haven: Yale UP, 1972

Watson, Anthony. *Juan de la Cueva and the Portuguese Succession*. London: Tamesis, 1971.

Webber, Edwin J. "The Literary Reputation of Terence and Plautus in Medieval and Pre-Renaissance Spain." *HR* 24 (1956): 191-206.

Weiger, John G. *Hacia la comedia: de los valencianos a Lope*. Madrid: Cupsa, 1978.

---. "Lope's Role in the Lope de Vega Myth." *Hispania* 63.4 (1980): 658-65.

---. *The Valencian Dramatists of Spain's Golden Age.* Boston: Twayne, 1976.

Weinstein, Leo. *Metamorphoses of Don Juan*. Stanford: Stanford UP, 1959.

Welles, Marcia L. "The Rape of Deianeira in Calderón's *El pintor de su deshonra*. *Gender, Identity, and Representation in Spain's Golden Age*. Ed. Dawn L. Smith and Anita K. Stoll. Lewisburg, PA: Bucknell UP, 2000. 184-201.

Wilkins, Constance. "Subversion through Comedy?: Two plays by Sor Juana Inés de la Cruz and María de Zayas." *The Perception of Women in the Spanish* Comedia. Ed. Anita K. Stoll and Dawn L. Smith. Lewisburg, PA: Bucknell UP, 1991. 107-20.

Williams, Robert H. "Francisco de Cáceres, Niccolo Franco and Juan de la Cueva." *HR* 27.2 (1959): 194-99.

Williamsen, Vern G., ed. *An Annotated, Analytical Bibliography of Tirso de Molina Studies, 1627-1977.* Comp. Walter Poesse. Columbia: U of Missouri P, 1979.

Wilson, Edward. "Estudios escénicos" *Cuadernos del Instituto del Teatro.* 6 (1960): 50.

---. "Calderón and the Stage-Censor in the Seventeenth Century: A Provisional Study." *Symposium* (1961): 165-84.

Wilson, Edward, and Duncan Moir. *Siglo de Oro, teatro*. 2 ed. Barcelona: Ariel, 1998. Volume 3 of *Historia de la literatura española*. 6 vols. 1998-.

Wilson, Edward, and Jack Sage. *Poesías líricas en las obras dramáticas de Calderón: Citas y glosas*. London: Tamesis, 1964.

Wilson, Margaret. "Some Aspect of Tirso de Molina's *Cigarrales de Toledo* and *Deleytar Aprovechando*." *HR* 22.1 (1954): 19-31.

---. *Spanish Drama of the Golden Age*. Oxford: Pergamon, 1969.

Worthen, W. B. "Drama, Performativity, and Performance." *PMLA* 113.5 (1998): 1093-107.

Ynduráin, Domingo. Introduction. *El gran teatro del mundo*. By Pedro Calderón de la Barca. Madrid: Alhambra, 1981.

Zabaleta, Juan de. "El Emperador Cómmodo, historia discursiva, según el texto de Herodiano." Appendix. *Theatro de los theatros de los passados y presentes siglos*. By Francisco Antonio Bances Candamo. Ed. Duncan Moir. London: Tamesis, 1970.

Zimic, Stanislav. "El pensamiento humanístico y satírico de Torres Naharro I." *Boletín de Biblioteca de Menéndez y Pelayo* 52 (1976): 21-100.

---. "El pensamiento humanístico y satírico de Torres Naharro II." *Boletín de Biblioteca de Menéndez y Pelayo* 54 (1978): 3-279.

---. *Ensayos y notas sobre el teatro de Gil Vicente*. Madrid: Vervuert, 2003.

---. "Estudios sobre el teatro de Gil Vicente: Obras de crítica social: El sentido satírico del *Auto de las gitanas*." *Acta Neophilologica* 16 (1983): 3-12.

---. "Estudios sobre el teatro de Gil Vicente: Obras de crítica social y religiosa." *Acta Neophilologica* 32 (1999): 39-50.

---. "Estudios sobre el teatro de Gil Vicente: Obras de tema amoroso." *Boletín de la Biblioteca Menéndez Pelayo* 58 (1982): 5-66.

---. "Estudios sobre el teatro de Gil Vicente: Obras de tema amoroso." *Boletín de la Biblioteca Menéndez Pelayo* 59 (1983): 11-78.

---. "Gil Vicente." *Sixteenth-Century Spanish Writers*. Ed. Gregory B. Kaplin. Detroit: Gale, 2006. 249-56.

INDEX

Zeitfracht Medien GmbH
Ferdinand-Jühlke-Straße 7
99095 Erfurt, Deutschland
produktsicherheit@kolibri360.de